Adland

Adland

Searching for the Meaning of Life
on a Branded Planet

James P. Othmer

Doubleday

New York   London   Toronto   Sydney   Auckland

⫲⫳ DOUBLEDAY

The events in this book are real. In some instances certain individuals have been given fictitious names and identifying characteristics.

Book design by Donna Sinisgalli

Library of Congress Cataloging-in-Publication Data
Othmer, James P.
Adland : searching for the meaning of life on a branded planet / by James P. Othmer
p.   cm .
1. Advertising. 2. Internet advertising. 3. Advertising agencies. I. Title.
HF5823.O83 2009
659.1092—dc22
[B]
2008046605

ISBN 978-0-385-52496-4

PRINTED IN THE UNITED STATES OF AMERICA

10 9 8 7 6 5 4 3 2 1

First Edition

For Judy, Isabel, and Jamie

Where you come from is gone, where you thought you were
going to never was there, and where you are is no good unless you can get away from it.

FLANNERY O'CONNOR

If God manifested himself to us he would do so in the form
of a product advertised on TV.

PHILIP K. DICK

Contents

Part 1

It's Hard to See the Writing
on the Wall of a Cubicle

On Moral Advertising and Other Corporate Oxymorons

Do you think it would be morally acceptable to work on a beer account? How about light beer? Or hard liquor? For instance, eighty-proof sweet stuff with a cool name that goes down easy, especially for those, ahem, new to drinking. Would you sell it with humor? Sell it with sex? Does alcoholism run in your family? Would you sell it to a younger, potentially underage demographic by casting older people who look young? Would you target a minority? What if it ran only on late-night cable channels?

What about tobacco? Would you make cigarette ads? Would you make cigarette ads if they had huge "YOU WILL DIE IF YOU SMOKE THESE!" warnings plastered across the bottom? Would you do antismoking ads paid for by big tobacco? Would you not under any circumstances do cigarette ads yet work for a company or holding company that makes hundreds of millions of dollars every year marketing cigarettes and selling them without communications restrictions to the third world? Does cancer run in your family?

Would you work on a military account? Would you if the assignment was to increase the number of eighteen-year-old recruits during an unpopular war? Does your 401(k) portfolio include any corporation or affiliate of a tobacco or defense contracting company?

Would you work on a political campaign if you believed in the candidate? Would you work on one if you didn't believe in the candidate, if, say, you are a Democrat and your boss (who you had thought was a Democrat) asks you off the record if you would like to fly to Maine to work on the campaign of a certain Republican presidential candidate? Would you play off the fears, anxieties, and prejudices of the public if it would sell your campaign and get you promoted?

Would you work on a fast-food account? Fried chicken? How about fried chicken with gobs of sodium and preservatives but no trans fats and they list the calories on the bucket and they do a separate "Hey, kids, don't be a fatty!" campaign and put jungle gyms and salad bars at select locations? Does obesity run in your family? Diabetes? Coronary disease?

Would you sell sugary children's yogurt to moms as a healthy snack choice? Would you bypass the moms and go right at the kids with animated spots starring skateboarding alligators and surfing polar bears on Nickelodeon programming?

How about an oil company? Would you take a creative director's position running the account of one of the world's biggest petrochemical companies if it meant a raise and an expense account and an office with eleven more ceiling tiles than that of your nemesis? Would you sleep better at night if your first assignment for mega-oil company was to do a global ad campaign about all the wonderful things it is doing for the environment, even if the media buy for the campaign cost more than the sum total of all the wonderful things they are doing for the environment?

Would the fact that you drive a Prius and intend to switch to compact fluorescent bulbs in less visible parts of your house make doing potentially award-winning work for the maker of an SUV that gets eleven miles per gallon easier to stomach?

How about a financial institution? Would you do ads for a bank encouraging people to refinance their homes even though you are a numbers-challenged liberal arts major with no house or savings of your own and if following your Live life to the fullest! *financial credo might actually lead families to lose their homes and, by association, cause a national lending crisis and, by further association, a worldwide economic recession?*

If you worked in advertising, do you know what you would and wouldn't do, what you could live with?

Would your "moral" choices vary depending upon your financial situation and/or your place in the creative pantheon of your current agency, that is, do you bend a bit more if you haven't sold a campaign in six months and you have a small apartment and a kid on the way and you're thisclosetobeingvested and you hear there may be yet another round of layoffs?

Do you still say, "Under no circumstances will I work on the farm pesticides/herbicides/insecticides business or the campaign for the latest miracle boner pill or sleeping aid pharma with thirty seconds of mandatory side-effect copy that includes death and blindness, not to mention a questionable FDA situation"?

Or do you get on your high horse and say, "Fuck you!" because last week you saved the $250-million-a-year Fortune 500 corporate consulting account and there's no way you're going to sell crap yogurt, beer, hard stuff, unfiltereds, troop surges, chemicals, or ideologies to anyone (this, of course, is before you happen to check out the Fortune 500 corporate consultant's client list)?

Do you? Will you? Can you?

Think about it. Because your boss wants an answer in two minutes.

The Death of Darrin Stephens

LARRY TATE: You look terrible. What's happened?
DARRIN STEPHENS: Nothing much. I just lost the Caldwell
account and my wife all in one week.
LARRY TATE: What? That's horrible.
DARRIN STEPHENS: I know, I can't believe it.
LARRY TATE: Your wife too, huh?

—*Bewitched* (1964)

Why a Dinosaur Has Never Won a Tony Award

Advertising as I knew it began its death rattle in the fall of 2000 in an old, dark off-off-Broadway theater on the far west side of Midtown Manhattan.

Over the years the theater had been the home to world-premiere performances of works written by the likes of Arthur Miller, Sam Shepard, Edward Albee, and August Wilson. But on this day the theater's modest stage was going to be home to a different kind of performance, a one-day-only world premiere written by a previously unpublished playwright, a nobody.

This performance would definitely contain elements of drama. And, almost certainly, tragedy. Most involved in the production, and by this time there were dozens of us, were fairly certain of this, but the degree to which it could be classified as tragedy or comedy would ultimately be decided not by the author (me) or the cast (two starving actors) or the producers (the Madison Avenue office of a global ad agency) but by the audience, which was expected to total all of five extremely impatient and not particularly happy people (our clients) absolutely predisposed to hate everything they were about to see.

We were in this venerable theater to make one last desperate pitch that promised a strategically focused, bright, shiny, globally synchronized, and brilliantly branded future to our multibillion-dollar banking client of several years who, by the way, desperately wanted to fire us.

If pressed to classify the type of production we were about to put on, I would have called it a farce.

Because I knew that even if Russell Crowe, Philip Seymour Hoffman, or Sir John Gielgud took the stage that afternoon and had channeled the spirit of David Ogilvy, Jay Chiat, and the original Young and Rubicam, our clients still would have hated it, still would have fired us. In their eyes we were too big, too slow to adapt to a rapidly changing financial and marketing landscape. Time had passed us by.

As the creative director pressed into supervising the assignment, I had come up with the idea of trying to sell this nontraditional, digitally inspired future to a financial mega-brand in this flesh-and-bones, sub-analog space. If they wanted nimble and out of the box, we'd give it to them live, in a theater, with real actors and stage props and lighting and signed black-and-white head shots of Pulitzer Prize winners on the lobby walls.

Why a theater? Advertising was entering a new age. Beyond the thirty-second television spot. Beyond print ads in *People* magazine. TV spots on *Friends*. Then of course there was that thing called the Internet. No one in big-agency advertising seemed to know what to do with it yet (beyond buying smaller digital shops that were better at pretending that *they* got it), so why should that stop us from pretending that *we* got it, that we were experts? We chose a theater because we felt that a live performance in an artistic environment was the last thing our clients expected from a dinosaur of an agency like Young & Rubicam, and onstage we could dazzle them with the countless unexpected, nontraditional, highly effective ways in which they could connect with their ideal customer.

Plus, all of our previous old-school, "traditional" attempts to save our asses had failed miserably.

Even though it was a daring idea, and even though I thought it had the makings of something special, I knew we were doomed. Mostly because I (as well as, I suspect, almost everyone else in the business at the time) had no idea what the bright, shiny digital future of advertising was. After all, in 2000, YouTube was years away from its inception, and the guy who invented Facebook was all of sixteen years old.

And did I mention that the client hated us?

In fact, if my voice counted in such matters, we wouldn't have been spending insane money, easily several hundred thousand dollars for a two-hour presentation, pitching an account to marketing officers who clearly did not want us anymore. I'd said as much six months earlier after they'd put us on notice. I'd said as much soon after that when they'd put us on double-secret probation.

And I said it again on the day of our last presentation two months earlier, another do-or-die, last-chance meeting during which we prostrated ourselves before them in another lavishly appointed conference room filled with motivational videos, PowerPoint decks, and stacks and stacks of foam-core storyboards, dozens of creatively inspired, insight-driven campaigns from the New York office's finest (bring in that funky young team . . . do we have any African American creatives?) as well as from our network around the world—London, check! Hong Kong, check! India, check! Australia, g'day!

But of course my voice didn't count in such matters. I was a slightly jaded creative director/copywriter, and slightly jaded creative director/copywriters with an aversion to leading large groups did not typically weigh in on high-level decisions, or run pitches for $500 million accounts, unless their superiors had already resigned themselves to losing said accounts.

We had gotten the mega-bank account in the first place because global capabilities had been the big thing in the merger-crazed 1990s (now, apparently, it's small and nimble and digital, but that could change by the time you finish this paragraph). Sharing ideas and resources with a far-reaching global network—satellite partner agencies around the world—had become an absolute necessity as brands themselves became more global. And our network had become so bloody global that there were times we could have used United Nations interpreters to have a simple strategic conference call between regional creative directors, which in retrospect probably wasn't a good thing.

Anyway, the result of the last meeting, which we had sworn would be our final attempt to salvage the business, was that they were not impressed. They were going to put the account up for review. They were going to open things up to other agencies.

This was a not particularly subtle way of telling us that we were history.

Being put up for review is akin to having your spouse announce in front of everyone you know that he or she no longer loves you and for the next several months he or she will be seeing other people—

dozens of smarter, younger, cooler people, many of whom, by the way, you know quite well—and then having all sorts of kinky, experimental sex with the most interesting and promising of them, probably no more than six, often doing many of the things that you may have once suggested but were never allowed to.

Sometimes during this process your spouse will describe his or her ongoing antics in excruciating detail for you. Sometimes you'll simply read a steamy, anonymous insider's account of it in the press. And then, after six months of this, six months of holding your tongue and continuing to do all the dishes and dirty laundry and seeing to the upkeep of the home you once shared, the children that mean so much to you, you will finally get your chance to say—after I've given you every ounce of my energy and passion for so many years, after trying to rekindle better times with romantic weekends and couple's counseling, after he or she has slept or flirted with just about every one of your friends and neighbors, not to mention several total strangers—"Here's how I've changed, sweetheart, and here's why and the extent to which I'm willing to publicly humiliate myself to win you back."

At that point, if you were the client (or spouse), would you want to take you back?

In 1985 the length of the average client-agency relationship was more than eight years. Today it is half that. In a 2007 poll taken by the Chief Marketing Officer (CMO) Council, more than half of the 825 CMOs surveyed said they planned to fire their advertising agency and change direction in 2008. This was before the markets collapsed in October.

Sometimes, in a rare instance, a client will put an account up for review to light a fire under its agency, secretly hoping that the agency will snap out of its complacency and produce brilliant, winning work. But this clearly was not one of those instances.

At that point, if our client was to light a fire under us, it would not have been with a match. It would have been with a flame-thrower, and we would have been lashed to a stake, neck deep in dead storyboard kindling.

In part this is because the people who hired us—old-school people with long-standing relationships with our senior management—were no longer there. They had been replaced on almost every level, most notably by a pair of young, progressive, meticulously dressed, and ambitious marketing executives who clearly wanted nothing to do with the likes of us—an old, stodgy advertising behemoth whose upper management was bloated on recent IPO cash (the agency had recently been sold to a large holding company) and had taken its collective eye off the ball.

What this new regime wanted was what every smart brand steward wanted in 2000: a smart, nimble, young, hip, hungry shop that had some kind of handle on global branding and the world of digital—a.k.a. new-media, a.k.a. nontraditional—advertising.

"We absolutely should not participate in the review," I told my boss (an executive creative director, who reported to a U.S. creative director, who answered to a global creative director), six weeks before the pitch. "They despise us. They sneer at the clumsy diplomacy of our global network. They detest our musty, 1950s-decor offices. They can't stomach our—okay, *my*—bad fashion choices. We embarrass them. We could show them the most innovative, strategically brilliant work possible right now, and they would not buy it."

What I didn't say is that I didn't blame them, because after many attempts we hadn't been able to get a consensus on a brand campaign from our global clients and even within the ranks of our own global satellite agencies.

Plus, we really didn't know the first thing about nontraditional advertising. At the time, asking an agency like ours to do nontraditional advertising was like asking Dick Cheney to be a contestant on—and win—*Dancing with the Stars*.

We were at the time a seventy-seven-year-old institution, an American advertising legend famous for building brands through solid, sometimes outstanding work, yes, but also through relationships (cocktails, favors, expensive dinners). We were the kings of the $2 million commercial shoot. We had offices in every corner of the world and profit centers, I mean subsidiaries, on top of subsidiaries. And of course, we could fill a football-field-size conference room with earnest, interested-looking suits and high-priced, jaded, arrogant creative talent like no one else.

The Internet? . . . Nontraditional? . . . That was beneath us.

"Don't worry," said my boss. "We just had a meeting. And we're totally not gonna pitch."

"Great," I said. "We get to leave with a little dignity. I really hope that this is our final decision. Because the only thing worse than starting a pitch now would be waiting until someone who never actually does the work decides two weeks before the presentation, 'On second thought, even though we have no chance of winning, maybe we should pitch.' *Then*," I said, "we'd be totally screwed."

Two weeks before the presentation, I was put in charge of the pitch that we swore we would not do.

Thirteen days before the presentation that we swore we would not do, my boss went on vacation. The next morning, a Friday, I decided, with apologies to Mickey Rooney and MGM, to put on a show.

I am not proud of this, but there were times in my twenty-year career in advertising when I would make a creative decision that had less to do with whether or not it was right for the client or the task at hand and more to do with whether it would be fun, preserve my sanity, or make an otherwise-miserable chunk of my life interesting. Especially if the task at hand held little promise in the way of any other form of fulfillment. For instance, the occasional inclusion of a palm tree in a storyboard for a retail ad that might be filmed between January and March. Or insisting on polka band auditions for the Minnesota vignette in a regional telecom commercial. Or proposing filming a man with a laptop sitting on an elephant (representing any-time, anywhere communications) for a B2B shoot in downtown L.A. Or asking Tom Selleck if he wouldn't mind recording a personal birthday message for my friend's answering machine. In advertising, if you keep a straight-enough face, it can and will happen.

Having actors do a pitch on a stage in an off-off-Broadway the-ater was one of those instances. I knew the process was going to be brutal and we were doomed to fail, but at least we'd get to play An-drew Lloyd Webber for a few days.

But it also made sense. Because we had tried everything else and this was the last thing mega-bank would expect from us. Even though we were far from experts in nontraditional advertising, couldn't we pretend we were? After all, wasn't advertising, as my for-mer colleague Augusten Burroughs wrote in his memoir *Dry*, "an in-dustry based on giving people false expectations"?

The theme of our performance, it had been decided by Friday afternoon, would be to show a day in the life of a young urban couple—mega-bank's bull's-eye demographic—and demonstrate through clever situations and witty dialogue how frequently and in how many nontraditional ways our proposed message would "touch" them.

The media department's term for this is "impressions." The more relevant impressions consumers see, the theory goes, the more loyal they will be to your brand.

After bitching and whining for a good half a day with the ac-count team, the planners and the creatives who would ultimately have to execute our plan, I took a semblance of a creative outline to the agency producer on the mega-bank account. An agency producer is someone who can make anything happen in two hours or less. Want to see snow in July? Or if the Coen brothers are interested in directing your spot? Need a pimped-out 1972 Caddy Eldorado this afternoon for a cheesy rap video for a client meeting? How about a soon-to-be Tony Award–winning director (whose name I will not mention, because we all make mistakes) who'd be willing to drop everything and put his career and reputation at risk by spending this weekend holed up in an unventilated room with your bitter, cynical self, vetting a poor excuse for a "script," discussing stage directions, trying to understand what you mean when you say things like "strategic intent," "target demographic," "guerrilla advertising," or "No matter what we do, they're gonna fire us"?

A good agency producer can make all of that happen, and more.

Within an hour, we had a director.

Throwing lots of money his way surely helped, as did the fact that he was between productions, but still, there he was the next morning, a gloomy Saturday, staring at a guy who wasn't exactly sky-high with optimism about this project or, for that matter, his career.

"So, is this how it was when you had to solve a problem with Arthur Miller?" I asked him later that afternoon during a mental-health walk around a deserted Midtown Manhattan. "You'd take a walk, bounce around ideas, maybe stop in a bodega to grab a six-pack?"

Soon-to-be Tony Award–winning director did not laugh. And to his credit, he took the writing and staging of the mega-bank skit as seriously as he would have taken staging a new play by Harold Pinter or Eugene O'Neill.

By Saturday night we'd fleshed out the lives of our characters and sketched out a semblance of a story. I went home and wrote it up that night, and by Sunday afternoon we had a working script and a good sense of set design, music, lighting, and the role of our secret weapon: the multimedia devices that our producer was procuring at that very moment.

Revenge of the Experientials

With script in hand, I sat down with my fellow members of the creative department the first thing Monday morning. In the creative department, first thing Monday morning means elevenish. Because of the variety of media involved, to get in the spirit of things and to demonstrate the extent that we were embracing the new advertising paradigm, I had invited our interactive agency to join us. In 2000, adding interactive messages to a marketing campaign usually meant slapping a Web address under the logo, or doing the occasional pop-up ad.

But these were extenuating circumstances. We were keen to do more.

During the previous year or so it seemed as if the mother ship (our holding company) had been buying or merging with a new Internet player every week. The interactive group had already gone through myriad incarnations. New names, new directors. New logos. In fact, they were no longer the interactive group. They were now an *experiential* agency. You can't say we weren't trying. Anyway, the people in the experiential group were really jacked up. Unlike my fellow creatives, who for several months had been thanklessly working on numerous campaigns for this account and had frequently been subjected to my sometimes too-frank opinion that this was the end of the line for this account (and perhaps all of us, because when a client of this size leaves, layoffs are sure to follow), the members of the experiential group saw this as a great opportunity.

I deduced this because they arrived early. They concentrated as they read through the brief. They actually listened when I went over the basic strategic and creative premise. They didn't roll their eyes when I read the rough, less-than-Shakespearean script. And when I was through, they asked a lot of smart, unexpected questions.

Unlike the rest of us, the experiential/digital group understood that this was definitely an instance where the right message combined with the right medium could be exponentially more successful than anything the old model of advertising—print, TV, and radio ads—ever turned out.

When I was through, they immediately began to brainstorm ideas. What if we were able to give our protagonist his latest mega-bank news on his pager (this was pre-BlackBerry, pre-iPhone)? What if we sent him customized video e-mails (pre-YouTube)? What if there were live actors on the billboard outside his apartment? Or if we created a micro–fantasy site (pre–Second Life) for their alter egos to visit and hypothetically spend all the money in their interest-free checking accounts?

The enthusiasm of the digital team was boundless. And why shouldn't it have been? They were creative. And they were hard-core techies. And they knew what the rest of us did not. For them, whether this pitch succeeded was irrelevant. They got it. They were part of the first wave of the next big thing. They had skills that were already in demand and would soon make many of them rich. They knew advertising. They knew the Internet and the magical potential of Flash video technology.

They knew that the culture of big-agency advertising as we knew it—a media constant, relatively predictable world of catchy jingles, celebrity endorsements, and expensive TV campaigns lionized by the fictional likes of Mr. Blandings (*Mr. Blandings Builds His Dream House,* 1948), Darrin Stephens (*Bewitched,* 1964–72), and Don Draper (*Mad Men,* 2007–2008, set in 1959–62)—was about to be blown into a billion pixilated, Nielsen-rating bits.

Make that bytes.

They knew that this was the death of Darrin Stephens and the birth of all sorts of crazy shit.

Who knew that in the coming years the major networks would lose so much of their audience that they'd resort to running ads to get people to watch their ads? Or that viewer attention spans would grow so fickle and the use of digital video recorders (DVRs) would double almost every year? Or that we'd see the advent of the five-second spot? Or that the future of broadcast television might be saved (or killed) by something called an iPod? Who knew that while network ad revenues continued to shrink, more than $25 billion would be spent online in 2007 (Bharat Book research) and that the line between what's digital and what isn't would literally disappear? Who knew that within a few years advertising on something called social-networking sites would surpass $2 billion annually?

Who knew in the fall of 2000 that something called Google would become one of the most dominant players in the history of advertising, or that advertising holding companies would gamble hundreds of millions of dollars on digital agencies in hopes that they wouldn't get left behind? Who could have imagined that a caveman from an insurance company commercial would get his own sitcom (although we all knew, once he did, that it would suck)? Or that millions of people would drop everything and visit Burger King's Subservient Chicken Web site every day? Or that consumers who zapped commercials on network TV would also use the Internet to seek and watch and rewatch and post and forward to friends other commercials tens of millions of times? Or that agencies that paid lip service to clients with a jury-rigged digital division were about to go out of business, replaced by exclusively digital agencies, or better yet, agencies at which every medium was treated equally, where digital was part of every creative person's repertoire and the transformative advertising idea was everything?

I'm pretty sure those guys did. Because that day, when most of us were dreading what lay ahead, they never stopped smiling.

Once treated like second-class citizens in the agency hierarchy, the unsung digital folks at agencies all around the country were about to change everything. They would not need to try to find a way to fit in at mainstream agencies; mainstream agencies would have to find a way to fit into the digital world. Call it the Revenge of the Interactives. I mean the Experientials.

But then a funny thing happened that day. My "traditional" team started smiling, too. They got into it. They fed off the experiential team's thoughts. They began to come up with breakthrough concepts that riffed off or perfectly complemented our other new-media ideas. Sometimes my team came up with the experiential component, and the experiential guys came up with the TV idea, or the headline, or the punch line. Sometimes they finished one another's sentences or turned the other's good visual or copy idea into a great, fully realized one.

This is what's amazing about almost all the good creative people I've ever worked with in advertising. They're handed a flawed strategy barren of insight for a thankless client, a ridiculous, personal-life-killing deadline, and a boss who tells them that no matter how great this work will be, no matter how flawlessly the presentation goes off, there is almost no chance at all of our winning, because the client is done with us. Time and again they're presented with situations like this, yet they throw themselves into the project with heart and soul. Sure, they will combine this with bouts of world-class bitching, a requisite period of eye rolling and cursing of the powers that be (account people, creative directors, clients, products, media buyers, and the Man), and sure they're getting paid good money to do this, but in two decades I rarely saw it get in the way of the work, and I rarely saw work presented that a creative person did not care deeply about.

When a brainstorming session is going well, the cynic (who harps on all of the above negative realities) goes into hibernation, and the believer becomes transfixed by the rush of unadulterated energy that can only come from the soul of an original idea. It is hard to explain. You don't have to like or believe in the product or client, but if the idea begins to make conceptual sense—creative sense— and if it has the scent of something that can be provocative and original and especially memorable, all negative feelings and distractions vanish and something else takes over.

I call it intellectual adrenaline. Yes, intellectual. With advertising there's something about the combination of having to solve a major corporation's strategic problem in a creative way, while a clock is ticking, the whole time knowing that others in your building and in buildings around the world are also trying to solve the same problem, with hundreds of millions of dollars at stake, that is thrilling and somewhat addictive. But it's not just the money or the ego-stroking salvation of a major corporation. Sometimes it's equally if not more challenging and addictive when the client has little or no money and the assignment is fund-raising to restore inner-city baseball fields, or a used-record store.

I'm not so sure that it's art. But it is creativity. And in the right environment it is contagious.

This is what happened to us that morning under the fluorescent lights at that ugly conference table. The intellectual adrenaline began to flow. The negativity of the cynic was replaced by the enthusiasm of the creative evangelist.

It's a great time. But it is also the most dangerous time for a creative advertising person or anyone in the business of creating ideas for others. Because it is when we begin to care.

The Profound Difference Between
Caring and Believing

We broke up around lunchtime, feeling good about our ideas, our possible creative executions, and our theatrical production. After the teams went off to flesh out their assignments, I met with my producer and my director. They'd already secured the theater. They had scheduled auditions for later that afternoon. And someone from the big-screen projection company that could turn this into a truly live, multimedia event was waiting in my office.

Between meetings, auditions, and run-throughs at the theater, I walked the halls of the agency, checking in on the work in progress, encouraging, redirecting, occasionally improving upon, but more often killing executions that didn't feel right before they went too far. If a team truly loved what I wanted to kill, I would hear them out and let their idea live for the time being, usually with the stipulation that they would need to have something else as a backup. From a creative perspective, there aren't a lot of pluses (other than the typically larger salary and production budgets) to working at a large agency. There's always a competition between teams and groups. There is a gauntlet of levels through which a winning idea must pass (for instance, work that I love or killed may be killed or given new life by someone whose office has a few more ceiling tiles than mine). Because of this you can often feel more like a part of a machine than a vital member of a creative group.

But when an agency of this size is engaged in a pitch of this magnitude, the machine cranks up to another level, a level that would be impossible to sustain at a boutique or even most medium-size agencies. And it is a thing to behold.

Individually and collectively, writers, art directors, producers, group assistants, strategic planners, and account execs all begin to interpret the work in progress for their own purposes. What's the overarching graphic glue or look for all components, right down to the PowerPoint deck? Is that the final tagline? Has anyone done a copyright check? How does it translate to Spanish? French? Has the lead art director chosen a storyboard artist?

Scraps of paper become 28-point headlines. A twenty-five-year-old copywriter's rant becomes a TV script. Pencil sketches become fully realized illustrations, and with final approvals it all gets scanned and shipped and sent (at least in the year 2000) to the studio. At my agency at this time a visit to the art studio would find anywhere from twenty to fifty designers and bull-pen artists finessing work for myriad aspects of the presentation. Day and night leading up to a pitch, a series of huge full-color printers churned out poster-size prints of storyboards, billboards, mock Web pages, and other key elements of the presentation.

This part of the process has its moments, but they're not nearly as satisfying as the original period of creativity that started everything. Seeing the work take shape is exciting, but at this stage the presentation looms over everything, and every ad, every line, every second of face time is fretted over and contested. Luckily in this instance, senior management, for reasons that I suspect had to do with knowing enough not to board a sinking, burning ship, stayed away entirely, or made the most cursory of inspections. Plus, my boss was on vacation. And her boss never asked to see so much as a coupon ad. Which was fine with me.

Days passed. Things seemed to be coming together. The traditional ads looked good. The digital stuff was different and promising. The actors were real actors, and in rehearsals they began to bring a touch of humanity to the script, a charming, slacker romantic comedy with an obscene amount of product placement. Kind of like most sitcoms on the networks today.

The director tweaked props, lighting, sound design. The theater looked great. We made posters for our production and hung them in the lobby. We made Playbills that served as agendas and experiential ads unto themselves. We even put a snappy headline on the bags of popcorn we'd be handing out to the clients. The bastards could fire us, but they couldn't accuse us of giving up or mailing it in.

It's around this time that we started allowing ourselves to say delusional, Cinderella-story-like things such as "This is going to blow them away," and "Wait until [insert agency or client nonbeliever here] sees this," and, the most dangerous of all, "Imagine if, with no help, no chance, we actually won this thing."

The only remaining problem was with the large projection screens that were vital to the production. They were supposed to work in perfect synchronicity with the actors and various digital devices, reinforcing strategic points and showcasing virtually every manner of mega-bank message that was burned into the script. We were going to show animated storyboards of TV spots on the big screens. We were going to show funny and emotional videos on the big screens. We were going to show the entire totally revolutionary, monumentally experiential Web experience on the big screens.

Only thing is, we didn't have any.

First they were late in arriving. Then, when they finally showed up and were installed, we couldn't get the screens to sync with our videos, our soundtracks, our computers, and our PowerPoint presentations. It was decided that we would need new big screens. This was no small matter in a presentation that was supposed to be all about the dawning of a new form of advertising. The commingling of the Web, the phone, the media, and the coolest and tiniest of gadgets.

In its present state, our digital presentation was sub-analog.

I wanted to ask the interactive/experiential dudes for help, but they had already delivered all of their work and had moved on to another account, another, more viable pitch.

At the time, the agency was losing pieces of business left and right, but suddenly the interactive guys, they were red-hot.

The screen crisis was frustrating because it was one of the few things that I felt I couldn't write, bullshit, or hustle my way out of. Everything was golden except for the tech, and I knew nothing about tech, especially making tech work.

On Friday night before the Monday afternoon presentation, my producer, who had never let me down, assured me that it would work out. Then she went home for the weekend. The rest of my team stayed and worked the weekend, improving the work right until the end, but every run-through was done without the accompaniment of the yet-to-arrive projection screens.

Opening (and Closing) Night

The screens finally arrived on Monday morning, several hours before the clients and just as senior management from the agency, after being invisible for several weeks, began to materialize.

We had time for two more run-throughs, neither of which went particularly well. I was not happy. But my producer said it would be all right.

The moments before the client arrives for a major creative and strategic presentation are surreal. Young junior account people scramble and fret and tend to get in the way. High-ranking executives who had no role in the preparation for this day begin to ask stupid questions and to make even stupider suggestions. Higher-ranking people who had no role in the preparation but who, in flashes of self-preservational inspiration, are beginning to think,

"Maybe this ship isn't about to sink, maybe this is something I ought to try to attach myself to," suddenly decide that perhaps they should make some brief introductory remarks, or at least be the ones to meet the clients at the door to pass a witty comment as they're handed their customized Playbills, their experientially branded bags of popcorn.

I tend to stand around, feeling angry and depressed, before meetings like this. Some of it is real, because of the above, and some is the by-product of having spent thirteen consecutive days and nights thinking of nothing but mega-bank.

"The things we have to do to impress these assholes. You ought to be ashamed of yourself for putting up with any of their shit— client, agency, any of them. And wouldn't it be great if we shocked the world and won this damned thing and then told them to fuck off anyway. If we said, 'Thanks, mega-bankers, but we don't want to do business with mega-assholes.'"

But when the clients arrived, for their second of what I believe was to be three agency pitches that day, trudging through the lobby as if about to witness a mercy killing instead of glimpse the future of advertising, I was all firm handshakes, smiles, and self-deprecating wisecracks.

After the clients were shown to their seats and our announcer in the PA booth jokingly asked them to please turn off all pagers and cell phones, the lights went down. The day before, I had written and recorded an introductory, sound-only piece that was designed to take the piss out of all the old, tired, expected ways in which brands the size of mega-bank used to tell their advertising story—grand vignettes, celebrity endorsements, and highfalutin language about so-called emotional truths that have nothing to do with the product—thus setting the stage, literally, for the way that global brands, global banks, and global souls will live in the future. Here it is:

Narrator (over house speakers):

Open. Open on a buttery gold field at dawn. An opal sea at dusk. Open with a helicopter shot of mist-blanketed mountains. Listen to the voice-over, the voice of God, your next-door neighbor. Your inner child. No. Listen as the vaguely recognizable celebrity voice of James Earl Kevin Costner Tom Selleck Zeta Jones speaks . . . about freedom and liberty and your inalienable right to revel in postmillennial, high-interest-bearing bliss. Speaks about the relationship between a smaller world, bigger dreams, and the whims of a skittish Fed. Hear the words, invoking Sartre and Keynes, Adam Smith and Britney Spears, likening the act of a simple credit card transaction to some life-changing gift from above.

Cut.

To the Great Wall. The floor of the Exchange. A New York–style pizza parlor in Sierra Leone. Cut to a hero shot of a banker shaking the hand of a cowboy client with embarrassingly shameful earnestness.

Flash cut. Jump-cut. Crosscut in black and white and slow dissolve to a slo-mo dolly pan of a lone old man enjoying the fruits of his retirement on a moonlit beach in Mykonos . . . on . . . a . . . unicycle.

Score it. To a world beat, a peppy salsa, a hip-hop-techno-polka fusion, a cappella, backed by Kid Rock, Celine Dion, and the Boys Choir of Harlem.

Now tag it. Sign it. Title it with a Web address and make it everlasting with a three-word, no-greater-than-twelve-syllable life-affirming wisp of marketing haiku . . .

And air it.

Air it on the Super Bowl. The Olympics. In theaters.

Air it on a very special episode of Everybody Loves Raymond.

Or . . . maybe not.

Maybe there's another way.

Meet Joe.

(SFX: The sound of a train clickety-clacking toward Manhattan. Lights come up on Joe, onstage, sipping coffee, reading his morning paper.)

Up to this point, we had them. Maybe not their hearts, or their $800 million in annual billings. But we had their attention. I'm certain. I was off to the side, watching them try not to look impressed. None of us had ever attempted or seen a presentation like this, but so far it was working.

So far.

Does it surprise you that the rest of the pitch was a disaster? That the big screens would never quite sync up with our actors, our presenters, and that the very thing we were counting on to be the coolest, most innovative part of our presentation came off as the most inept, the least inspired?

It didn't surprise me, but to this day that doesn't make me feel any better. I was prepared to lose the account, but I wanted us to do it on our own terms, to make them think that their ex had really changed and had gotten his act together. New clothes. New attitude. New possibilities. Open, even, to a threesome.

But instead of going out with a flourish, we lost it spectacularly. There were seemingly endless moments when the screens blinked on and off, or an actor awkwardly stood waiting for a visual cue, or the guitar player (did I mention that we had a singing guitar player onstage to help move things along?) began to play during a very important video.

There were other similarly disastrous moments, during each of which everyone looked to me, as if I knew what the hell had gone wrong.

———

Does it matter that within days (thus confirming our suspicions that our fate was sealed before they even saw us) mega-bank would move its business to a very fine medium-size creative shop that would, to my dismay, do terrific, beautifully written, highly visible work?

Does it matter that later that night in a West Side theater-district bar I could be heard lamenting, like Barton Fink or any of a thousand real writers who had lost a part of their soul on the Great White Way, "If only we had one more day of rehearsals," or "The screens! The screens! The horror!"? And then later telling my loyal creatives that I loved each and every one of them and they should all have a plan B because this is "a vile, vile business" while running up an unauthorized $1,100 bar tab?

Does it matter that I was hammered on single-malt scotch, breaking my own rule about not getting drunk when I'm down? Or that I was breaking that rule with the people who had gone to advertising war with me for years, old-school print and TV people, and several members of a new generation who got it, for whom it might not be too late, all of whom deep down knew that we had no chance but had worked their asses off anyway?

I guess not.

I guess what mattered in the fall of 2000, when the lights came back up in that old theater and our somber (not a good sign) clients left their Playbills on their seats (definitely not a good sign) and shook our hands for the last time, is that we all knew that we had just been part of a profound paradigm shift. In advertising, someone says paradigm shift every time a client checks his BlackBerry, but this was real.

Lines had been drawn. Advertising would never be the same again. Time had passed my agency by, and for the next seven years, like many agencies large and small, we would struggle to catch up with it.

Some kind of torch was about to be passed, but not to or by me.

I was angry because I knew I had seen the future of advertising. I just hadn't quite figured out how to make it work.

One Huckster's Beginnings

It is better to know some of the questions than all of the answers.

—James Thurber

Charo as Guidance Counselor
Mahopac, New York, Spring 1978

"What about advertising?"

My sister Karen posed this question to me one spring night after dinner while I was a senior in high school. After the plates had been cleared, we remained at the table with my mother to discuss a topic to which I hadn't given much thought since, well, I had discovered sex, drugs, and alcohol*: my future.

Some teenagers would dread an encounter like this. But as the youngest of four children, and the last one living at home, I was excited that anyone was paying attention to me at all. My older brother had recently joined the navy, and both of my sisters were married and living in homes of their own.

---

*Not simultaneously, or necessarily in that order; plus, actually having sex versus being obsessed with wanting to have sex is a distinction that must be made.

Another bonus was that my father wasn't part of the discussion. His participation in such matters usually concluded with a deep reddening of the face, a bulging of the eyes, and a look of shame-inducing disgust. It's not that my father had anything against college or my having a fulfilling future, but he had made it clear that after my negligible academic and social performance of the last few years, he wasn't about to spend a cent sending me anywhere. At the time, his vision of my future entailed my spending another summer, and perhaps more, working for his masonry business, laying block in a mental institution.

So, sure, my future. Let's discuss. Let's break out the Devil Dogs and figure this sucker out. Besides, what else was I going to do, go to my room to listen to an eight track of Jethro Tull and think unsavory things about Charo's appearance on *The Mike Douglas Show* that afternoon?

"What about advertising?" I repeated, but with skepticism rather than Karen's enthusiasm.

"You know, like *Bewitched*."

I wriggled my nose. "But I have no supernatural powers."

My sister did not smile. She had recently graduated from college. She knew that I was teetering on the vocational brink, and I should have known better than to give her a hard time. After all, this is the person who had taught me an entire year's worth of algebra in one week before my Regents exam. This is the person who still saw a glimmer of promise in my slanted stoner's eyes. "Like Darrin Stephens, jerko." She's also the person who once found me so irritating that she kicked me through the glass of a storm door. "Darrin Stephens writes commercials and snappy jingles for a living." I nodded. Of course I was familiar with Stephens's work. He was the hybrid account/creative guy at McMahon and Tate. Wore a suit, kowtowed to his blustering boss, Larry Tate, and tried to keep his wife, who was a witch, from getting him in trouble.

From what I could discern, besides the witchcraft issues, Darrin Stephens's world seemed to revolve around schmoozing clients, enjoying cocktails, and coming through with the occasional burst of ass-saving inspiration.

I also knew why my sister had suggested Stephens as a mentor: her little brother was a liberal arts specialist with a smart mouth, so why not advertising? But still, I just couldn't see myself . . .

She raised a finger to make one last point. "Of course, you know that there's no math whatsoever in advertising."

Hey now!

This is the first time I had officially thought of advertising as a career. In fact, it's the first time I'd thought of any career other than professional baseball player since I was eight. That was the year I had requested and submitted an application to Harvard. That was also the year in which someone from a technical institute knocked on our door one night during dinner to speak with Mr. James P. Othmer about his application (procured via a matchbook-cover ad) and pursuing a career in mechanical drawing. My father, who was not amused by this aspect of my precocious ambition, sent all fifty-three pounds of me out to apologize to the man, who had driven all the way from lower Westchester County to recruit me.

Back to advertising. It didn't sound half-bad. It also didn't hurt that Elizabeth Montgomery, Darrin's on-screen witch-wife, was a serious hottie. I imagined (to a certain extent, correctly) that thinking up ads was probably a lot like signing yearbooks. And I absolutely was a gifted signer of yearbooks!

It was true. The odd, experimental, and occasionally obscene passages I'd been regularly churning out transcended the more pedestrian "Have a great summer," or "Remember what happened in Mr. So-and-so's class," or the inside-cover-spread, cliché-ridden "Best friends/soul mates forever" offerings of my peers.

My passages were sought after by friends and strangers. Students and parents commented on my unique turns of phrase. My postmodern riffs on classic themes. My clever use of the eraser on teacher photos. Clearly, I had a special talent.

So, yeah. Shit, yeah! Advertising! Then it's settled. Westchester Community College, here I come. Thank you, Karen. Thank you, Mother. Now, if you'll please excuse me while I grab another Devil Dog and retire to my room to listen to *Aqualung* and contemplate the beautiful, multitalented Charo. No, make that Elizabeth Montgomery.

Academia and Asteroids
Valhalla, New York, 1978

Did I choose advertising, did advertising choose me, or did I simply stumble from job to job until I found something that I didn't hate, that paid well, and that had medical?

After another summer of mixing mortar and laying block with my father at the mental institution, on my sister's advice I went to community college. Since it didn't have a two-year degree in advertising, I inexplicably thought the next-best move would be to enroll as an accounting major. I believe this is because one of my older sister's friends was an accountant, and apparently he was doing well, meaning he wasn't mowing lawns or flipping burgers or picking up trash in a neon orange vest on the side of the road, so that's how that happened. One month later, beaten down by debits and credits, I switched out of accounting (or perhaps was asked to leave, the memory fails here) and thought that maybe English or journalism would be a better major.

Also, I decided I had to make a change because one month into my collegiate career, I wasn't exactly thriving in any class. I'd been commuting thirty miles each way with two high school friends, and some days we never made it to campus. Some mornings we would park outside a White Plains liquor store, waiting for the owner to open the doors at nine. Some days we would skip out early to go bowling, or I would accompany my friend to various bars where, after getting high, he would play high-stakes ($500 and up) games of Asteroids against the area's top gamers.

Once, after a morning visit to the liquor store, at my suggestion, we found Babe Ruth's grave in the cemetery of the Gate of Heaven in Hawthorne, where, after recounting his legendary on- and off-field career, I toasted the Sultan of Swat. Later that same day we were at a hilltop park overlooking the site of the Battle of White Plains. I grew excited as I described for my friend Washington's maneuvers and the manner in which Howe and his Hessians had outflanked the American positions. That night, semiconscious in my room before eight o'clock, I finally saw the irony in the fact that while I was passionately describing American history and giving a comprehensive sports report to my friend, I was cutting American History and Journalism 101.

I stopped commuting with him after that and never went back to the liquor store. At least during school hours.

I was determined to make a comeback. I was seventeen.

A few weeks later in a creative-writing class, we were asked to read our favorite poem out loud. To eye rolls, snickers, and sighs of highbrow community college artiste disgust, I read this:

The Men That Don't Fit In
by Robert W. Service

There's a race of men that don't fit in,
A race that can't stay still;

So they break the hearts of kith and kin,
And they roam the world at will.
They range the field and they rove the flood,
And they climb the mountain's crest;
Theirs is the curse of the gypsy blood,
And they don't know how to rest.

Clearly, in those days I wasn't reading a lot of poetry (my alternate choice, which I suspect wouldn't have fared much better, was *Desiderata*). This was the first thing that came to mind, if only because I had "discovered" it on a Yukon Jack whiskey poster that was tacked on my brother's bedroom wall. Previously, I had recited it for my friends while drinking Yukon Jack in a moonlit field, and they seemed to enjoy it, to embrace being a member of the misfit tribe.

So for my first assignment in creative writing, I had brought in not a poem but a piece of guerrilla marketing. While others in class had recited Sylvia Plath, Dylan Thomas, and Allen Ginsberg, I read a liquor ad.

The Antithesis of Having a Distinct Sense of Anything
Boston, Massachusetts, 1980

My first day as a transfer student at Northeastern University was my first day in Boston. Six months earlier I had read a magazine article that said Boston was a great college (read: party) town. Northeastern accepted me, presumably based on my academic renaissance at community college and, I like to think, the emotional power of an application essay whose title could have been "I Don't Want to Spend the Rest of My Life Laying Block in a Mental Institution."

During my first week at Northeastern, a counselor asked me about my co-op plans. When I asked her what co-op was, and then assured her I wasn't kidding, I was told that co-op was the reason most if not all students went to Northeastern. She said that 95 percent of the student body worked a co-op job related to his or her major every other quarter, creating a résumé and making money at the same time.

Ohhhh. Co-op. Yes, I absolutely had co-op plans, I told her. I'm all about the co-op.

A week later I was sent on my first co-op interview, make that my first interview of any kind, at the *Boston Globe* sports department. I was told that the *Globe,* and the sports department in particular, was the most sought-after job in the journalism program. It had national gravitas, and it paid well, especially for journalism.

I was up against more than twenty other students. With no familiarity with the paper and having done nothing in the way of preparation, I went to the interview in a flannel shirt and work boots that went especially well with my Charles Manson beard. I winged it in the interview. I told jokes. I said that I hated the Red Sox. I said the word "fuck." Not because I didn't care or wanted to come off as a rebel, but because I didn't know better. I didn't know about Woodward or Bernstein, Red Smith, or the First Amendment. Besides, the assistant sports editor who was doing the interviewing had said "shit" a few seconds earlier, so why the fuck not?

Despite or perhaps because of the above, I got the job, and it changed my life. In part because I wouldn't have been able to pay my tuition or graduate if not for the money I made working full-time (thanks to overtime and covering for others) year-round. My tenure at the *Globe* also changed me because I was suddenly hanging out with (okay, getting coffee for) the best sportswriters in the country: Peter Gammons, Lesley Visser, Bob Ryan, Leigh Montville, Bud Collins, and many others.

They called my young coworkers and me Nighthawks. At first I took scores and dictation and answered the trivia questions of

Boston drunks over the phone. Within weeks I was being sent on photo runs, sitting underneath the hoop or on the catwalk high above the parquet floor of the old Boston Garden, watching Larry Bird and Dr. J while waiting to rush the staff photographer's film back to the paper in time for the first edition. I sat ringside for the Marvin Hagler versus Vito Antuofermo middleweight championship fight. I took dictation from and line-edited Bud Collins live at Wimbledon and shot the shit with the old-school pasteup guys wearing folded newspaper hats putting the paper together on the lower level. Some nights after we put the paper to bed, we would hang out on the roof of the building and talk and drink and sometimes shoot fireworks out high above Dorchester's Morrissey Boulevard until dawn. This is where I was told that if I played my cards right, I would be given a chance to be a reporter for high school games in a year or so. But it was not a sure thing. There was a waiting list, a pecking order.

Then one day for journalism class I wrote an essay about a seventy-mile canoe race I'd participated in—the World Flatwater Championships*—that spring in Cooperstown, New York. On a whim I submitted it to Bob Duffy, a cantankerous, hilarious editor who also happened to be an exceptional writer. Duffy ran the piece, "Paddling into the Past," accompanied by a pen-and-ink illustration, in the following Saturday's Sports Plus section. They paid me $75, and my favorite writer on the paper, Leigh Montville, went out of his way to congratulate me. This was the first time—okay, at least since my yearbook-signing days—that I felt the satisfaction and pull of being a writer.

---

*For the World Flatwater Championships, a.k.a. the General Clinton Canoe Regatta, my brother, two friends, and I used borrowed battleship-heavy Grumman canoes, did zero in-water training, and drank until 2:00 a.m. the night before the 6:00 a.m. start. In the world's longest flat-water canoe race we finished a mere six hours off the pace.

Soon I was bumped in the cub-reporter pecking order, and I had a regular byline in the paper, mostly covering high school sports. This led to another part-time job, as a stringer for the Associated Press, covering Boston Red Sox home games.

The extent of my responsibilities for the AP job at Fenway Park was to hustle up and down stairs between the press box and the winning and losing clubhouses to record quotations for an aging beat writer to slug into the second version of his wire service story. At first I was impressed by the effortless way in which he would sometimes dictate a game story in his Boston Irish twang seconds after it ended: "The Bahstan Red Sawks, cawma, led by Cahney Lansfud's three RBIs, cawma . . ." But then, after realizing that he had been at it for more than forty years and that within a few weeks I was able to do the same thing in my head, I wasn't so impressed. For this (and keeping said writer's gin-and-tonic glass filled) I got $50 a game, all the food I could eat at the press buffet, and the privilege of leaning against the batting-practice cage for three hours before first pitch and watching players, reporters, coaches, vendors, and owners prepare for the game. Often I found watching these hundred-year-old rituals unfold as the antique ballpark came to life more fascinating than the game itself.

In two years I'd gone from drinking on top of Babe Ruth's grave while cutting class to covering the likes of Carl Yastrzemski, Jim Rice, Cal Ripken, and Reggie Jackson and listening to the likes of the diminutive, beer-drinking, corn-on-the-cob-eating Baltimore Orioles manager Earl Weaver spew a poetic litany of profanities while he was sitting behind a postgame clubhouse desk, naked.

However, even though I was a lover of baseball and the beat was fascinating, especially for a twenty-one-year-old, the Red Sox clubhouse was not the most hospitable place in the world, and with a few exceptions the players treated most writers (and often with good reason) as something (not infield clay) to be scraped off the bottom of their spikes.

Without a doubt it was easier and more glamorous than mixing cement, and it certainly had its moments, but after a while I decided that writing my canoe trip essay had been more fulfilling than all the game stories and features I'd done since then.

I'd already begun to wonder if this was what I wanted to do, if this was how I wanted to be treated, for the next twenty-five years.

Three Jobs That Would Never Appear on My Résumé
Yonkers, New York, 1983

"I spoke to someone in the laborers' union, and if you go up to Peekskill first thing tomorrow morning, there's a good chance he can pull some strings and help get you a card to join."

I had just graduated from college, where I'd spent the previous three years writing for one of the country's best newspapers. There, I'd earned scholarships and a steady paycheck, and thanks to student loans, a loan from my uncle, and a loan from my soon-to-be wife, Judy, I'd paid for every cent of it. The problem was, once my co-op gig ended upon graduation, the *Globe* could only offer me a part-time job and no future guarantee of full-time employment. So I was back in New York, engaged to be married, and, because I was without a job, feeling particularly vulnerable.

Hence the sage advice of my father, who at the time, with the mental institution job finally over, was laying brick on lower Manhattan skyscrapers by day and driving a New York City cab at night. And hence my actually considering said advice.

I realize now that this was a particularly difficult time for my father, a child of the Depression, a self-made man who once had a thriving construction and paving business. He was only trying to protect me from the disappointments he'd experienced. To my father at that time, my not failing was what mattered most.

I get it now, but still: thanks for believing in my hopes and dreams, Dad.

Prior to the laborers' union offer I did a short stint as a reporter at the *New Haven Register* covering sports and, briefly, metro news and politics. But the uneasy feeling that had first revealed itself in the locker rooms at Fenway Park had become more manifest. It was one thing to be looked down upon by a future Hall of Famer, and quite another by a minor-league hockey player, or a corrupt East Haven councilman. I decided that covering regional sports and uncovering small-time campaign improprieties, an understandably admirable and rewarding job for some, weren't for me. I liked newspaper work, but not enough to work nights and weekends for $189 a paycheck. So there we were, my wife-to-be and I, sitting in our Plymouth Turismo on a gray winter's day, staring at the long line of men in work boots and Carhartt jackets with sweatshirt hoods pulled over their heads waiting, presumably, for the same thing that I sought. The coveted union laborer's card.

To me the situation didn't seem out of the ordinary. I'd been mixing cement and hauling block for my father since I was fourteen. But to Judy it was something altogether different. I imagine in that line of somber men leaning into the wind she glimpsed an aspect of a future she had never planned on. I imagine that to her the line of unemployed would-be laborers represented not a temporary job but a scene straight out of *The Grapes of Wrath*.

"You're a writer," she told me. "Not a laborer. You've been looking for a job for what, a month?"

"Six weeks. It's just to get some cash coming in."

"I don't care what your father thinks," she told me. "If you get out of this car, I will never speak to you again."

My first job in New York was for a forty-five-year-old man who published a respected wine magazine out of his Upper East Side apartment. Every day I copyedited his forthcoming book on wine, laid out his monthly magazine, and printed up ads on some kind of tintype press while he usually did nothing. Most of the day I sat next to an older Trinidadian woman, an administrative assistant who either was not one for small talk or for some reason detested me.

It was boring, tedious work, a far cry from the excitement of the *Globe* and Fenway Park. However, I knew it was a place-holder job until something better came along. And on the plus side, I wasn't hauling twelve-inch block in the dead of winter, and for the six weeks I worked there, Judy and I enjoyed some of the world's finest wines in our apartment in Yonkers.

One day Wine Man came back from a two-hour lunch in his full-length mink coat and asked me to move the tintype press to another part of the apartment. The machine weighed several hundred pounds and was difficult to grip. "How about on the other side of the room? Nah, how about behind the couch?" This went on for some time. It bothered me because I could tell he thought I was a hick, and I didn't like the way he was getting off on having me muscle things around. Perhaps the laborer's job looming as a dreaded option exacerbated my sensitivity to this circumstance. Perhaps I felt it was important that I distance myself from physical labor to prove that I was capable of better, more cerebral things. I was a writer, after all, not a moving man. Plus, the full-length mink coat, which he still had not taken off, wasn't helping things.

Before the fifth move I asked if he was sure that was where he wanted it. "Yes, I'm quite sure." During the sixth move, after I'd smashed my hand on a doorjamb, I calmly told him that if he didn't make up his mind, I was going to throw him, his printing press, and his mink fucking coat out of the twenty-third-floor window.

My next job was with Dell Publishing. While I was with the wine magazine, I'd interviewed there for a job as an editorial assistant but didn't get it. I wrote back to the HR person saying that I was shocked. I thought I'd killed in the interview (during which I didn't utter one obscenity). This follow-up letter didn't get me the editorial job, but it did lead to a position in the publicity department, and soon my first taste of advertising.

Five Things I Wrote Before Attempting My First Ad

1. Book-jacket copy for a romance novel about a woman who was "an accountant by day and Fatima, the exotic belly dancer, by night."
2. The premature obituary for the former Boston Red Sox favorite Tony Conigliaro.*
3. A script for a training film for New York City hospitals titled "Creating a Sterile Field for Basic Gall Bladder Surgery."
4. Copy for Wacky Packages stickers for the Scholastic Book Club.

*I was the only person on the sports desk at the *Globe* the day in January 1982 that Conigliaro, a onetime beloved Red Sox superstar whose promising career had been cut short by an ugly 1967 beanball incident, had collapsed in an airport and slipped into a coma. When famous people have near-death experiences or live a certain lifestyle, obits are written and standing by. I imagine, for instance, that there were times when someone was updating Britney Spears's obit every hour on the hour. Conigliaro died in 1990.

5. A halfhearted letter of apology to the publisher of a
   certain wine magazine, asking for forgiveness and
   (unsuccessfully) a second chance at employment.

Feh!
New York, New York, 1985

Turns out I wasn't a very good publicist. I wrote a hell of a press release, but I wasn't especially gifted at convincing, say, the producers
at *Good Morning America* or *Oprah* (before she became "OPRAH!")
that I had the perfect author for them. So after a less-than-amazing
go at booking tours for commercial authors such as Joan Rivers and
Danielle Steel, I was assigned more literary authors, including Kurt
Vonnegut and Richard Yates. Which was more than fine by me.

But still, I had no idea what I wanted to do with my life. For a
while, I thought about going to law school to study environmental
law. But my brother tried to talk me out of it. He said lawyers were
soulless scum.* The same week I signed up for the LSATs, I also
filled out an application for NYU's MFA Creative Writing Program.
As luck or fate would have it, NYU accepted me first, and I quickly
abandoned any ideas of attending law school. There was no future
in environmental law, anyway, right?

Soon my press-release-writing skills (combined with my subpar
booking skills) led to a request by the head of advertising and promotion to compete with Dell's outside ad agency to think up a campaign line for a book by a gonzo movie critic named Joe Bob Briggs.

My line was eventually chosen and used on everything from
bumper stickers, ads, and brochures to the cover. The book would
prove to be a flop, but by then I had been moved out of publicity to

*Several years later my brother would defy his own advice and attend law school.

a better-paying job in the marketing department, churning out catalog copy and promotional brochures and occasionally rewriting trade and consumer print ads and radio spots submitted by Dell's ad agency.

My boss at the time was a smart, tough woman who was a champion of my work and a harsh, moody, and often brutal critic. One early piece of copy I submitted to her for a brochure about a glorified Irish romance novel came back to my in-box with one word grease-penciled across the lede: "Feh!"

I was perplexed. What to make of "Feh!"? Perhaps in Hebrew (which I assumed it was) "Feh!" represented the highest of praise. After all, it was capped off by an exclamation point. Moses was *Feh!* My body copy was *Feh!* My future was totally, undeniably *Feh!*

However, since I was too embarrassed to ask anyone, and judging by her surly mood that day, I concluded that maybe "Feh!," exclamation point or not, wasn't such a favorable comment. So I rewrote the piece for the glorified Irish romance novel.

One day in my office I received a call from the president of Dell's outside ad agency. He told me, "Since you've been rewriting most of our ads for the last few months, we want to offer you a junior copywriter's job so you can get them right the first time."

When I found out that the position paid $10,000 a year more than I was making, the decision was easy. However, my boss went beyond *Feh!* when I gave her the news. She slammed her door and told me I was making the biggest mistake of my life and it was important that I understand there would be no turning back. No crawling back. If I went through with this, I would never, ever work for her again.*

I didn't care. I was leaving Midtown for the West Village to work at an actual advertising agency, and I was getting a raise. Sure, it was

*This, interestingly, would not be the case.

a small specialty agency, I had never heard of most of their non-publishing clients, and my salary was still a fraction of what I'd have made as a mason's laborer. Plus, at the time I had no idea that the creative director had one foot out the door and the whole damned place was on the verge of bankruptcy. Even if I had known, it probably wouldn't have mattered. I was going to make ads for a living.

It's Hard to See the Writing on the Wall of a Cubicle
New York, New York, 1986

My final interview for my first agency job took place in front of a big-screen TV in a conference room with the principals of the agency. Part of the screening process apparently had to do with my ability to drink beer and watch the Mets play the Houston Astros in the play-offs, a skill at which I was particularly gifted. In 1986 few people knew more about my beloved Mets or were as adept at the consumption of beer.

No one asked me any questions about where I had gone to college, where I saw myself in five years, what my favorite campaign or agency was, or if I had ever committed a felony. What they wanted to know is what I thought of Gooden, Carter, Strawberry, and Hernandez, and if I wanted another beer.

At one point someone clinked my bottle and said congratulations, which is when I began to suspect that I'd gotten the job.

The agency had about a half-dozen book publishers for clients as well as a handful of smaller "mainstream" accounts. My creative director had worked at large full-service agencies and made it clear that he was going to focus on new business and non-book-related ads. Much of the book stuff was beneath him and would be my responsibility. For the next eight months I wrote between three and six ads a day. Most were for book sections in newspapers and magazines. For each assignment I would simply scan the sales sheet or read some or, if I liked it, all of a manuscript. Typically, I'd give the account person a choice of three headlines—straightforward, clever, and unexpected—but eight times out of ten the client would simply ask for a quotation headline.

I wasn't working on a big account, doing high-profile TV spots, or crafting traffic-stopping print ads. I rarely got to meet, let alone present my work to, a client, and 99 percent of the time I didn't even work with an art director. Basically, I was holed up alone in a windowless work space, all day, every day, while my boss in the corner office overlooking the Hudson across the hall, in addition to being focused on nonbook ads, was mostly focused on the acquisition of luxury items. New Volvos. Vacation homes. Leather jackets. I could hear it all quite clearly as I pumped out more and more copy. If this sounds inhuman and grueling, it's because it was. But I also found it exhilarating, and a tremendous learning experience. After all, I loved books, and if a creative director at an agency this small could afford that kind of lifestyle, why not aspire to it?

So I was making ads like a demon. Often writing fifty or more headlines a day. Block after block of body copy. I was experimenting with styles, from bold and brash to highbrow and witty, to staccato, jazzy, and unabashedly sentimental. I got the bad pun and wordplay phase of my career out of my system in a matter of weeks. I saw what types of ads got a rise out of clients and could enhance your reputation, even if no one had the guts to run them. Then I started doing radio, which was a whole other way of thinking and writing. I learned to write for the ear and to a clock, and to edit on the fly with a pissed-off voice-over talent (Lawrence Taylor, Bowie Kuhn, Suzanne Somers) sitting in a booth waiting to get to his or her next gig.

For the most part, as long as the clients were happy, I was left to my own devices. Soon I got a raise. Then the creative director, out of laziness and respect, began asking me into his office to brainstorm real, nonbook ads with his art director.

One night he asked me to hang around to meet two guys who had a few small accounts of their own, and who might be interested in merging their fledgling agency with ours. Deep into the next two nights we created ideas with them for a campaign for a brand of Italian condom (this is before every aspiring and junior creative felt compelled to have a condom ad in his or her book). These guys were smart and funny and passionate. I'd never seen people get passionate about ads before, and I was transfixed by the process and feeding off the vibe.

I wanted to be funny and passionate, too. When it's working, brainstorming fuels a unique kind of rush: at once competitive, entertaining, surprising, and intellectually stimulating. Sometimes it's like an intense game of *Jeopardy!* or Pictionary (interrupted by jags of late-night dorm room small talk); other times it's like being an inventor perpetually on the cusp of discovery. Those two nights had elements of all of the above, and if this is what it was like to work at a real agency, I wanted in. Ultimately, we came up with dozens of concepts, several of which were mine.

After a week passed without any word from our prospective partners, I stood outside my creative director's office and waited for him to get off the phone with the travel agent who was securing a personal chef for his Caribbean vacation villa. I asked what happened to the other guys, if they were still thinking of merging with us. He told me it wasn't going to happen. Richard Kirshenbaum and Jon Bond had decided they were going to start an agency of their own. Within months their headlines were making headlines, with a series of controversial, industry-shaking ads for Kenneth Cole that had fun with of-the-moment pop-culture characters like Imelda Marcos, Ivan Boesky, and Corazon Aquino. Twenty-two years later Kirshenbaum Bond is a global agency whose work is part of the advertising

canon and still going strong. Often in the years that followed, especially when things would get trying for me in adland, I would wonder what could have been if I'd just written a more provocative
Italian condom headline.

A few weeks after the encounter with Kirshenbaum and Bond,
my creative director resigned to take a big job at another, "real"
agency. Several weeks after *that*, the president of the agency saun-
tered into my cube for the first time since I'd been hired.

He told me I was being laid off. He assured me that had nothing to do with performance and everything to do with the state of the
agency, which was not good. I immediately called my former creative
director, who was already at his new agency.

He was not at all sympathetic. "You should have seen the writing on the wall," he said. "The place is an inch away from foreclo-
sure."

How was I supposed to know that? What writing? What wall? I
was a junior copywriter holed up in a cubicle all day. "Why didn't you
tell me?" I asked. He laughed. It wasn't really a mocking laugh, but
more of a knowing, condescending chuckle. There was a reason he
had that vacation villa, and it wasn't solely creative talent.

Having learned my lesson about burning bridges from the mink-
coat-wearing wine magazine editor, I took a different tack and asked
for a job. I thought about the laborers' union and my father saying I
told you so. I thought about my old boss in publishing and that this
is what you get when you're disloyal. My former creative director
said he would look into it.

After I hung up, I immediately started dialing. Not to tell people that I'd been fired, but to find a job. Within two hours I had one,
with a raise. It wasn't at an agency (the one that had just fired me,
incidentally, would have chains and padlocks on its doors by the end

of the month) but as a senior copywriter for another book publisher. The person who hired me was my old boss, the queen of *Feh!* The woman who told me eight months earlier that I had made a horrible mistake, and had no sense of loyalty, and would never work for her again if I left, had left for greener pastures of her own and wanted me to come back to work for her.

A few months after that I got a call from a creative director at another small agency. A former client had recommended me, and he wanted to know if I'd be interested in doing some freelance ads on the side for him. I thought about the boss who'd just fired me and the hypocritical tendencies of the one who had just hired me. "Sure," I said. "A guy's got to make a living, right?"

He liked this answer so much he hired me.

When Agencies Fall

Keeping everlastingly at it brings success.

—*Francis Wayland Ayer*

Casualty of the Phone Wars

The fall of the first American advertising agency began on a sunny morning in 1994 in a corner office on the thirty-fifth floor of the Worldwide Plaza tower on the west side of Midtown Manhattan. We were gathered in the spacious executive suite of Jerry Siano, the CEO of N. W. Ayer, dozens of anxious, optimistic employees who had put their outside lives on hold for the previous several months to work on a pitch to defend our most important client, American Telephone and Telegraph.

We were anxious because not only was Ayer the first and therefore the oldest advertising agency in America but its relationship with AT&T was also the nation's longest-running client-agency partnership. Ayer was the agency that had created AT&T's famous "Reach Out and Touch Someone" campaign, the agency that had introduced long-distance telephone service to America and, more recently, had taken on the upstart MCI Communications in a series of hard-hitting retail "phone wars" campaigns. More recently, Ayer had also created the acclaimed, futuristic, David Fincher–directed "You Will" campaign and was in the process of shepherding AT&T through the complex waters of deregulation. With more than seventy-five years of a shared history, for Ayer to lose lead-agency status on its charter account would not only be a huge financial loss for a company that in recent years had lost a number of high-profile accounts, including Citibank, Seven Up, the U.S. Army, and Burger King; it would also be a crippling public relations blow.

The reason for the confidence, and some might say arrogance, that day in Siano's office was that we'd put together a hell of a presentation for AT&T several days earlier in our conference room. Smart, tight, strategically illuminating, and creatively compelling.

Plus, after all, we were N. W. Ayer: one of the largest and most respected agencies on the planet. America's first and oldest. Founded in Philadelphia as N. W. Ayer and Son in 1869.* Moved to New York in 1973. Originator of some of the most famous lines ever burned into the consumer soul:

When it rains it pours (Morton Salt, 1912)
I'd walk a mile for a Camel (R. J. Reynolds Tobacco, 1921)
A diamond is forever (De Beers, 1948)
Be all you can be (U.S. Army, 1981)
And, of course, *Reach out . . .* (AT&T, 1979)

My partner Kenny and I had several storyboards in the mix that depicted a humane and humorous version of the future of telecommunications. At the time it seemed as if the group of assembled

---

*Actually the agency was founded by Son only. But since Francis Wayland Ayer was only nineteen years old when he decided to invest $250 and open an advertising agency and he was smart enough to realize that no one would take him seriously, his first brilliant piece of branding was to name the agency after his father, Nathan Wheeler Ayer, and relegate himself to the title of Son.

clients liked our spots and the presentation in general. I remember a lot of talk about anytime, anywhere communication, and lots of commercials that showed people from around the globe coming together via twisted-copper, fiber-optic, and wireless connectivity.

After our portion of the presentation, my partner and I squeezed into the dark, glass-enclosed production booth in the back of the room and watched the smartest and most dedicated group of account execs, planners, and creative people I'd ever worked with commence with the closing of the deal. Of course, as we watched, we were brutally critical of one another—"I can't believe she said that!" and "Will someone shut him the hell up!"—but the feeling was that we had put together something special.

The clients seemed to agree. You can tell in meetings like this. They were nodding along, laughing at the appropriate times. There was definitely chemistry in that room. I remember eight clients sitting rapt in the front row. Perhaps there were more in the back rows, but in the front row there were representatives from the corporate group, the regulatory/public-policy group, the consumer group, the collect/800-number group, none more important at the time than the man in the middle, AT&T's rising star Joseph Nacchio. And during my part of the presentation, Nacchio (who would soon become the CEO of Qwest Communications and be convicted of insider trading for his curious selling of $52 million of Quest stock) seemed to be laughing, too.

After the meeting had ended and the last client got on the down elevator, we reconvened in the conference room. We felt good. So good that we had a party, celebrating the presumably good meeting.

I learned many valuable lessons during my eight years at N. W. Ayer, but one that I will never forget is not to throw a victory party until after you've been told the account is yours.

In the days that followed, there was more reason to be optimistic. Someone heard that Y&R had bombed during its pitch.

Someone at AT&T called one of our account people and said that we
had blown them away, that we were golden.

The creative director of the agency said as much to me that
morning, the day of the phone call, when he passed me in the hall.
"It's a done deal," he said, on his way out to a long lunch. "We're
golden."

That kind of talk, in sports, school, business, and relationships,
always made me superstitious, but I had to figure: Who would
throw a party, say we're golden, and then invite dozens of people into
the office of the CEO of the agency unless we were, indeed,
golden?

I was sitting on a radiator against the far wall of Siano's office
when the phone company called to tell us that after three-quarters
of a century, we were being disconnected. When I tell this story, I
usually say that I could see the blood drain from Siano's face, but I
was probably too far away for that. What I saw was a man sitting
alert behind his desk and smiling when he picked up the phone.
Then I saw him nod yes, yes, yes as he slowly turned away from us
and looked out his window toward the Hudson River. Then the
smile disappeared. Then his shoulders sagged, and when he glanced
back at one of his senior-management partners, the muscles of his
face had gone slack. His look said, "There's been a tragedy, get the
children out of the room," and before anyone said anything to us, we
knew enough to leave.

Later it was confirmed that we would no longer be the lead
agency on AT&T. Of course, out of some strange allegiance or perhaps to hedge its bets, the company would leave us a few scraps,
their CALL ATT business, some corporate bullshit. But for the most
part, it was over.

Of course this is only my opinion, that the phone call in Siano's
office was the beginning of the end of Ayer. Others who had worked
at N. W. Ayer much longer than I had, many of whom had preceded

the move from Philadelphia to New York and who held higher-level jobs and were privy to behind-the-scenes information, surely have a different take from mine on why the agency fell. I know this because over the years I've spoken with them. Some blame other events, other reasons, and other people. Others feel that at that point it still wasn't too late, that the once-great top-five agency could still have been saved. And I have to admit that more than once in the immediate years after we shuffled out of Siano's office that day, I thought it could be saved, too.

In retrospect, I couldn't have been more naive.

Beware the Golden Boy (Especially If It's You)

My boss was coming my way again, stumbling across the bar at the posh Midtown eatery. It was 1993, still several years before posh had worn out its welcome. We were at the after party of the Christmas party for our biggest client, and he was happy, my boss. And drunk.

He was particularly happy with me, not because I had been making and selling great ads, but because of my recent extracurricular client-nurturing activites, most notably a just-recited, shamelessly bastardized version of Charles Dickens's *A Christmas Carol* that had made these clients laugh.

With accounts of this size, at an agency of this size, I was quickly learning, making high-level clients laugh could be infinitely more important than actually writing and producing a great ad. Apparently, the only thing better than making big clients laugh was making them feel special. This could be achieved by having a party in their honor at a posh Manhattan eatery. By ordering six $200 bottles of wine for their table. Or by commissioning (forcing) a young writer on the rise to spend billable hours rewriting classic holiday tales in their likeness.

On this night, we had done all of the above, and everyone was happy (except for the young writer on the rise, who, despite enjoying the hell out of the $200 bottle of Bordeaux, was on some level deeply ashamed).

On nights like that there were moments when it almost felt as if we were all in it together. "Partners" was the new name we'd taken to using with clients and even inside the agency: N. W. Ayer & Partners. On nights like that, at least before it got too late and they started passing around shots, you almost forgot about the layoffs, the shake-ups, the way some of your best work was often so rudely, summarily dismissed. You almost forgot that billings were down and accounts (including this one) were in review, and what client was banging what account person. On nights like that you thought perhaps we could still be a great agency.

The boss came closer, and I prepared myself for another kiss. The first had come fifteen minutes earlier, after I'd read my story (which, incidentally, he had no interest in or time for when I'd stopped by his office that morning), and since he had the same look on his face, I assumed it would be another. Which was fine, I guessed, as long as it wasn't a kiss on the lips. We weren't those kinds of partners. For a kiss on the lips, I'd need some serious stock options, maybe a spot bonus. Now his hands were on my shoulders, and as he leaned in, I closed my eyes and waited.

But he didn't kiss me this time.

He head-butted me.

I opened my eyes. *What the fuck?*

Then he kissed me.

"We're going to make a lot of fucking money together," he told me, punctuating the sentence with a second, softer head-butt. Even that hurt. If he'd had hair, maybe not so much.

"If you keep head-butting me, I won't be worth much to anyone."

He laughed. Leaned closer. Kiss or head-butt? Christ, if it's another full-on head-butt, I wasn't sure if I could stop myself from punching him in the mouth, promised riches or not. I was fairly drunk myself. I mean, do you think I could have read that shit in front of a crowd—Marley is this client, Ebenezer is this account guy, the competition is want and pestilence, *har-har-har!*—if I was sober? Then again, he did have a bottle of the Bordeaux in his hand and my glass was just about empty.

But this time he simply whispered, "You are gonna be a star, and we are gonna make a killing."

This is the same man who would later tell me that the AT&T win was in the bag, golden. The same person who will be fired somewhere in the middle of the next anecdote. But of course, I didn't know this. And what was I supposed to say: "No, we're not gonna make a killing . . . We're gonna run this venerable ship into the ground and then proceed directly to hell"?

I rubbed the small knot forming on my forehead. Then I looked in the mirror behind the bar at the Ghost of Adman Yet to Come, held out my glass, and said, "You got that right, partner."

Madison Avenue Invades Normandy

One of the benefits of working at an agency in decline is that opportunities abound for the young, aggressive, and resourceful because the old, vested, and powerful are preoccupied with spending their money and/or saving their respective asses.

At N. W. Ayer in the mid-1990s my partner Kenny and I frequently benefited from the turmoil of huge account losses and upper-management turnover that in many ways allowed us to work like a creative boutique, creating and selling smaller-budget, unorthodox work that our bosses were not interested in. This included a series of quirky, down-and-dirty TV ads for the Philadelphia-headquartered auto-parts retailer Pep Boys and an unheard-of one-day, $80,000, four-commercial TV shoot for the housewares chain Lechters, in which during one spot a grown man wore a gingerbread-man suit and in another a dedicated Lechters employee (played by the then-unknown comedian Jim Gaffigan) recited a disturbingly earnest ode to a tea ball in which he described the steeping perforations of said tea ball as "tiny portals to the soul."

Ironically, the most unexpected and unforgettable experience of my entire career came in the spring of 1994 from an assignment that no one wanted for a client that would soon become an ex-client of ours: AT&T. The project in question was an extra-credit/pity thought that a client had suggested on a whim at the end of an otherwise-depressing meeting: think of ways to link the phone to significant cultural events. It was such an out-of-the-blue throwaway that it never made it into a conference report, and no one ever followed up. But my art director/partner Kenny and I didn't forget it. We were hungry to make ads, and this seemed like a great opportunity to us precisely because no one else thought it did.

We made lists. The anniversary of Rosa Parks. The Olympics. Jackie Robinson breaking the color barrier—was there a phone involved? But none of the dates lined up. Then one day in February it hit us: D-day. That coming June would mark the fiftieth anniversary of the Allied invasion of Normandy. Clearly there would be a lot of media attention around this. Tens of thousands of veterans (then in their sixties and seventies) would surely go to commemorate the hallowed event, and surely the president would go, too.

So we put together a spot, the basic premise of which was: a group of American D-day veterans call one another to arrange a reunion in Normandy. To our next meeting, for something entirely different—a print ad for some telecom legislation—we brought the D-day spot with us in our back pocket. At the end of the presentation we shared it. The client liked it. His boss liked it.

Within days we were told to go shoot it.

Back at the agency, other than the creative director we reported to, no one was paying much attention to the project (there was a new CEO, a rift in the creative department, a pitch, another account loss—in other words, the usual), which was fine by us.

Next we found a talented director, Marcus Stevens, whose reel demonstrated a capacity to capture truthful individual moments as well as scenes of great natural beauty. In April we began to cast veterans during a week in New York and then for a long weekend in Washington, D.C. I complemented a decent grasp of World War II history with additional cramming for the sessions, reading as many books as time allowed on the subject. But nothing prepared me for sitting across from these men and listening to them detail the most seminal event of their lives, if not of the twentieth century. I did the interviewing, but it didn't require much skill beyond prompting them to describe from a personal perspective what happened that day. Many men walked into our studio stoic and taciturn but within minutes began to cry. Others told their stories with such rehearsed precision that I would become skeptical, only to be convinced of their authenticity later when I saw their names in the history books, among the first to parachute into Normandy early that morning, or to take out a Nazi gun emplacement on the cliffs of Pointe du Hoc. Sometimes, especially near the end of our sessions, I would have to leave the room to compose myself. And often, for no reason other than that it made me feel good, I told them that my father had also served in World War II, and had been blown off a landing craft during a different, equally monumental naval invasion, at Leyte Gulf in the Pacific theater.

It quickly became apparent to Kenny and me that we were doing something that transcended advertising, and that the conceits of advertising could only ruin. This was before Tom Brokaw's *The Greatest Generation,* before *Saving Private Ryan.*

With Stevens we made our final casting choices and had our final preproduction meeting. In the first week in May we were to spend a day shooting a scene in Rockland County, New York, and after that we were off to Normandy.

The shoot in Rockland County was hardly spectacular. It basically entailed filming a group of older men who had never been on camera talking on various telephones, saying things such as "So you're going to the reunion, aren't cha?" Fairly straightforward, but especially notable for me because it's the only time my father would ever see me at work. When I told the director and his crew that my father was also a veteran, they treated him as if he were a king. They walked him through the storyboard. They gave him a special seat in video village to watch the proceedings on a monitor linked to the director's camera. They brought him snacks and drinks and things to read all day long.

I'd like to think my father was impressed and, because of the subject matter, even a little proud, despite the fact that on the way home that night the first thing he told me was that never in his life had he seen so many people scrambling to accomplish so little.

Then a funny thing happened as we were preparing to leave for France. Back at the agency, people began to ask about the spot. People other than Kenny and me, our creative director, and the junior account executive/producer who had been attached to the spot from the start. The head of the account wanted to see the storyboard. The creative director of the agency wanted to take a look at the schedule for the French part of the shoot. People who had never so much as looked at the script, people who had denied most of us raises for years because of difficult financial times, were now calling the corporate travel agent to check on the availability of seats on the Concorde.

Despite the protestations of the senior producer, Kenny and I brought our wives. "The wives will be trouble," he told us. "They will get in the way." I didn't care. Judy had tagged along with me for a number of shoots, often in sunny California but also in the most god-awful of places. This time we were staying in Paris and at a thousand-year-old castle in Normandy. She was coming.

The castle rose up out of a verdant field, its towers and parapets flanked by a moat and lined with a string of stunning, if unkempt, gardens. Other than Cinderella's digs in Orlando, Château de Canisy was the first castle I'd ever seen, and it was stunning.

We arrived just before dark. Over introductory glasses of estate (as in, grown out back) bottled Calvados, our host, a twitchy yet amiable long-haired man named Luc, told us that the castle had been in the family for nearly a thousand years and was now owned by his cousin, otherwise known as the count.

Over a simple late snack Luc told us how the family had avoided execution by hiding here during the French Revolution and how, prior to the Allied invasion on D-day, the German field marshal Erwin Rommel (who, incidentally, was home visiting his wife on D-day) had used the castle as his headquarters. After dinner we retired to the parlor for more drinks. Then we took a tour of the rooms. Apparently, the production company was able to secure the estate for us at a reasonable price because it was being renovated. Some rooms were gutted or being used for storage. Others were simply locked, and the bathroom faucets, when they worked, spit brown water. But we didn't care. It sure beat the hell out of shooting a diaper commercial in Queens.

Upstairs on our way to our rooms we stopped at the end of a long hallway and looked through closed double doors (what do you call French doors in France?) into a grand library that Luc said we were not allowed to enter under any circumstances because it was filled with antiquities.

"Do you live here?" I asked Luc.

"Oh, no," he said. "I am just visiting."

Then, changing the subject, he looked at Betsy, one of our production assistants, a cute woman in her early twenties who was on her first shoot. "And you, Betsy," Luc said, so lasciviously that it made me giggle. "I know that Jeeem and Kennee are married to these beautiful ladies, but you . . . are you married?"

Betsy shuddered, blinked her eyes, and reluctantly shook her head.

Later in our room, just before my wife turned the light out, there was a knock at our door. It was Betsy. She said she was scared.

"Of ghosts?"

"No," she said. "Of Luc."

On the third morning we were up early and out of the castle to scout locations. The D-day veterans, who were staying in a separate location nearby, joined our caravan. First we stopped in Sainte-Mère-Église, the small town near Utah Beach into which one of our veterans (along with about fifteen thousand others in the 101st and 82nd Airborne divisions) had parachuted in the early morning darkness of June 6, 1944. His younger brother, who was part of the beach assault, would die later that morning a few miles away on Omaha Beach.

Next we went to the cliffs at Pointe du Hoc. On D-day the Germans had six massive 155 mm cannon emplacements on top of the cliffs, smack in the middle of Omaha and Utah beaches. Today many of the massive concrete German observation posts are still intact, and the ground is pocked with hundreds of thirty-foot-wide craters from the American naval bombardment.

Two of the veterans we'd brought with us had been part of the U.S. Army Rangers assault team charged with climbing the hundred-meter cliffs—mostly with muddy rope while being fired upon—and taking out the gun emplacements. I was familiar with Pointe du Hoc from my research, from preliminary interviews with the Rangers, and from the film *The Longest Day*. But while most movies overdramatize moments and places like this, seeing it in person, with the men who'd actually done it fifty years earlier, was beyond compare.

Since this was days before we were to commence filming, and we were in lo-fi mode, there was time for us to linger. I watched the two old Rangers drift off, one limping so badly that his wife was near tears with worry, the other tough and fit enough at seventy-five to easily kick all of our asses. They pointed out landmarks to each other. An observation bunker. A bomb crater. A gap in the hedgerows behind the guns. Then both gestured past the cliffs to a point far out in the English Channel.

At the base of the cliffs I found another one of our veterans looking out at the channel. He was a small, quiet man in his midseventies. His right shirtsleeve was pinned to his side, customized because his right arm had been amputated just above the elbow on June 6, 1944. Unlike the more animated Rangers, who had previously returned to Normandy several times and had formed a sort of collective narrative of their heroics for historians and spoke of the days that followed in terms of D-day Plus One (June 7), and so on, he was making just his second trip to Normandy. The first had barely lasted a day.

After some small talk, he pointed to where his sensibly shod feet were presently touching the beach and told me that this was exactly where it happened. He was a navy frogman (a precursor to today's Navy SEALs) on D-day who had come ashore in darkness, before the Rangers, long before the rest of the invasion. His job was to quietly emerge from the water and blow up beach obstacles—barbed wire, steel crosses or "hedgehogs," and Belgian gates—to clear the way for infantrymen, tanks, and other vehicles.

He told me that soon after he had detonated his first explosive, a Bangalore torpedo, German machine-gun bullets tore through his right arm. As more guns bore down on him, helpless and almost alone with the sun not yet risen, he crawled to one of the obstacles he was to destroy and sat with his back to the German army, facing the sea as the greatest naval invasion of all time revealed itself with the dawn.

"All I could see were ships, ships, ships," he told me (and later said the same thing on film for our commercial). "I sat there for hours, crying and watching our soldiers land, and so many got shot down. At some point someone must have come up and tied a tourniquet around my arm. I really don't remember, but I imagine that saved my life."

He was the same age that Francis Wayland Ayer had been when he started America's first advertising agency: nineteen.

Our final stop on the most profound location scout of my life was at the U.S. military cemetery at Colleville-sur-Mer, whose entrance sits on a cliff overlooking the left flank of Omaha Beach. I had seen plenty of pictures of the cemetery, the seemingly endless rows of white crosses, and I had tried to prepare myself for the experience. Nearly ten thousand American soldiers, most of whom had died within a week of June 6 fifty years earlier, are buried here. I was prepared for the eerie symmetry of the crosses. And I knew enough to look away with the rest of the crew while our paratrooper friend and his wife were taken to the grave of his brother for the first time. What I wasn't expecting, however, was to see so many members of our crew—from twenty-year-old production assistants to hardened account execs—wiping tears from their eyes.

Not a day went by in advertising when I didn't question some aspect of my job, but on this day it was hard to find fault with any of it. Even if this commercial turned out to be a disaster and never made it onto the air, it would be an undeniable success. It changed my life, and I'd like to think it made the lives of the men we brought there somewhat easier to bear.

That afternoon was unforgettable.

But that night was just plain freaky.

The Longest Night

How did the most profound and moving experience in my professional career devolve so rapidly? How did a day that began with the remembrances of a group of proud, emotionally overwhelmed veterans in one of the world's most hallowed cemeteries turn so bizarre so quickly?

The easy out would be to blame it on Luc. Or the homegrown Calvados. Or the fact that for the last three weeks we were working incredibly long hours with little sleep. Or the fact that when things are going well, I'm always ready for a party. But most of it can be blamed on the excesses and unpredictability of American advertising, particularly at its first and oldest agency, on D-day plus fifty years.

When we got back to the château, Luc was there to greet us. He shepherded us into the parlor, where portraits of the count's predecessors hung on the walls and a table was adorned with a fresh bottle of Calvados and several magnums of the count's homegrown bubbly. We'd had parts of the previous two days off and had spent them (when we weren't sitting in a service station because I'd put the wrong gasoline in our car) visiting Caen and the monastery at Mont-Saint-Michel and Bayeux, where we saw the famous tapestry. The night before we'd had an amazing group dinner at a Norman farmhouse restaurant (during which our creative director more than earned his keep with his deft handling of the wine list), and the night before that we even got to meet the count, who had driven up from Paris for a meal.

During our dinner with the count (a nice, fashionable man, not at all count-like), Luc was a clump of Norman nerves. He didn't touch a drop of alcohol and hardly spoke. But tonight, with the count back at work in Paris, he was clearly relieved. For starters, he was drinking, and talking, and flirting with Betsy again. Because my wife and Kenny's wife were going to be leaving in the morning, before our afternoon preproduction meeting and the actual shoot was to begin, Luc had planned a special dinner.

But first we had more drinks. I raised a few glasses—okay, shots—of Calvados with Luc, who continued to regale us about the history of the place. At dinner, we drank more estate champagne and wine. Luc was buzzed. Everyone was. Other than a steady rain that had been blowing in off the Channel for days (similar to the conditions that had threatened the invasion), things were going exceptionally well. Marcus Stevens, our director, was more logistically buttoned up and artistically passionate about the project than any other director I'd ever worked with. The locations were stunning. The client was happy. The commercial that no one wanted was going to kick altruistic ass, and our bosses weren't scheduled to fly over on the Concorde and screw things up for another day. So far, so good.

After dinner we went back into the parlor for more drinks and stories from Luc about the paintings of dead people on the walls. I asked Luc to point out some people from his side of the family. He stared at the portraits in their gilded frames and then into his empty tumbler. Then he said that he wasn't really the count's cousin but was perhaps a very distant relative and that he was at the château not out of entitlement but to do faux-marble work in the old wing, as long as he didn't screw things up. The fact that he was telling us this, a direct contradiction of his earlier, sober claims, led me to believe he was about to screw things up.

Royally.

Soon Kenny and I had to step out. We had a call to make back to the States to brief the composers Tom and Andy of tomandandy, the music company that would be scoring the finished commercial. Our producer suggested that we use the phone in the kitchen. But Luc wouldn't hear of it. He stood up, staggered a bit, and waved for us to follow him. We went down a long hall to a back stairway. As he walked, Luc continued to mumble and gesticulate, but we couldn't understand any of it. At the top of the stairs he took us down another abandoned hallway and then stopped outside a pair of large glass doors. French doors. We were at the entrance to the forbidden library.

"But I thought we weren't allowed to go into the library," I said.

Luc waved me off. That was the old Luc. The sober Luc. That was before we'd bonded, before the count had come and gone back to Paris. He pushed open the doors and pointed to a table. "Speakerphone," he said.

The call took all of ten minutes. I was fairly drunk, and there wasn't a lot to say other than that it was going to be a great spot and, yes, we'd bring the composers back a wheel of Camembert cheese. When we hung up, Luc walked over to the table and plunked down a massive book of maps alongside my brandy glass. "Zees, ees a souzand years old," he said. But what he meant was "Let's mess around with zee count's antiquities."

We looked at the thousand-year-old map book. We looked at five-hundred-year-old history books. Luc handed us Roman coins from Julius Caesar's time. An ancient sword. He unlocked boxes of more coins and jewelry. He opened an armoire filled with garments that people wore only in places like Versailles, or a Madonna video. We chased one another around with the swords. We tried things on. It was surreal.

At one point Luc dropped something breakable. Glass, crystal, ceramic—I don't remember. But he was fairly devastated. The count would not be happy. As he cleaned up the mess, to cheer him up, I may have intimated that Betsy thought he was cute.

Back in the parlor downstairs Luc set to formally wooing Betsy, who was clearly disturbed by this development. Soon after our return the phone rang. Luc answered. It was someone back at the agency in New York. Luc said that they wanted to speak with my boss. "They probably want to know if we can arrange a horse-drawn carriage to meet them on the tarmac when they get off the Concorde," I said. Everyone stopped to see how the call went down. No matter what, it was a major buzz kill. Because things were going so well and we were having such a good time, we felt New York could only ruin it for us. Plus, we were dreading the ostentatious show of force that was about to descend upon us.

Or not.

Soon after he picked up the phone, my boss's expression changed. He stopped smiling and his eyes widened. Not with fear, but certainly he looked surprised. "Uh-huh," he said. And, "You're kidding me?" And, "Her, too?" And, "What about Keith?" And, "Who else?"

When he hung up, our boss stared at the wall for a moment. "What happened?" we asked. "Who's coming?"

"No one's coming," he answered. "No one is taking the Concorde or any flight from New York to Paris. They've all been fired."

While we had been drinking with Luc and the count and prepping for our shoot, everyone who mattered back at the agency—the president, the creative director, the head of account services, and more—had been whacked. The new management that had recently been put in place had begun a reign of terror. I looked at the count's family portraits on the walls. Like them, we had temporarily escaped the revolutionary carnage by hiding in the country behind the moat of the Château de Canisy.

The news triggered a flurry of wild speculation about the fate of the rest of the senior management, ourselves, the commercial we were shooting, and the agency itself.

And of course it led to more drinking.

After a while it was as if the call had never happened. Fire everyone as long as we get to stay a few more days in Normandy. It was about this time that Luc began to chase Betsy around an antique dining table and then down a hallway. Later she would knock on our bedroom door again, terrified again, claiming that she could hear Luc breathing in the hall outside her room. I told her not to worry, although earlier I'd thought the eyes in one of the family portraits had followed me across the parlor.

It was like starring in a very special episode of *Scooby-Doo*.

On acid.

With subtitles.

The next day Kenny and I got up early to drive our wives to a train station twenty kilometers away. We got lost. They missed their train to Paris, and would probably miss their flights back to New York. We had four hours before what is probably the most important part of any production, what my yogurt client used to consider a binding contract between agency, client, and production company: the pre-pro meeting. Paris was two and a half hours away. We decided to drive them. Four hours later, after a harrowing trip during which I drove in excess of two hundred kilometers an hour, we barreled around a corner and squealed to a stop in front of the café in which our pre-pro was just beginning. We looked at our executive producer, who had warned us that "the wives" would be a problem and that there was no place for them on a shoot, and we smiled.

The shoot went even better than we'd expected. One poignant moment after another beautifully captured, framed by sea and cliffs and monuments to freedom and the fallen. Going back to New York, we knew that unless we really botched the edit and postproduction work, we'd have the powerful commercial we had hoped for all along. What we were less sure about was what kind of agency we were returning to.

The D-day spot was a success in all respects. It won several awards. It won us a chance to do more business for our increasingly estranged client. It raised awareness and money for World War II veterans. Also, it won me a promotion, a token raise, and more opportunities.

The agency, however, continued its death spiral.

In the next few years after that fateful call from AT&T in our CEO's office, we became a shell of the organization we had been. A slew of senior executives had come and gone. More clients had followed AT&T's lead and were jumping ship, and new business prospects were being steered away by their pitch consultants, the client advisers who, rightly, saw our instability at the top as a risk not worth taking.

At one point in early 1996, I was offered a creative director's job and a substantial raise at the agency Wells, Rich, Green, working for Linda Kaplan Thaler (now head of the Kaplan Thaler Group). I was doing well at Ayer and I liked and respected my coworkers, but Ayer was obviously in decline and Wells, Rich, Green was not,* and raises were especially hard to come by at an agency on a losing streak.

I went back to Ayer and gave my boss (who would later be my boss at Y&R) the news. She in turn called Mary Lou Quinlan, our new president, who barely knew me. Quinlan was in a town car on her way to a client meeting with our new CEO, who knew me even less. Considering the dire circumstances at the agency and my relationship with its new leaders, I was expecting that to be my last day at Ayer. But I was surprised when, a few minutes later, my boss called back to tell me that they wanted to match Wells's offer. Quinlan said they were determined to turn the agency around and wanted me to be a part of it. Plus, she said, "Wait till you get a load of the guy we're going to bring in here as the next creative director, it will blow your mind."

Back then I was a sucker for that kind of talk.

Greetings from the Nincompoop Forest

"You are all lost in the Nincompoop Forest, and I am the only person who can show you the way out."

It was October 1996, and Mark Fenske was standing at the front of a conference room filled with the leadership of the once-outstanding and presently struggling New York advertising agency

---

* Ironically, the seemingly stable Wells, Rich, Green turned out to be more volatile than Ayer. It, too, went out of business, four years before N. W. Ayer, in 1998.

N. W. Ayer & Partners. There were dozens of us, many of whom had had long and successful careers, and here was this West Coast guy telling each and every one of us, by way of introduction, that we sucked.

Fenske had just been hired as our chief creative officer and was charged with nothing less than overhauling our entire creative output, and saving America's first and oldest advertising agency from extinction. He was wearing an untucked flannel shirt and blue jeans, and he held a large leather-bound journal, much as a preacher would hold a cherished copy of the Good Book. Standing more than six feet four and built like a retired offensive lineman, Fenske was a former creative star at shops like Wieden+Kennedy and his own agency/commercial-production hybrid, the Bomb Factory. He has a basso voice that is easily recognizable from the number of commercials he's read for, and which only enhanced his aura, depending on whom you speak with, as either a purist creative guru or a surly, bullying ass.

Several weeks earlier, when Quinlan had told me on the down low whom she had hired as chief creative officer, I was surprised, then concerned. Fenske was already something of a legend, a writer-provocateur who had created some of the most memorable and award-winning ads of the previous five years for clients like Nike and Levi's. His work at the time had a weight to it, a combination of the personal, social, and ethical, and unlike anything I'd seen in advertising. He'd also been doing some directing, most notably Van Halen's at-the-time-ubiquitous "Right Now" music video, which had earned him MTV's video- and director-of-the-year awards. More than once back then, my partners and I would say things like "Imagine if we could get Fenske to do the V-O on this spot." But what we should have said was "This spot is so derivative of Fenske's work it would only be fair to have him read its voice-over."

So on that level, as a writer, fan, and plagiarist, I couldn't help but be excited. But as an employee of venerable old N. W. Ayer, whose client list at the time included the less-than-edgy brands AT&T, General Motors, Folgers, and KitchenAid, I was deeply concerned.

"The Nincompoop Forest," a senior planner with more than twenty years of experience whispered to several of us in the back of the room. "My God, our new boss is a megalomaniac."

Still, I thought, there was reason to be optimistic. The agency had been losing huge hunks of core business (the U.S. Army, Seven Up, Burger King, parcels of AT&T) with alarming regularity for several years, and a kick in the ass from a creative star might actually be a good thing for all of us.

Plus, while the agency had been in decline, I'd actually been able to thrive despite, or perhaps because of, the chaos. With upper management preoccupied with saving their jobs, my partner and I, relatively young mid-level creatives, were having a nice run under the radar, selling decent work without adult supervision to a range of clients, from AT&T to Pep Boys, and assuming more and more responsibility. Perhaps, I thought, Fenske would recognize our entrepreneurial creative natures and make us an integral part of the new regime. Also, I thought, he must be smart enough to realize that running an agency like Ayer would be radically different from working for a West Coast boutique, or on a high-profile, edgy account like Nike. He'd even acknowledged as much in an interview in the *New York Times* announcing his arrival: "It's time for me to grow up, take a stand, play on the big stage," he said. After reading this, I thought that Fenske's influence at Ayer might lead to something special after all.

But I was wrong.

Soon after the Nincompoop Forest speech, I went to Fenske's office to introduce myself and offer to give him a status report on my account. Outside his office was a doormat that said, "GO AWAY." Inside his office, to further discourage visitors who got beyond the doormat from lingering, there were no chairs. I felt like Dorothy on her first visit to the wizard's chamber. But still, I was a creative on the rise. One of the D-day guys.

"For the last year I've been the creative director on the AT&T corporate business," I told him. "And if you'd like, I'd be happy to brief you on what's been going on with the account and what I think about the new assignment."

Fenske looked up from the sheet of paper he was reading (script? pink slip? birthday card from Eddie Van Halen?) and said, "That won't be necessary."

I stood for a while, waiting for an explanation, a sharing of his master plan, perhaps an offer of some kind of lieutenancy. But none came. I was no longer a promising young creative director on the AT&T corporate business. From that point on I was something less than a writer. I was an apprentice, a lowly scribbler on trees deep within the Nincompoop Forest.

Fenske, he was the creative director of everything.

Later that week, Fenske pulled me aside after a grueling presentation. "Your words," he said, "are good." I'm ashamed to say that, briefly, this made me happy. "But your partner . . ."

"A lot of those words are his, too," I told him.

Fenske groaned. "Does he have any children?" When I nodded, Fenske groaned one octave deeper. "That," he said, "will make him more difficult to fire."

The next few months didn't get much better. Other than a handful of mostly younger creatives who had become his disciples, carrying around little idea journals of their own, sitting at his feet while he dispensed pearls of truth, we were all miserable. People were eviscerated in meetings. Women cried. Grown men felt like . . .

well, the opposite. My misery had less to do with the type of work I was doing than with pride. It's one thing to be twenty-five and learning from a master. It's another to be thirty-five, seemingly on your way to having a fine career and being told that everything you've done to this point is banal.

And it is something altogether different to realize that maybe the son of a bitch is right.

One way I responded was to totally dedicate myself to the creative work while dismissing his "way" and what I considered the sycophantic behavior of his followers. After all, wasn't copying someone's every belief and gesture the opposite of the subversive creative ethos he espoused? The quest for originality and individuality?

"You should get yourself one of these," he said to me one day, tapping his journal. By now everyone, even some account people, were diligently filling Fenske-approved journals with collages, poems, and art. Some were quite beautiful, but I resisted.

"No," I said. "Pencil and a yellow legal pad works fine for me."

I smiled. Fenske groaned.

Another day, one of the many Saturdays and Sundays we were required to work then, he looked me up and down outside his office. "You're built like a wrestler," he said. "Were you a wrestler?" I hadn't wrestled since high school, but I wasn't going to miss an alpha opportunity with the man who had derailed my career and turned my life upside down. In addition to being wealthier, more famous, and a better writer than I was, he was big enough to squash me like a ladybug. "Yeah," I said. "I've done quite a bit of wrestling." So sad. So insecure. But it's all I had.

I was miserable, resentful, and filled with self-pity. We worked late every night and most weekends, which was just great for my marriage and made my sixty-mile commute from the northern suburbs all the more fun. Fenske had taken up residence in a corporate apartment next to the agency and seemingly lived in the office. He watched football (with a group of Fenske-ites) in the conference room on Sundays. He had a margarita machine installed in his office and gave well-attended parties every Friday.

To many, these gestures signified change and a real chance for our agency to overcome its old, faltering image and show the world that we could make ads with anyone. For me, Fenske's social events felt more required than optional, and signified that now there was no need to ever leave the office.

And yet . . . during the brief time I spent with Fenske, I learned more about copywriting and editing and professional standards and what makes an ad great than I would learn from everyone else combined in my career. Until that point I'd never written anything remotely like the scripts I was turning out under his watch.

It was Fenske's contention that we were wizards, that we were making art, and he compelled each of us to take chances and plumb depths we had never reached. In some cases my ads had become more provocative and bizarre than any of the fiction I was wrestling with on the side. Advertising, Fenske said to a trade journal at the time, "may be the most powerful art form on earth," and while I didn't necessarily believe it, his words (an act of persuasive advertising unto themselves) did propel me to dig deeper and reach higher.

Fourteen years later, I still have some of the scripts: A young skier thinking of a long-distance phone call to his girlfriend while being swept away by an avalanche. An aging actress leaving a tummy-tuck emporium and considering her face in the polished steel coin flap of an AT&T phone booth. I wrote about aliens and unrequited love and the relationship between God and dishwashers. For each assignment I would submit dozens of scripts. Fenske would casually scan them before dismissively shaking his head and saying, "Keep going." But sometimes he would pencil the words "This one" on top of a script buried in a stack of rejections. In this regard it was perversely exhilarating, because there were moments when I would suspend rational thought and allow myself to daydream. If the client ever buys this, a Fenske-approved ad, life will be sweet.

But in every other regard it was depressing. Because, unlike the young writers and art directors who were, at the very least, building great spec portfolios that could lead to a job at a more creative agency, most of us who had hoped to stay at N. W. Ayer for a while knew better. We knew that our clients, with whom some of us had been working for more than a dozen years, would never go for this stuff. We knew that the future of the agency was hanging by a thread and what Fenske was attempting was audacious and reckless.

And, ultimately, a failure.

Despite writing hundreds of scripts, I never sold one ad, one headline, while working for Fenske. At first he convinced AT&T to give us another chance, but the work he did for them was inconsistent, occasionally brilliant, and ultimately the type of work they would never be brave enough to buy. Finally they deprived us of the last scraps of their business, tossing it off to BBDO.

One day, after a particularly bad internal meeting in which our work, especially the art direction, had been brutalized, I told Kenny, my partner and friend, what Fenske had said about his being harder to fire because he had kids. I suggested that maybe he should cover his ass by getting his portfolio together and testing the waters for another job. Within a month, my friend, who had loved his job at N. W. Ayer, left. Fortunately, with his portfolio, he had no problem landing a job.

Of course, soon after he left, Fenske left, too.

Something Amish

In 1997, after AT&T had cut its final ties with us, we were determined to find another phone company, preferably one that would
appreciate an agency with almost a hundred years of telecommunications experience. We targeted one of the Baby Bells, US West, a
Regional Bell Operating Company (RBOC) that had been spun off
from the AT&T mother ship after the industry had been deregulated.
US West, which serviced more than a dozen states in the Southwest
and the Northwest, had recently put its account up for review and
was about to break out national offerings.

Since at the time of the US West pitch we were an agency without a creative director (a makeshift creative board had been formed
in Fenske's absence) and our newest CEO incarnation was the passionate and ambitious but relatively inexperienced Quinlan, it
should have been a disaster.

But of course, this being advertising, it was the opposite.

This was largely because the people left at N. W. Ayer were sur-
vivors of a long series of wars, internal and external. We had won and
lost cherished accounts together. We had weathered one series of
layoffs after another. And we had worked for every management type
in the books, from tyrants and taskmasters, to cokeheads, executive
greenhorns, and the occasional fair and talented leader, which made
all the others that much harder to endure. And my creative peers,
while not yet top-level executives, were for the most part skilled veterans who knew good work and formed a group unlike any I'd ever
been part of, not only because we liked one another, but because we
trusted one another.

Additionally, whether we wanted to admit it or not, the last creative director for whom we'd worked, Fenske, had changed every
one of us. Yes, he was probably a bad choice for an agency like Ayer,

and he had told us we all sucked and had made most of our lives a living hell, but he had also made each of us a more provocative, progressive, and personally and collectively demanding creator.

And finally, despite and because of our relationship with AT&T, when it came to telecommunications, no agency on the planet was more informed or experienced.

For all these reasons, the creatives decided that rather than split up into classic art-director/copywriter teams, we'd jam as a team and make decisions as a team. I can think of no other time or place I'd worked where this kind of experiment would have succeeded, but at that agency, at that moment, it worked beautifully. We staked out a creative war room and talked for days. If someone had a good thought or an interesting visual idea, someone else would write it on a piece of paper or the occasional paper plate and stick it on the wall. Then we'd riff on it some more until it became something else entirely.

Somehow, because we didn't have to worry about anyone higher up judging or killing or bastardizing our work, individual ownership had become less important than winning the account, saving our jobs, and keeping the agency alive.

One afternoon, buzzing with creative adrenaline and camaraderie, one of us decided that if we were to succeed at all, our group needed a name, a gimmick, and an ethos. We weren't laid-back cool like some of the newer West Coast shops, nor were we slick, ponytailed, Armani-wearing East Coast sharks. What we were doing was fairly socialist, but it was agreed that quoting Karl Marx's manifesto and using hammer-and-sickle imagery probably wasn't the way to go with blue-chip clients in a society that, last we checked, was still based on capitalism. We were hardworking and selfless craftsmen and craftswomen not prone to the gimmicks of the moment. Then someone blurted it out: "Like the Amish!" So from that point on we called ourselves, for internal purposes only, the Amish Group.

To differentiate ourselves from the pack, someone suggested

that we grow chin beards (the women would be permitted to wear fakes), wear black suits and hats and white shirts, and travel to client meetings by horse and buggy. In the days that followed, when passing one another in the halls, we'd say things like "How goes the visual harvest today, Brother Magee?" Or "Your (hideous) chin beard is looking especially handsome today, Brother Othmer."

It was working. The work on the wall was getting good. And the account team and planners, feeding off our energy or perhaps riding a caution-to-the-wind, *fin du monde* vibe of their own, wasn't just liking our work; they were making it better. Not only that, but they were bringing in provocative and unexpected consultants for us, from experts on the western mind-set to the Internet futurist George Gilder, who told us that the future would be built not on twisted copper but on magic fibers born of sand and glass.

What is interesting to me now about the work we produced for that pitch is that it reflected the spirit in which it was made. The campaign or tagline, "Life's Better Here," was consistent with the boom mentality of the mid-1990s American West, and was supported by ads that were based on an ethos, an idealistic, patently western telecom manifesto about what people deserve and should demand from their phone company. "Here, Josey Wales has a pager," and "Here, a handshake still beats an e-mail," and "Here, work and play don't argue." It was good stuff.

I was chosen as one of two creatives from the Amish Group to present the campaign (sans chin beard) in Denver. It went well. Within days we'd been told that we'd won their business, that US West's next ad campaign would be "Life's Better Here," and I was told that I'd been promoted to senior vice president and would be the creative director on the account.

This was the type of opportunity that I thought I'd wanted for years and absolutely felt I was ready for. A senior position running a major account. After years of paying dues and suffering and benefiting from the myriad managerial styles of my superiors, especially my creative directors, I would have a chance to do it my way.

Our campaign launch, a rearticulation of the "Life's Better Here" manifesto, with Kris Kristofferson as our wise and weathered cowboy voice-over, was a fine piece of branding and positioning. But I soon found out that high-end branding—my strength—was only part of the assignment. The bulk of the assignment on the account would be coming not from US West headquarters in Denver but from its products and retail team in Phoenix. And it was also revealed to us that the retail team had been quite happy with its former agency and thought our "Life's Better Here" strategy was all hype and no substance. I also soon discovered that the retail people pretty much couldn't stand their own brand people.

So, to hear the retail folks out and hopefully ingratiate ourselves to them, I was instructed to fly my newly empowered ass to Phoenix once a week to try to discern how to do ads that would bring the disparate aspects of their business together. Often I'd stay for several days, but as much as possible I'd fly out and back on a red-eye in the same day. After almost fifteen years of marriage, my wife and I were expecting our first child.

In the months that followed, we created some great retail spots that were built upon the "Life's Better Here" brand foundation that the brand people loved and the retail people hated. Then we created some great hardworking retail spots with considerably less attention given to the "Life's Better Here" credo that the retail people loved and the brand people hated. Each group accused us of pandering to the other. I'm sure there was a way to make them all happy, but after three months on the business it was eluding me. High-end branding may have been my specialty, but being a corporate mediator clearly was not.

———

Youth is a wonderful thing in a profession known for eating its old. But if a young person in a position of leadership, especially creative leadership, begins to falter, he can quickly become the meal, too.

The clients from both camps stepped up their complaints about the work. It's amazing how many times I've seen agencies fired because of infighting within the client ranks, and this seemed to be one of those times. At one point, two young creatives who worked under me produced, with my guidance and encouragement, a very funny retail long-distance commercial featuring Rock 'Em Sock 'Em Robots that, in retrospect, probably wasn't the best fit for any part of that client dynamic at that particular time. Too quirky. Too much fun.

Part of the "Rock 'Em Sock 'Em" fallout was that I was told I should stop managing the work of others and do what I did best, which was to create more of my own. I did. Then, just before Christmas, my partner and I sold a flight of new work, a three-spot campaign, that we were scheduled to shoot for three weeks starting on New Year's Day. My wife was eight months pregnant at the time, and neither of us was thrilled by the prospect of another long-term separation.

The lifestyle of an executive at that agency at that time was 24/7/365 (the day I got the new title, I was handed a new phone and a pager, and I'm fairly sure some kind of tracking chip was implanted under my skin). Because my account and the agency were constantly on the precipice of disaster, my days and nights were filled with anxiety. Sometimes I'd wake up at 3:00 a.m. thinking about a line in a commercial for voice messaging (based on the ironic strategy that this communications product would give you more freedom and control in your life), and then, more out of the grip of addiction than the siren call of curiosity or responsibility, I'd check my e-mail.

Invariably, there were messages. An account exec half-drunk in a Denver hotel room setting up a meeting or relaying comments on our latest work, the CEO parsing some upper-level client angst. And of course, I would answer their messages, an act that I'm still ashamed of.

But the only thing more disturbing than answering someone's e-mail at 3:01 a.m. EST is getting a response at 3:02 a.m. EST.

On one flight home from Denver, after an extremely trying series of meetings, I was seated directly behind the indefatigable Mary Lou Quinlan. I ordered a glass of wine, reclined my seat, and opened a novel. The plan was to read and drink myself to sleep, but Mary Lou kept turning around and speaking between the seats, dissecting the day's events. When she sensed that the people around us weren't about to put up with four and a half hours of inter-row ad chatter, she scribbled a note and lobbed it over her head into my lap. The second note landed in my wineglass.

The first sign that I was completely burned-out occurred when, after getting a call on Christmas Eve telling me that the CEO of US West had canceled the best two commercials in our three-spot, potentially career-enhancing shoot with an A-list director (the talented photographer and director Peggy Sirota), I wasn't crestfallen. I was relieved. I would have to be away from home only half as long as I'd imagined. Soon after this I found out that management was bringing in a senior creative executive from Ogilvy to take over the account. I was angry and jealous. The move was clearly a reflection on my performance. The second sign that I needed a time-out was how quickly my anger and jealousy again turned to relief.

Sometimes I wonder how my life would have turned out if we had been wildly and immediately successful with the US West business. If I had solved the retail-brand problem and shot the rest of those spots with Peggy Sirota and made all the clients happy and won awards that would have won us new business, and perhaps helped turn America's first agency around.

But of course, that wasn't the case. Before my daughter was born, I did something that was not common for a male advertising executive in 1998. I told my ambitious, driven, unyieldingly dedicated boss that I was going to take an unpaid yet totally legal three-month paternity leave. I told her I was going to stay at home and enjoy fatherhood. I was going to take a break, a sabbatical, catch my breath, recharge the old batteries.

I knew this would not be a popular or particularly smart career move. Although I was legally entitled to it, it screamed *I give up* to my creative director and to Quinlan, a young (by CEO standards) woman passionately trying to make the most of her shot at advertising stardom and not known for her tolerance of outside commitments, let alone breaks or sabbaticals.* Plus, she was embroiled in high-stakes internal and external political battles that I was oblivious to, and she was fighting for her job every day. Shit was hitting fans of every size and oscillating range in every part of the agency and I was going home to change diapers? So it's understandable to an extent that she would not be pleased, that her response to my words could best be described as looking at me as if I no longer mattered.

Ayer's management team was even less pleased when, three months later, I came back to visit the office to announce that I was going to further exercise my rights under U.S. law and take an additional three months of unpaid paternity leave.

My creative director, who would soon be let go, folded his hands on his desk and told me that this was not a good thing. He told me that because of the way the agency was structured and its current fi-

* More irony. Quinlan would soon stop to smell the roses herself, as evidenced by her 2005 book from this very publisher: *Time Off for Good Behavior: How Hardworking Women [NOT MEN!] Can Take a Break and Change Their Lives.*

nancial situation—not, lawyers note, because of paternity leave!—
they were going to have to let me go. I knew this was coming. In fact,
I already had a job lined up at Y&R. But still, it was no fun being let
go. It had been a flawed, difficult place to work for some time, but
I knew that I'd had my chances—chances that few people my age
were offered at a major agency—and I had failed.

Before I left his office, my creative director, one of the most in-
telligent people I've ever met, said, "You know, at some point you've
got to decide whether you want to be a great adman or a great novelist." Despite his intelligence, I still think this is one of the dumb-
est things anyone has ever said to me.

Three months later I was hired as a creative director at Young &
Rubicam, with the understanding that I would not have to work on
the AT&T business. Three months after that, with the AT&T business on the bubble, I was writing phone ads.

Within three years, and completely unrelated to my departure,
America's first and oldest agency would no longer exist.

A Tale of Two Chickens

Sticking feathers up your butt does not make you a chicken.

—*Chuck Palahniuk*

The Bucket, About to Be Kicked
September 2000

When in the Greater Louisville area, joking about the late Colonel Harland Sanders, let alone expressing a mock desire to break into the corporate vault and steal his secret "original recipe" of eleven herbs and spices,* is akin to joking about yellow-cake uranium on the security line at LaGuardia Airport. And having any kind of fun at the expense of the Colonel at Yum! Brands headquarters, home of the iconic global quick-service restaurants (QSRs) Kentucky Fried Chicken, Pizza Hut, Taco Bell, Long John Silver's, and A&W restau-

---

* According to online conspiracy theorists and fast-food chicken freaks, the ingredients for the recipe are assembled at multiple locations, and the only known copy of the recipe is indeed kept in a vault in the Louisville headquarters. However, most hypothetical versions of the recipe posted online specify that no fewer than three of the eleven herbs and spices are (surprise!) sodium based (table, celery, and garlic salt) and the fourth is that family spice cabinet favorite, MSG (monosodium glutamate).

rants, is the ideological equivalent of handing out wacky caricatures of Muhammad in downtown Riyadh during Ramadan.

I speak from experience.

Not only was I the infidel who made the mistake of saying the unthinkable inside KFC's global base of operations; I had done it within the hallowed halls of the in-house KFC museum, in front of a life-size statue of the Colonel himself.*

The head of the account at my agency shot me a look, as if to say, "What the hell are you thinking?" He had been in the business long enough to have met (and, I imagine, crisply saluted) the Colonel, and he was not pleased. The $175 million account, which our agency had serviced for twenty-three years, was on life support. Sales were down, and the franchisees, dozens of whom were gathering in a conference room on the other side of the building to see the rough cuts of our latest and probably last chance (but my first) at retaining their business, were not happy.

The chief marketing officer looked at the head of the account and shook his head: "That cynical shit won't fly with the franchisees. Mind your smart-mouthed new creative boy."

I held up my hand, a gesture of guilt and apology. "My bad." I assured the account guy that once I got in front of the franchisees, it would be nothing but Kentucky Fried respect and positivity. If necessary, I would prostrate myself before a sarcophagus of the Colonel, the recipe, the franchisees, and the iconic chicken bucket. Plus, fresh off the huge loss of mega-bank, it was in everyone's best interest that I dial down the cynicism.

If necessary, I would even eat and claim to enjoy the taste of their product. This is because, as I'd been briefed, the franchisees

---

* The Colonel, incidentally, did serve in the U.S. Army, but as a private stationed mostly in Cuba during World War I. Sanders, an Indiana native, was given the honorary "Kentucky Colonel" title in 1935 by Governor Ruby Laffoon.

controlled everything. The advertising, the meal combos, and, no matter how much the chief marketing officer or the CEO liked our commercials, the fate of the account.

With fifteen minutes to go before the screening of the new work, I hung my head and moved on to the museum's not-to-be-missed pressure-cooking exhibit.

The Chicken That Changes Everything
April 2004

The chicken that changes everything exists in the living room of a generic, sparsely furnished apartment. Technically, it is a person in a chicken suit rumored to be inspired by the markings of a Rhode Island Red. It stands waiting for your command, flanked by two red easy chairs and a red love seat. There's a scrap of white carpet beneath its ugly chicken feet (is that a silver parolee tracking device wrapped around its left chicken ankle or the more poultry-specific touch of a standard chicken farm leg brand?), a modest TV rests on a stand to the chicken's right, and there's nothing on the walls. To be sure, there's something creepy about the whole thing, which is happening seemingly in real time on your computer monitor. Creepy, yet compelling. Compelling enough to make you type something in the prompt box that urges you, "Type in your command here."

You type: "Dance." The chicken, by God, it starts to dance. Nothing terribly fancy or graceful. Not the moonwalk, or even the chicken dance. More like a drunk forty-seven-year-old at a wedding. In a chicken suit.

You type: "Lay an egg." And there it goes, squatting, miming the laying of an egg. Even if you hate mimes, you decide that this is different: chickens miming on command on your computer should be given a pass.

Next you type: "Choke your chicken." And it cleverly avoids any perverted connotation of the euphemism and grabs itself by the throat.

Then you type: "Masturbate." And the chicken walks the high road directly toward you, leans into the camera, and waves a chicken finger. *Shame on you.*

Welcome to Burger King's Subservient Chicken Web site (subservientchicken.com). To most advertising people, Subservient Chicken, cocreated by the Miami agency Crispin Porter + Bogusky and the interactive wizards of the Barbarian Group in Boston, is a known entity, a frequently cited case history. But it is also a landmark in advertising history, the moment that turned every notion of contemporary branding on its ear, legitimized viral advertising. The day the chicken followed its first command is the day when two of the most dynamic companies in the industry came of age.

Subservient Chicken launched on April 7, 2004. This, technically, is when the Barbarian Group's cofounder and chief operating officer, Rick Webb, posted it on his blog one evening after work. Within forty-eight hours almost fifty million people had visited the unbranded site and had asked the chicken to do everything from the charming to the expected to the obscene.

The average time spent per visit was seven and a half minutes. In other words, people were voluntarily spending the equivalent of fifteen thirty-second TV spots with the Subservient Chicken.

The site, technically for BK's Chicken Tender Crisp, dominated industry talk in the months that followed, and, predictably, the reaction was mixed. While most applauded the gaudy numbers, many questioned the site's relationship to the brand and, more important, its ability to sell chicken. One week into the campaign, the veteran *Advertising Age* columnist Bob Garfield praised the overall creative idea but ultimately panned BK for intentionally obscuring the connection to the brand (for example, no logo, product shot, or tagline) "in order not to seem too commercial and uncool."

By the time Garfield's column ran, visits to the site were being measured in the hundreds of millions, and few people seemed to give a crap if it translated into sales of additional chicken tenders sandwiches. Pundits began talking less about individual product sales and more about "capturing the mind share" of BK's desired audience, specifically the tough-to-reach eighteen- to thirty-four-year-old male.

That year, Subservient Chicken went on to sweep every major interactive award in the industry, Crispin Porter + Bogusky solidified its reputation as one of America's most innovative agencies, and the tiny Barbarian Group was suddenly getting calls from the biggest brands and agencies in the world and being asked to prove time and again that it was anything but a one-hit wonder.

"The chicken was the watershed moment that put us on the map but also the first project that proved that interactive worked," Webb told me during the first of my several visits to the Barbarian Group's new offices in lower Manhattan. "Everyone had these academic theories about viral marketing, but nobody had proven it. They needed a case study that proved that VM could have an impact on the scale of other advertising. The chicken did that."

As we spoke, I thought of the first time I had visited the Subservient Chicken site in 2004. While sitting in my office at Y&R and still smarting from my tour on the KFC account, on a whim I commanded the chicken to eat KFC. The chicken briefly stared at me, then slowly stepped forward, put its finger down its throat, and pantomimed vomiting.

The Author Knowingly Invites His Nineteen-Year-Old Nephew to a Gang Bang
Spring 2000

When an account that has been at an agency for twenty-three years threatens to leave, and that agency is struggling, the agency doesn't put one or two top teams to work on the problem. It has a full-blown gang bang, with every available creative person and team in the agency network working, if things are especially desperate, against multiple strategies. This is how I got recruited into the KFC mess. This is also why I recruited my favorite creative team to work with me and how, once we had a semblance of a half-assed idea, I decided to enlist an advertising virgin into the mix, my nineteen-year-old nephew Joey, who was on summer break from classes at Florida State University and who happened to be a precocious singer, songwriter, and guitarist.

The idea was to create a series of quirky "Chickenquest" visual tales starring a younger slacker demographic. But rather than have on-camera dialogue or a lot of clichéd announcer voice-over, they would be backed by crude musical ditties performed by a comedian/musician, like Adam Sandler. Before we pitched the unformed concept within the agency, I called my nephew, who was mixing cement for my brother at the time, gave him our thoughts, the Adam Sandler–esque direction, and asked him to crank out a few rough demos in his garage that night.

The next day, I played a song called "Dem Bones" for the agency's chief creative officer. It was about an everyman who never went anywhere—art galleries, weddings, romantic dates—without a bucket of original-recipe chicken.

He smiled. "Got anything else?" We did. I played another track called "Chicken Strippy Rendezvous" about love and chicken strips in a tollbooth setting. He smiled again and told me to get my nephew into the agency the next day to do more.

In all, the four of us came up with a half-dozen ditty-backed scenarios that would form one of several campaigns to be presented in the meeting. I was pleased to help round out the presentation. But I was convinced we were a token novelty act whose role was to show the wacky extremes to which our agency was capable of going, mere placeholders for a more conventional agency recommendation turned out by another team. It wouldn't be the first time my work had been used for such a purpose.

On the day of the pitch, when I was called into the room, I did a simple strategic and visual setup for the grim, poker-faced clients gathered in the conference room. Then I told them that ideally we could enlist someone like Adam Sandler to perform the music, but for now I was turning the rest of the presentation over to my nephew, on break from classes at Florida State University and hours removed from a stint as a mason's laborer. When Joey walked into the room with an acoustic guitar over his shoulder and a harmonica around his neck, a funny thing happened.

The stone-faced clients smiled.

Later that day, around 7:00 p.m., long after Joey had taken the train north to my sister's house in the suburbs, the chief creative officer came into my office. "Good job today," he said.

"Glad I could help. How'd it go?"

"They liked your ditties."

"That's good. Are they still gonna fire us?"

"No. They bought your campaign."

"No shit. Did they buy Adam Sandler?"

He shook his head. They didn't like the campaign enough to spend millions on a celebrity. "They bought your nephew."

"Holy shit."

"They're all yours now," he said, and then started to walk away.

"But I don't want them," I called after him. "I never did fast food before. I was just helping out."

"Don't fuck it up," he said.

B.C./A.C.
October 2007

My first visit to Barbarian's new office on Broadway in lower Manhattan, on Halloween, began with my sitting on a lobby couch a little too close to the receptionist, who was coolly trying to locate the cofounder and COO, Rick Webb, who had apparently vapor-locked and was late for our appointment. Just to make sure I wasn't the one who vapor-locked, I opened my laptop and checked some of the lively e-mails we'd been exchanging over the past few weeks, including one from the night before:

ME: We still on for tomorrow?
WEBB: Totally. And I will totally rock.

Not exactly the type of terse online dialogue one would expect from one of the principals of a company that's a frequent cover story in the marketing trades and has won every major advertising award for work above and beyond Subservient Chicken, including *Creativity* magazine's Interactive Agency of the Year (even though Barbarian doesn't consider itself an interactive agency) and the Cyber Lions Grand Prix at Cannes. Then again, the theme line beneath the logo on TBG's Web site reads: "It's gonna be awesome."

All of which is why I didn't mind waiting. I was content to hang out and observe details that I probably wouldn't have noticed if I'd been fully engaged in conducting an interview with someone who was one of the best in the world at something about which I had little understanding. Details such as the work permit posted on the first-floor entry door, or the scrap of tape on the lobby intercom with "Barbarian" penned on it, which denoted that, at least in New York, the Barbarian Group was very much a work in progress. And then there was the young man in the blue tights, cape, and red flower-speckled mask of a superhero whose powers I was not familiar with who rode up in the elevator with me but, alas, got off to fight crime, or pollinate flowers, or make pop-up ads on another floor.

Barbarian's interior decor was similar to that of so many of the newer agencies and production companies I'd been visiting: open floor plan, lots of long, shared worktables covered with Macs and iBooks, conference rooms flanking the sides of a stark communal kitchen tucked into a corner in the back, all somehow projecting a vibe of being progressive, cool, important, socially transparent, and totally perishable, all at the same time.

My second visit to Barbarian began on a better note, in large part because this time my interview subject was actually in the building. When Webb came across the room to meet me, a mop of curly sandy hair, dressed in a baggy black T-shirt and jeans, looking not unlike the actor Seth Rogen in the film *Knocked Up*, he decided that our first nonelectronic communication should be not a hand-shake but a hug.

A group was brainstorming in the main conference room, so Webb took me into a smaller "conference room" that was curiously furnished with two white plastic Ikea chairs that happened to be facing a video monitor with an Xbox 360 and two gaming controllers. Twice while we spoke, twosomes of young employees walked in on us, then pretended they were looking for something other than a gaming fix before glancing longingly at the idle controllers and leaving.

When Webb and the Barbarian cofounder and president, Benjamin Palmer, discuss their company's beginnings, they'll occasionally frame it in terms of B.C. and A.C. Before (Subservient) Chicken and After Chicken. Because, while the Barbarian Group was a viable and emerging young company when it created the chicken work for Burger King, Webb and Palmer are the first to admit that the chicken changed everything. So, in the year 2½ B.C. (November 2001), barely two months after the attacks of September 11, while most of the American business world was hunkered down, trying to figure out what to do next, six talented, disgruntled, and potentially visionary young men, several of whom had been working on the digital side of the highly acclaimed Volkswagen account at Arnold Communications in Boston, decided to open a digital production company. Before settling on the Barbarian Group, the names Pixel, Vector, and Jones were strongly considered.

"We were all fed up with our jobs," Webb explained to me, fondling a gaming controller. "I loved Arnold and VW. They did great work and were the reason I wanted to get into advertising. But we became bored working on one account, just doing the same site over and over again. We had a lingering malaise we couldn't identify, then Ben said: 'This is the wrong model for this work. [The commercial and feature-film director] Michel Gondry isn't bored or sitting at an agency. When he's needed, he's called by the agency and has the freedom to do work for anyone.' "

At first, they worked out of Palmer's loft in Roxbury. Three days into the new venture they got their first assignment, from the Portland, Oregon, agency Wieden+Kennedy, to create a site for its Nike client. On their first company trip the entire staff of seven went to Nike World Headquarters in Beaverton. The night before the meeting, they prepared by attending a Motörhead concert. The next night they went as a group to see *Star Wars: Attack of the Clones*.

Doing work for Wieden+Kennedy and Nike gave Barbarian instant credibility. Also, having Robert Hodgin, one of the most talented people in the country working in the emerging medium of Flash animation, as one of their cofounders helped. The Nike job also validated Barbarian in the eyes of Webb and Palmer's former employer, Arnold, who began to feed them work. This begat an assignment from another elite agency, Goodby, Silverstein & Partners in San Francisco, to create a site for General Motors' Saturn business. Soon they were getting calls from digitally savvy art directors at the most creative agencies in the country to work on premier accounts.

The Barbarian Group had become successful enough that a decision was made to upgrade its office space. So, post-9/11 economy be damned, in April 2002 the staff moved out of Palmer's loft in Roxbury and into Webb's apartment in Allston.

"Actually, the economics in 2001 made the uncertainty of having all of these digital people sitting around an agency very manifest," explained Webb, who had worked as an economist before turning to advertising. "In some ways the downturn helped us, because this whole outsourcing of interactive creative production the same way you do broadcast [television and radio] happened because agencies realized they had to do some belt-tightening."

In many respects, the B.C. years at the Barbarian Group were idyllic. The group was working with a creatively and technologically enlightened cadre of clients and agencies, all of whom "got it": the technology, the Internet, and, most important, the possibilities of the medium. Plus, their new model, which sometimes meant fleshing out an interactive element that complemented an agency's traditional idea for its client and sometimes meant creating an entirely new interactive idea, was working.

Coincidentally, at the same time that Barbarian was seemingly breaking new digital ground every day, on the eve of the chicken that would change everything, I was working at an agency that was not yet getting it, for a client that barely had a Web site, my face pressed against the gates of retail chicken hell.

Don't Be Blaspheming the Colonel
July 2000

For my nephew Joey, this was a special time. Not only had he gotten himself out of a summer in the sticks mixing cement for my brother, but he was working in Manhattan and being paid $350 a day to write silly songs about poultry.

For me, it wasn't quite as special.

We had sold a campaign idea, but we hadn't finalized the individual executions. So this meant spending many hours circled around a speakerphone debating the concepts and the semantics of sweet and tangy and hot and spicy and the difference between crispy and crunchy. Every call began with the lead client telling my team that even though we'd been on the account for a little more than a week, sales were down and the franchisees were getting restless. Every call ended with the head of the account in the agency double-checking that the speakerphone was off before telling us that sales were down, the franchisees were getting restless, and we were all going to be fired if this campaign didn't work.

"Maybe their problem is beyond advertising," I said. "Maybe it's their scuzzy restaurants and incompetent employees. Maybe it's their unhealthy menu, or people are just sick of the Colonel, live, dead, or animated."

Veteran account guy glared at me. I had forgotten that he had met the Colonel and the experience had apparently been life changing, similar to meeting the pope, the Dalai Lama, or Hannah Montana. "Don't you bad-mouth the goddamn Colonel, Jimmy." *Jimmy*. "Listen, I know this business. I know the way chicken works. And I know what the franchisees want."

"Maybe what the franchisees want," I said, "isn't necessarily what is best for them."

In addition to my nephew, some of my favorite people were working with me, good friends but also exceptionally capable professionals, including a young writer and art director team, a producer I had known since my start at N. W. Ayer, and a film editor with whom I'd been friends for more than ten years. Turns out that this was a mistake.

In part, this was because exceptionally capable professionals were not what the account as it was then constituted called for. But more so because it's one thing to be reamed out by an arrogant, ignorant client in front of strangers, and quite another to have it happen in front of respected peers, friends, and relatives, including a nephew who once looked up to me and my supposedly flashy ad job. Several times a day, for several months.

Finally we settled on concepts for three spots, versions of two of the original spots—"Dem Bones" and "Chicken Strippy Rendezvous"—as well as a promotional spot with a jingle that someone else had presented and the client had us shoehorn into our campaign. Next we found a director. Two directors, actually. One was to shoot the live action, and the other, a first for me, was a tabletop specialist, hired exclusively to have his camera make intimate, close-up love to the chicken.

The first part of the filming, for the promotional spot, was at a modest house in a middle-class neighborhood in Rockland County, about fifty miles from Manhattan. We were scheduled to film some interiors, a few backyard-party/eating scenes, and a sequence of teenagers munching out in a moving car we'd tow around the neighborhood in a camera car.

The call time was to be on set at 8:00 a.m., but the client didn't arrive until after 10:00. His plane was late; his driver had gotten lost. He was not happy, and it was obvious that he was not happy with Rockland County or our set, either. If he was going to get out of Louisville, he wanted to be in L.A., staying at Shutters on the Beach or the Sunset Marquis. And if he was going to have to film in New York, a less than spectacular ranch house in the suburbs wasn't going to cut it.

He lit into the set design. The wardrobe. The lighting. The texture of the chicken. The bucket's lack of ubiquity. The account person looked at me. It was usually her job to put him at ease, to change the subject, offer him a fresh smoothie from crafts service, or take him to a nice restaurant. But at times like this the hand-holding job was mine. I explained that we wouldn't see any of the downscale imagery that was troubling him. We were framing the shots to maximize the more interesting aspects of the location. And of course, the chicken. The chicken was looking fantastic. After I said this, the director yelled, "Cut!" and the on-camera talent, a young woman who had just taken a bite of a drumstick, bent over and spit out the half-chewed food. Into a KFC bucket. Which I thought was hilarious. The client, alas, did not.

Next we showed him an abundance of wardrobe and set decoration options. I promised to lose the party streamers, the pink flamingos on the lawn, and the scruffy-faced kid who looked like a junkie. Too downscale. Then we had a sit-down with the line producer from the production company and the food stylist to go over the difference between crispy and crunchy for the millionth time.

It didn't matter. This wasn't L.A., and he did not want to be here. I was surprised, not about the L.A. part, but because this was supposed to be the easiest of the three commercials, a fairly straightforward, quick-turnaround promo spot that we had to get on the air to keep the franchisees at bay until our silly-song campaign was ready to save the day. Simple. No on-camera dialogue, just a bunch of young people at a party getting orgasmic about fried chicken strips and mayo-like goop wrapped in a tortilla. We'd add the food cutaways from the tabletop shoot and score it to the campaign theme song the agency had created, and that would be that. Or not.

After watching another bite-and-chew take that culminated in another contribution to the spit bucket (a sequence we found so hilarious we would make a separate video, scored to the same theme song but for agency eyes only, of pretty people spitting half-chewed chicken into a bucket), the client stormed across the set to accost the director. I turned to the account executive. "How about a cocktail?" I asked. "Is it too early to have crafts service mix him a drink?"

She shook her head. "He's an alcoholic. Recovering. You don't want to go there."

I nodded. Fair enough. "How about a masseuse? Or a hooker?" I asked jokingly. I think. "Or is he a recovering sex addict, too?"

I had never been to a tabletop shoot before. Every spot I'd ever made up to that point had been with a live-action director, or animation, and if a product shot was necessary, the director would simply take extra care to light and shoot it as well as possible. But food is different. QSR is different. And the way the food looks is everything in an ad for a QSR. Even if Scorsese were to shoot the live action, he'd have to defer to a tabletop person on a QSR shoot. Because a good tabletop director can make even the most overprocessed, chemical-laden food appear on your TV screen looking like something you may even want to eat.

So I was semi-excited, or at least mildly curious, as I walked upstairs and into the Chelsea loft to join the tabletop shoot already in

progress. And I use the term "progress" very loosely. When I'd originally looked at the food section of the director's show reel (one of
approximately fifty that we'd screened and debated), I was transfixed
by a montage of glistening shrimp dancing on barbecue grills, monster burgers flipping over open flames, succulent fruit falling from
the sky in erotically choreographed formations. On his show reel,
movement was everything, and it seemed to occur with a freewheeling grace and spontaneity, tossing, spinning, whirling, tumbling, siz-
zling, dripping, and plumping, at once mouthwateringly tempting
and strangely beautiful. So, naturally, I expected to walk in on a carnival of flying food, bass-thumping house music, and a flurry of activity.

Instead, I found the silence of a hospital surgery room and three
account people, an agency art director, and a junior client staring
blankly at a tiny video monitor that had no picture. On a food shoot,
I would soon discover, there was no freewheeling spontaneity; everything was meticulously coordinated and painstakingly considered.
On a food shoot nothing moved. Least of all the camera. I took a seat
next to the zombies and opened a beer. At least the senior client was
gone for the night, back at his Manhattan boutique hotel, prepping
for a gourmet meal with the heads of my agency.

At 7:00 p.m., after two hours of prep, we were invited to look into
the camera to check the lighting and composition of a shot of a
wooden honey dripper seductively rolling a bead of golden honey
along the ridge of a fried chicken strip. At 8:00 p.m., they finally
rolled film, securing the honey-drip shot. At 10:00 p.m., after eating
my sixth (chicken-free) crafts-service meal of the day, I was asked to
sign off on the composition and choreography of the dancing-chili-
pepper shot. At 11:00 p.m., just as we were capturing that small
piece of cinema magic, the studio phone rang. It was the senior

client, back from his exorbitantly priced meal, calling to say that he was on his way downtown to see how things were shaping up.

I looked around, hoping to find a bucket to spit into.

If the World Economic Forum Asked the Subservient Chicken to Solve Earth's Financial Problems, What Would It Do?
Fall 2007

The Subservient Chicken will respond to more than three hundred commands, but when I order it to "deal with sudden fame," it stares at me, shuffling its synthetic chicken feet. When I type "Deal with big-agency, digitally clueless fools who repeatedly ask you to rip off your own idea for their clients," it . . . well, it won't let me type that many characters.

While I was sitting with Rick Webb in the tiny Xbox-equipped conference room, Ben Palmer, Barbarian's president and cofounder, stepped in to ask Webb a question. "First," Webb said, "tell the story about how our clients changed after the chicken."

"Well," Palmer began, "we had started under the assumption that our clients had heard of the Internet and were smart. But after the chicken this was no longer the case."

Webb added, "Our clients started out as ten guys around the country who got us. Then it all changed. It went from 100 percent of the clients getting us/*it* to only 20 percent who actually knew what to do with the Net."

After the chicken, the Barbarian Group was written up in *BusinessWeek,* the *Wall Street Journal,* the trades. "We had grown organically for two years," Webb continued, "working with [progressive, creatively driven agencies like] Crispin and Fallon and Wieden and Mother, but everything changed when the mainstream found us."

"Our whole M.O. was to be really excited about everything," said Palmer. "But because we actually were, we overdid it and gave too much." Coming from any other ad-type executive, a statement like this would smack of insincerity, but when almost whispered by the slight, sleepy-eyed Palmer, whom one agency head who has worked with him described as "a lovable guy who looks like a stoner but who just blurts out these amazing, visionary things," it's almost believable.

"We weren't set up to deal with ad people in big agencies that didn't get the Internet," Webb explained. "We had never worked with any of them, and most were using broadcast [TV and radio] producers to oversee interactive projects . . ."

Palmer finished Webb's thought: "Which is fucked."

"We hadn't set out to, but we were starting to become like one of those agencies. We never got into business to get as much work as we can. My business plan was in five years we sell to Omnicom. We've long since abandoned it."

"In part," Palmer said, "because I'm ridiculously unemployable."

Webb shook his head. "Dude, you were on the cover of *Ad Age*. You could get a job."

"Oh, yeah. I could get a job. But I would totally quit. I want to make money in a way that is enjoyable. Work with cool people who are inspired. This is like a big sandbox where we can experiment with the future, with computers and brands, which are really exciting."

Before he left, Palmer tugged at his T-shirt, then showed Webb something he'd made for the company's Facebook page. Watching them, I found it hard to believe that these two had as much if not more influence on the future of advertising as any suit in a Madison Avenue corner office.

"Anyway," Webb continued after Palmer left, "we had reached a point where we needed to do a lot of soul-searching. Were we kind of blindly turning into an agency, or a production shop? Plus, the digital realm was changing. We were one of the first, but now there's like forty digital production companies. Then factor in outsourcing to India or Brazil, where they turn out some of the work for a quarter of the money. We were busy, but it had totally become a race to the bottom where we were just underbidding each other."

So rather than sell out to a conglomerate or soldier on as a thriving, successful digital production company serving mostly agency clients looking for Chicken 2.0, Barbarian's five partners spent more than six months trying to figure out what they wanted to become next.

"We figured we might as well go for it and do what we believe in," Webb said. "So in the last six months we've been broadening our interests, and have almost sold as much in the first quarter of '08 as we did in all of '07."

Webb said much of this had to do with letting the leaders of the company do what they do best. For instance, he said, "With Ben. He is so good at inspiring people. Agency people. VPs at Viacom. He'll just blow people away in meetings with these extraordinarily visionary ideas—for instance, we just spoke at the World Economic Forum in Tokyo—but we needed someone to follow up and close those deals, which is why we've hired a corps of client-service people."

The World Economic What? In Tokyo? I tried to picture Webb and Palmer in T-shirts and jeans speaking in front of the most powerful financial figures in the world. "No fucking way."

"Way."

"About what?"

"The convergence of media, entertainment, and advertising. And it was awesome."

"So then," I asked, "what are you now, if not a digital agency, after the six months of soul-searching? And what is it that you're 'going for,' that you believe in?"

"Oh," Webb said, smiling, rubbing his hands. "So many people are terrified of all of this, convergence, digital advertising, the future of TV and music, because they don't completely understand it. But that's exactly what makes us so excited, the uncertainty. We want to play in all of those areas, media, entertainment, and advertising. And it's gonna be . . ."

Critical Mass
August 2000

"Fucking horrible."

We were sitting on couches at the editor's suite in Chelsea. The client, my boss, the head of the account, and a managing partner at the agency were there, too, and we had just previewed rough cuts of the three commercials. I waited for someone to speak, but no one did. Finally I said, "I think they're really funny. In fact, I think they're unlike anything in the category."

The senior account guy shot me another look. The managing partner glared at me. Who wants to be unlike anything in the category? The goal, I was beginning to realize, was to be just like everything in the category, which, with this account, would be a marked improvement.

According to the client, the basic problem was too much humor and story, not enough food. The logo was too small, the price point came up too quietly and was also too small. And the food, there was not enough footage of the food. Where was all that beautiful film we'd shot of chicken and honey and chili peppers? After some discussion, the editor, my friend, trimmed some of the scenes that the client called superfluous. We lengthened food shots, zoomed in closer on the chicken, and increased the size of the price offer of so many pieces for $3.99. Still the client was not satisfied. "This isn't

working," he said. "And we have to get this in front of the franchisees in a few days."

We spoke some more. I stood up for the work. "We can't just run
thirty seconds of food footage, can we?"

He looked at the people in charge of me and then at me. "I've
got a flight to catch. You know what I'm looking for."

This is probably a good time to discuss why many, if not most, ads
suck.

Why don't we see clever, entertaining, Super Bowl–quality,
award-winning work all the time? Why didn't the leaders of the
agency take a stand, as they seemingly do at all the great agencies,
and tell the client to chill out, to fuck off, to trust us?

In this case, I imagine that at more than one time during the
long relationship between this client and our agency, when sales
were up with the client and the agency was thriving, people would
have taken more of a stand. People would have said, "Trust us, we
know best." But, as previously mentioned, sales at KFC had been in
the tank for a while, and my agency, once a blue-chip new-business-
winning global force, was on a prolonged losing streak. On top of
that, my group within the agency had already recently lost the huge
financial-services mega-bank client, and our once independently
owned company was now part of a holding company that answered
to stockholders.

People had told me more than once that in the current climate,
this would be an especially bad thing, to lose a high-profile, longtime
client. "Whatever it takes" are three words that were often spoken in
my presence.

But what about me? Just because the agency was willing to
lower its standards and subject itself to daily humiliation, putting
profit before integrity, did that mean I had to as well? Good ques-

tion, and one I asked myself on my way home from Manhattan every day. One answer is that I set out, as I always did, with the best intentions and goals: do great work and make the agency money, and hopefully some of it will trickle your way. When we sold the initial work, I was wary but excited. It wasn't groundbreaking, but it was different, and fun, and potentially very good. When it became apparent that most of the originality and humor of the presented work were going to slowly be sucked out of the campaign, I protested, but I probably could have protested a bit more, or at least more convincingly. Or I could have asked off of the account. Or I could have quit, leaving behind my friends, my peers, and my nephew to clean up the mess.

But I didn't bail, in large part because I didn't want to let down my friends and coworkers and I had a family and a mortgage and I knew that there were not many places left out there that would pay me enough to support the lifestyle we were enjoying. Also, I'm fairly sure none of my solutions would have mattered.

I knew I was in this position as a direct result of every assignment I had ever taken, every job I had ever held, every raise I'd ever accepted, and every time I declined an offer to move to another city, to take a pay cut to work at the hot shop du jour, or to break free and open up a shop of my own. I was hardly a victim.

Somehow my once-thriving agency had become one of those agencies that had given Webb and Palmer the chills, too big, too comfortable, and not particularly innovative, and somehow I had become one of those guys who worked at one of those agencies.

A Barbaric Vision of the Future

On my final visit to the Barbarian Group, I was met in the waiting area by a woman with two black eyes wearing a black short-peaked cap. In addition to being Barbarian's director of public relations and new business, Eva McCloskey is also a member of the Boston-based Roller Derby league the Boston Derby Dames. After telling me that Rick and Benjamin would be with me shortly, McCloskey, who skates under the name "Evilicious," explained that she injured her nose in a bout several weeks earlier but hoped to be back on skates soon.

When I told McCloskey that I'd returned to check up on the progress of several ongoing projects, but mostly to pick Webb's brain about some of his and Barbarian's provocative views on the future of advertising and branding, she took a deep breath as she considered the combination of a writer with a micro-recorder and her outspoken visionary partners. Keeping them in line (not insulting current clients) while discussing their views of the future would take all of her Roller Derby jamming expertise. "You know what?" she said. "I think I'll join you."

Back in the mini conference room I asked Webb for an update on the non-advertising projects Barbarian was working on. In short order he rattled off a handful of projects, including an installation art exhibit, a collaboration with twelve agencies for UNICEF's 2008 Tap Project water-conservation effort, a plan to save the music industry, and the2husbands.com, an irreverent Web reality show in which two men, one of whom happens to be gay, seek the perfect wife.

"Advertising was the first mover to worry about the Internet as a revenue-generating platform," Webb explained. "It didn't have to work transactionally for advertisers at first, but they knew they had to be there. But there are many other industries that need help with interactive. The networks. The movie houses. Publications . . . periodicals are totally screwed on the Internet. So we thought, 'Why are we limiting ourselves to brands when all these other industries need help?' Agencies don't touch them. It starts at the consulting level and then goes further. Online-marketing strategy, developing content and properties. Plus, there are whole industries that don't talk to each other. Some have content but don't know where to go. Others have brand equity but don't know how to use it on the Web."

Why? "Fear. Uncertainty freaks so many people out, but we think it's fucking awesome, all the changes happening because of the Internet. We love change. That's why we decided to become Internet geeks."

This is reiterated in a call-out on their new Web site that reads, "An almost radical devotion to Internet culture and nice red Swedish Fish™."

This all sounded cool and empowering and, as the kids like to say, hep. But, I asked, isn't all this digital work actually more intrusive and dangerous than "traditional" ads? Isn't the Internet just another pipe through which marketers can pump more insidious, nuanced, and targeted messages?

Webb shook his head. "To experience a traditional ad, all I have to do is open my eyes. In an airplane, car, bedroom, work, et cetera. I just have to look, and there it is, screaming at me. On the Web, aside from banner advertising, I pretty much have to *decide* to experience a marketing message. I have to click on that banner, I have to visit that Web site, I have to add that Facebook app or watch that viral video. I have to start the engagement. And therefore advertisers have to incent me to do so, the same way they incent me to visit their showroom. Think of VW ads—jarring, in-your-face, edgy. They have to be, because they have to catch my attention. Now think of their showrooms. Clean, friendly, inviting, with nice couches and coffee. Because they have to be, because they have to convince me to come in. Interactive advertising *is* the showroom.

"This manifests itself in gifts of entertainment, branded utilities, coupons, discounts, honest information, helpful tools like configurators and comparison guides. Things I need and want. Things that would sway me to take action. This is what online advertising is all about."

Do most brands look at it this way? Do most brands get this?

Webb laughed, and now Palmer, who had just entered the room, laughed, too. Palmer said, "I see the Internet as a way of taking advertising back from the evil assholes," and McCloskey shuddered just a bit.

I asked where they thought the next breakthrough in online marketing would come from, and Webb said, "MMO: massively multiplayer online gaming. Go online and check out World of Warcraft. Eighty to ninety million people are spending like seventy dollars a month to be on it. Billions of dollars is in play every month, and everyone is trying to crack it, to apply a marketing model to it."

To a game?

"The whole concept of brands and branding is somewhat archaic," Webb said. "In fact, I think that branding as we know it is gonna die."

The Death of Branding?

It sounds radical and subversive, but when I think about the etymology of the word "brand" in contrast to the evolution of digital advertising, Webb and Palmer's hypotheses are worth considering: in Old English, the noun *bround* is first attested from the epic poem *Beowulf*, meaning "destruction by fire." In the old West, cattle were branded with the mark of a specific ranch. Brands were originally created as labels of identification and ownership. For hundreds of years, brands have spoken to people, and people have not been invited to speak back.

Now with the Internet, people are speaking back to brands. The smarter brands are listening, while others are choosing to ignore or suppress the input of consumers, especially dissenters. Commercials are critiqued online. Products are reviewed online. "It's getting to the point," Webb said, "where you have to wonder why companies are spending a hundred thousand dollars to focus-group a commercial when a hundred thousand people are already blogging about it online. Branding as we know it is gonna fade away."

"In some ways, I agree," I told him. "I can see the death of branding, the verb. But brands and the word 'brand' will live on as a noun. Coke won't go away. The Golden Arches won't die. But those brands/nouns won't just be defined by the company that owns them, but by the consumers who interact with it as well."

We agreed to continue this conversation, fittingly, online.

"Agencies have spent the last few decades refining brands," Webb wrote. "But no matter what they did, in the end, wherever they netted out, that brand became inviolable. It was enshrined in a 'bible'—I have literally dozens of these sitting in my office. And each one shares the same basic belief: that the brand can't be violated."

Once, Webb spent six months trying to get a logo approved on a pixel-animated-style video game for a major brand. "Six months. Because they were totally freaked because their brand bible had not accounted for a pixel version of the logo."

Analog brand rigidity will not cut it in a digital, transparent world. With the Internet, consumers suddenly have the ability to talk back in numbers too vast for PR and advertising to control. "We still see companies grappling with this now. PR firms are abuzz with new techniques on how to handle blogs, and CMOs are wigging out about the bad PR a blog can generate."

What's a brand to do? Openly enter a dialogue with consumers online, embracing transparency and hopefully nurturing goodwill? Or go the Whole Foods route, where the CEO unsuccessfully masqueraded as a regular blogger trying to influence opinions? " 'Engagement' is starting to come up as a buzzword," Webb continued.

"But I think it's something more. When I think of 'engagement,' and when I hear a CMO use it, I generally hear it in terms of time someone is thinking about my brand. I don't hear it in the context of *dialogue*. We're going to have to accept that this dialogue is more important than anything else. This dialogue is, in fact, the new brand. The way you converse and communicate with your consumers *is* your brand positioning."

Webb then recounted a recent brand experience of his own with the Zipcar rental company. He complained via e-mail that if he could no longer get a car on weekends, he would abandon the brand. He told me it was the kind of e-mail that "most companies ignore and most consumers seethe inwardly over about how useless the exercise is. But amazingly, the freakin' CMO of Zipcar himself e-mailed me back. Not once, but something like ten times. One customer. I will never leave that company."

Rather than pass the e-mail along to someone in PR, or make up an excuse, or ignore Webb's complaint completely, Zipcar engaged in a conversation. "No brand bible can guide this," Webb said. "Principles guide this. Communication principles that accept, encourage, and reward conversation."

Rigid, one-way, inviolable branding is no longer possible. The Internet killed it. Interesting stuff from someone who doesn't think of his company as an ad agency or an interactive agency.

And not one word about chickens. Kentucky Fried, subservient, or other.

The Bucket, Kicked, Repeatedly
Fall 2000

I have presented work before CEOs of Fortune 500 companies, four-star generals in the U.S. Army, hundreds of salespeople at soft drink bottlers' conventions, and even George Steinbrenner, but nothing quite prepared me for the more than fifty KFC franchisees gathered in the main conference room at Yum! Brands headquarters in Louisville.

They had been arriving all morning, some in white stretch limousines, some in Cadillacs, many in personal cars adorned with some iteration of a chicken-themed vanity plate. Senior account guy presented himself before them all as if they were visiting heads of state. Sometimes he would turn to me and whisper, "He owns more than a hundred," or "He controls the entire Southwest voting bloc," or "Make sure you make eye contact with that one when you speak . . . he's already pushing for a move to [Pizza Hut's agency of record] BBDO, and a no vote from him can bring the whole thing down."

We had to wait outside while the franchisees discussed and voted on a number of business issues. After a half hour the double doors opened and senior client guy looked at me and said, "You're on." The first thing I noticed when I walked inside was that they had changed the configuration of the entire room. They had moved the conference tables into a square. So instead of standing at a podium in front of the assembled purveyors of poultry, I was ushered into a small, podiumless square through a gap in the tables that closed behind me. Like a trap.

I looked out at the franchisees and made a joke about feeling as if I were testifying before both houses of Congress. Of course, no one laughed. Moving right along, I began to deliver a short talk about the work they were about to see, how excited we were about it. I shared what I erroneously thought was a humorous anecdote from the set. I had been certain that I could charm them and win them over before they even saw their commercials, but I was interrupted by a voice to my right. It was the known enemy of the agency, He Who Had the Power to Bring It All Down. "Just show us the danged work," he yelled, even though I was less than six feet away. I smiled and attempted to continue, but someone else spoke. "Yeah. Let's see the commercials." I'm fairly sure that someone said, "Hear! Hear!" and I'm absolutely certain that several of them began rapping on the table.

I pushed play. But what I was really doing was pulling the trigger on a pistol pressed against the temple of the account.

To avoid rewinding, I'd had the commercials looped so we could watch each one three consecutive times. There was grumbling midway through the first spot. By the middle of the second commercial, the grumbling had risen to a low roar that made it difficult to hear the words to the songs, the silly chicken songs that were the campaign's main creative idea. But they didn't care about music, or words or stories, they wanted to see chicken and price points, and what was on the screen before them was not at all acceptable. Even though we had already zoomed in on and extended every bit of chicken footage and bumped up the type size of their offers several times, it was not enough for the franchisees. No one even bothered to listen to the commercials as they played a second time. Bedlam had broken out. Factions formed. Franchisees shouted one another down like senators in the chamber on the eve of the Civil War. Senior account guy glared at me. Senior client guy glared at me. "I told you so." I snuck out of the square and out into the hallway. The doors to the franchisee meeting closed, never to open for me again.

A week later we ran the straightforward, heavily edited commercials. Rather than showing charming stories set to quirky music, they were almost wall-to-wall chicken, backed by songs that made little sense taken out of context. It may take several weeks to declare a winner of a presidential election, but in the fall of 2000, franchisees could report on in-store sales at the end of every day that the commercials ran. And sales were not good. In fact, they were flat or down across the country. It could have been the economy, or a change in America's eating habits, or a changing perception of the chain that had been developing for years. But in their eyes, it was all about the ads. Every morning we gathered around the speakerphone for the bad news and then set out for the editor's studio in search of a Kentucky Fried miracle.

Thankfully, by this point, my nephew had returned to school.* So at least I could take solace in the fact that a good portion, if not all, of his tuition was being paid for with chicken money. A few weeks later, just before we were about to leave for Vancouver to shoot their next commercial, we got the news. After twenty-three years at our agency—from "Finger Lickin' Good" through our latest theme line, "How good is that?"—they were firing us.

Out of curiosity, while writing this, I went to KFC's Web site to see if they had evolved and were having what Webb called real dialogue with consumers, or if they were using twentieth-century branding in a twenty-first-century medium. One of the first pages I saw featured a chicken bucket filled with roses and the headline "Take a Tour of the Hippest Shop on the Block."

Incidentally, in China, where there are now more than twelve hundred KFC franchises, "Finger Lickin' Good" translates to "Eat Your Fingers Off."

How good is that?

*My nephew, Joey Spallina, despite numerous warnings against it, has gone on to become a successful commercial composer and sound designer, not to mention a solo recording artist.

The Healing Power of Yogurt

My job was to make logos bigger. Once the logo got big
enough, they would have a meeting. Then I would move the
logo up or down, or to the right or to the left. Finally, I would
be told to make the headline bigger. Because compared to the
logo, it was now too small.

—*Hal Riney*

Only the Muffin Remains

One afternoon in the winter of 2001, shortly after the Kentucky
Fried Chicken client had fired us, which was shortly after our mega-
bank client had fired us, ending what for me had been six months of
unprecedented daily torture and humiliation, my boss called me into
her office.

Her boss, the creative director of the agency, had left her office
just a few minutes earlier, so I knew something was up. While I
stood in her doorway, waiting for her to get off the phone, I peeked
down the hall to see if there were any clipboard-toting HR geeks
coming to make sure that my exit interview would be done in a
legally safe way, or if they had security guards at the ready to escort
me from the building, or subdue me in case I went bonkers. But the

coast was clear, and since I was white, straight, and not yet forty years old, I guess they felt I wouldn't have a whole lot of ammunition for any kind of discrimination case.

As usual, my boss was smoking a cigarette, even though smoking inside corporate office spaces had been banned in New York City buildings for years, and as usual upon her desk sat a blueberry muffin that looked as if it had been briefly nibbled upon by a sparrow.

So, I thought, this is the end. The end of this job at least, and perhaps the end of something larger. Advertising. Commuting. Climbing. Hell, it had been a good run. That's what I'll tell her, after she gives me the news. Some high-road shit like that.

And maybe it was time for a change. Maybe it was the proverbial blessing in disguise. Blah, blah, blah. Plus, I couldn't really blame her for this. She'd hired me, and for the last few years she'd done a decent job of protecting and compensating me. Often that meant having me work on things she'd told me I'd never work on, but shit happens. Everything changes when you lose business, and in the past year our group had lost two of the agency's largest accounts.

"Maybe I'll get a good package." Looking for a place to sit, I wondered why every day she had her assistant place a blueberry muffin on her desk even though she never ate it. Wouldn't you think at some point one of them would have put an end to it, or at least switched from blueberry to carrot?

"Maybe I'll make more and stress less doing freelance."

Usually I plopped down on a couch as far away from the smoke as possible, but that wouldn't do for this kind of conversation. This time I decided to sit on the other side of her desk, within pecking distance of the muffin. Before my ass touched the chair, I had already determined that after she gave me the news, I would take the damned muffin with me on the way out the door.

"I guess you saw who just left my office."

I nodded. "The grim reaper."

As she puffed her cigarette, I thought of the first time we'd met more than ten years earlier, when we both worked at another agency, N. W. Ayer. She was the young creative star of the place, smart, energetic, always laughing, and selling good work to big clients. It was no surprise to any of us when she left the agency to assume this powerful new job. When she called to ask me to join her at Y&R, I was flattered. But in the two years that I'd worked with her, although she was still full of energy, her laughter had changed. Less joy and more anxiety. In the two years we'd been together, a series of grueling battles to save disgruntled accounts, frequently working late nights and weekends, we had both aged like wartime presidents. "Well," she continued, "you know we haven't exactly been on a winning streak."

I nodded impatiently. Just tell me. I can take it.

"The bank. Now KFC."

"I know. I understand."

"So . . . I'm going to be leaving the agency." ·

"You mean *I'm* going to be leaving the agency."

"No, I am."

"But me too, right?"

She dragged on her cigarette, pecked at her muffin for the second-to-last time. "No, you're staying. You're gonna work on yogurt."

Several weeks earlier I had jumped in and contributed some work for a pitch for a diet-yogurt presentation. My storyboards didn't win, but the head of the account and the client liked my presentation enough to ask me if I wanted to run the business.

"I'm shocked," I told my soon-to-be ex-boss. "I thought if anyone, it was gonna be me. Are you all right?"

She smoked, then picked at but did not eat any more of the muffin. "I'll be fine," she said. "How about you?"

"Yogurt?"

"Yep."

"I don't think it's a very good idea. I think they saw me on a happy day, when I decided to ramp up the charm."

I stood up. She came around the desk and we hugged. We respected and liked each other, but the hug, it was awkward. After we let each other go, she noticed me looking at her desk, at the muffin.

"You want?"

I sure did. But I thought it best to leave it where it was.

Active Cultures

The client was in Westchester. Less than a half hour from three things I had not seen much of in the last several years: my house, my wife, and my two-year-old daughter. So for the first time in my career, after avoiding unnecessary client interaction at all costs, I became a big believer in going to meetings at the client's place. Instead of schlepping an hour and a half each way to Manhattan every day, I had a nearby alternative. At the time they had at least five active sub-brands and another three in development, and they had meetings for everything. Package design. Rough cuts. Voice-over recommendations. Testing results. I needed to be there. I was all over all of it.

The client applauded my attention to detail. The head of the account applauded my commitment to the business. And my family applauded the fact that I was able to join them for the occasional dinner before 8:00 p.m.

Who cared if the account was looked upon in the agency as a creative wasteland, a packaged-goods penal colony run by detail-obsessed brand managers, fastidious logo police, and a den-mothering account supervisor? I was beginning to feel half-human.

———

My first task was to oversee production of a commercial for the client's flagship fruit-on-the-bottom product. The ad had been created and presented before I took over the account, and in focus groups its animatic—a rough cartoon version of the spot we'd eventually film—had scored higher than any other spot they had ever tested. The reasons for the high score were not hard to figure out: it featured a bunch of handsome construction workers sitting on a girder (sex), plenty of close-ups of the yogurt (taste), and an upbeat popular song from the 1970s (fun).

After a meeting in which the client agreed to go ahead and full-up produce the commercial, I asked the creative team, two women who had been on the account for a while, to keep me updated as the production progressed. I told them I would try to stay out of their hair. They had more than enough talent and experience to handle it.

One day they came to my office with their producer and told me that they had found a director.

"Great."

"He's from South Africa."

I'd worked with lots of directors from South Africa. "Okay."

"And he wants to shoot in Johannesburg."

"Why? We could shoot that spot on a lot in Queens, at Silvercup [Studios]."

The producer spoke up. "If we shoot over there, they'll save more than two hundred thousand dollars in talent. There's no on-camera speaking parts, and if it pisses off the unions, they can't do anything, because technically it's a global spot."

The three of them were single, and friends. If they wanted to get a trip out of this, and save money, who was I to stop them? I watched the director's reel. It was decent. A little artsy for a packaged-goods spot, but if he wanted to shoot it, good for us. The producer told me that the agency had recently used the production company for a shoot for another client and everyone was happy.

"Fine. Only thing is I'm not gonna fly seventeen hours to Johannesburg just to go to a pre-pro meeting, so you're on your own." This news did not seem to bother them.

The next day the creative director of the agency, the man who had recently laid off my boss, knocked on my door. "So how's the construction-worker shoot going?"

I gave him an update and offered to show him the director's reel, but he waved it off. He said he totally trusted me. Which meant he'd already had the producer run it by him without telling me. "So when are you going to Johannesburg?"

"Actually, the client will only pay for two creatives, and I thought it was only fair that the team that did the work should make the trip."

He stood up and looked out my window. Obviously he knew all of this and had discussed it with the head of the account, who, because of my newly acquired obsessive desire to attend client meetings, was still under the impression that I was a responsible adult and therefore my presence was essential to the success of the shoot. Under normal circumstances I would have jumped at a trip like this and would have tried to bring my family with me. But not this time. My wife was in the middle of a major work project. Plus, we weren't thrilled about the prospect of having to get shots for our two-year-old, or that we'd be going to Johannesburg and not the safer, more tourist-friendly coastal city of Cape Town. Also, it meant I'd be gone for Mother's Day, and in my wife's family every holiday—Christmas, Easter, Groundhog Day, and especially Mother's Day—was sacred. So for all these reasons, I did not want to go.

"Do you want me to go?"

"That's your decision," he said. He walked back into the hall and turned. "But if it fucks up in any way, it's your sorry ass."

A week later me and my sorry ass were on a jet headed to Cape

Verde and then on to Johannesburg while one very pissed-off copy-writer and my slightly less angry family ("On Mother's Day—and you said you could shoot it in Queens!") were back in New York.

There wasn't a lot for me to do once I got to Johannesburg. A few hours a day for the first two days I hung out with the agency producer, the agency art director, and an account guy, watching casting sessions, picking through wardrobe possibilities, and checking out the location, which in our case was the roof of an abandoned parking lot in the burned-out center of downtown Johannesburg. On the second prep day the director shared his shooting board with us. The rest of the day was all ours.

The production company had assigned us a young chaperone named David who drove us throughout Greater Johannesburg, taking us to quirky restaurants, out-of-the-way art galleries, sporting events, and markets that we would not have dared to visit on our own. As he answered my questions about politics, music, writing, and America, the adman never stopped scribbling notes, like a journalist, and then, later in my room, I'd ponder their meaning, like a novelist.

The next day we had our preproduction meeting via videoconference with the clients and agency folks back in the States. This included the mandatory passionate discussions about quotidian things like how scuffed the work boots should be, how many days of growth construction worker number four should have, and, of course, the many ways in which the product would be filmed.

If my presence in South Africa was at all justified, it was because of the way I coached the director about how to talk yogurt footage with the client. "You cannot spend too much time talking about color, texture, and consistency. The way the spoon dips in, the swirl, the drip, should be discussed with love and a touch of eroticism. To the client this is a ten-second piece of soft-core pornography about a camera making love to a seven-ounce cup of yogurt, book-ended by a logo shot and sixteen seconds of incidental human activity." He nailed it. The picture quality coming from New York was fuzzy, but I was fairly sure that when the director lovingly described the succulent fruit spooned up from the bottom of the yogurt cup, a tear rolled down the chief marketing officer's cheek.

Next Stop, Hell

Even in the most exclusive neighborhoods of Southern California, a full-blown commercial television shoot can seem decadent and excessive.

Now imagine taking a set with all the perks and trimmings of the most lavish of American productions—air-conditioned trailers, an on-set masseuse, and a gourmet crafts-service staff that hand-delivers everything to you from fresh smoothies and sushi to wine and lobster tails—and plunking it down on the roof of an abandoned parking garage in a decimated section of downtown Johannesburg.

Now imagine that you're on just such a set, and from America, circa 2000, and slightly disoriented, and completely hungover, and you're looking over the edge of said parking garage at thousands of black workers waiting in maddening queues five stories below for buses to take them to low-paying jobs in the white suburbs, and try to keep yourself from feeling like you will soon be going straight to hell.

Hypothetically, of course.

It went on all day, the desolation below and the $350,000 production above. There were arguments, of course, about the level of love and attention given to the swirl shot of the yogurt, or whether or not someone would use silverware on a construction site. Sides were taken. Interventions were made. Entreaties for peace went ignored. The client felt as if I had let him down. The director didn't want to talk to me anymore. In the eyes of the client I was afraid of the director. In the eyes of the director I had sold my soul to the god Acidophilus.

Between setups I called my wife. As we spoke, I looked across the street at a billboard next to a burned-out building, squatters gathered around a campfire below. The billboard featured a picture of glistening skyscrapers and had this headline: JOHANNESBURG CENTRAL BUSINESS DISTRICT: THE FUTURE IS NOW!

I asked to speak with my daughter, and told her that I'd be home soon. When I hung up, I took out the tiny Instamatic camera I'd purchased at the airport and aimed it over the side of the building, away from our production. I wanted to get the juxtaposition of the squatters and the bullshit billboard. I clicked, even though I knew it wouldn't come out. I knew it would develop as a vague speck in an undefined space.

From Russia, with Nanoabsorbers™

> The greatest problem with communication is the illusion that
> it has been accomplished.
>
> —*George Bernard Shaw*

Hello, Kitty

Turd-shrinking cat food.

This was what six relatively sane adults and I were talking about,
or getting an education about, at seven o'clock at night, hunkered
over a tinny speakerphone as siren wails rose up from the gloomy
crevasse of Madison Avenue seven floors below, drowning out the
voices of six other presumably sane adults, enlightened turd-
shrinking-cat-food experts all, hunkered over a tinny speakerphone
of their own. In Tokyo.

It's a big deal over there, a Japanese-accented speakerphone
voice told us, the shrinking of the animal turds. I thought that this
is probably because they live in cramped quarters in Japan, tiny, im-
maculately maintained structures where every extra fecal milligram
matters. I thought for a moment about the brilliant, white-smocked
team of scientists and chemists who had been charged with creating
the product—the careful measuring of the various turds with

calipers, comparing and contrasting shape and consistency with previous samples—I decided that their job was only slightly more humiliating than the one I was about to be given.

As the briefing continued, I began to conjure a product demo. I envisioned an animated shot of the inside of a cat's intestine, where an alarmingly inflamed log magically shrinks, changing from an angry, large, home-wrecking orange mass into a tranquil, adorable little lavender-colored turd that wouldn't think of encroaching upon one's precious Japanese personal space. I thought of *Turd vs. Godzilla*, engaged in mortal (to the extent that shit has a life) combat, high above the flashing video billboards of the Ginza district.

Maybe, I thought, we could ask the animators behind *The Powerpuff Girls* to design it. That could be cool. Then a more rational part of me thought, no. It would not be cool. It could never be even remotely cool. There is nothing cool about cat shit or, for that matter, anyone who has anything to do with the calibration of its size or shape or the style in which it might be animated.

Technically, I was in this meeting because my new boss, a Manhattan-based French global creative director, liked the doctoring I had performed earlier in the week with a Brazilian hair-ball-formula script. I wish I could remember more details about the Brazilian hair-ball-formula script (did it involve a thong, caipirinhas, and hair balls at Carnival?), but sometimes the brain does the conscience a favor and builds a wall around moments that can potentially destroy the soul.

Technically, I was there because my Brazilian hair-ball scriptectomy was all the proof my new boss needed to get me on the phone with a group of people from an island nation six thousand miles away who were breathlessly waiting to hear my thoughts on how to save their bullshit cat-shit commercial.

But the real explanation for how I ended up in this meeting is much more complicated. Twenty years' worth of complicated, the short version of which is that a once enthusiastic and promising young copywriter turned cynical, existential creative director was in his mid-forties and burned-out, his 125-year-old telecom client gone (recently absorbed by another telecom client with an agency of its own), the person who courted, hired, and championed him long gone, and his employer had run out of places to put him.

More than once I had mentioned to the manager of the creative department that if there happened to be another round of layoffs coming, and if they were looking for volunteers to take some kind of package, I had a "friend" who might be interested in starting another chapter in his life.

But I was told, "No way." After years of thinking I was going to get laid off, I was suddenly, if not indispensable, at least worth keeping around. Maybe I wasn't an ad legend, but I was a "writer's writer." An "in-house poet." And suddenly deemed beloved, apparently, by someone who mattered. It's as if they thought that anyone talented or crazy enough to want to leave a high-paying job in this economy must be truly special and just the kind of person they couldn't afford to lose.

The plan, I was told, was to put me to work as the North American creative director for our huge packaged-goods client—a.k.a. the world's largest maker of stuff you put in your medicine cabinet (not to mention turd-shrinking, hair-ball-eliminating cat foods)—where there was plenty of work and a short-term need for senior leadership, until another assignment came along that was a better fit for my skills.

So there I was, thinking, "This cat food is not about the cat at all. It's all about the owner, who could care less about what chemicals his beloved Tuffy-san ingests as long as the turds are tidy." Thinking, "These people are incredibly stupid, but then again they were smart enough to figure out how to make me fix their 'Honey, I Shrunk the Turd' spot." And thinking, "In addition to going to People Hell for this, now we'll surely have to do time in Pet Purgatory."

And this favorite, even though I knew the answer: "How did I end up here?"

I looked at the account guy next to me who had multiple degrees, had done some kind of fellowship in London, and had a sharp, seemingly rational mind. Then I looked at the creative team across from me that had been led to believe that the cynical old bastard across from them was going to become their boss, their unwanted mentor, two funny, talented, and much-abused young men, one of whom had hung out in college with the guys who made the film *Napoleon Dynamite* and who could make art out of an e-mail newsletter about a Central Park kickball league, and I wondered what they thought of all this: Why were *they* here?

Packaged-goods work is created and judged differently from other forms of advertising. The strategic briefs are concise and demanding, requiring in our allotted thirty seconds myriad talking points (problem/solution, unique attribute, key emotional takeaway, and so on), numerous product mentions, and one overt and heavy-handed product demo (the magical whitening of the teeth, the efficient genocide of the germs, the time-elapsed shrinking of the turd/stain/prostate), and so it is hard to find room for creativity. The truly driven will always try to do creative work that transcends the category—work that's "great for a feminine hygiene product" or "really funny for a laxative commercial"—and those that do are heralded in the trades and at awards shows. But in addition to being truly driven, those creatives must also be truly thick-skinned and unflappable, since in the land of packaged goods great work often dies because it diverged half a degree away from the path of the brief.

My problem was I was no longer thick-skinned or unflappable. And the thought of ever having to celebrate one of those incremental, "in-category" triumphs made me want to blow my head off. After twenty years of shoveling concepts into the idea furnace, I was done.

It helped just a bit that I had recently finished a novel and had gotten an agent. This was indeed promising, but I had finished novels before and had agents before, one of whom died, one of whom quit weeks after I signed with her, and one of whom told me that she was leaving the industry to go to clown school.* So it's not like I was all set or anything.

Near the end of the conversation with the Japanese, I looked up to see everyone on our end of the call staring at me. The turd baton was about to be passed to the U.S. team, and I was to be its anchorman.

"Do you have everything you need?" asked someone from the other side of the world.

I shook my head no, but couldn't stop myself from asking, "Does anyone?"

The Last Shoot

The assignment, my last, was to do an Americanized remake of a men's deodorant commercial that had tested well in that hotbed of advertising excellence . . . Russia.

* Perhaps the lowest point of my literary career was when I asked her if she could, "you know, do both." Represent me in between tiny-tricycle riding and clown-makeup-application classes. As long as she remembered to take off the red nose and giant floppy shoes for face-to-face meetings, it was cool with me. This was also, in some ways, a high point. Because if you're still compelled to write after your agent has abandoned you for a remote chance at a career in the circus, it's not because you think you're going to be a best-selling author. It's because you like it.

To the best of my knowledge there was no precedent for this, no legacy of killer creative coming to the States via the Siberian pipeline. And to the best of my knowledge there was no rational reason to believe that this exercise was even remotely a good idea.

"What form of testing was it subjected to in Russia?" I asked.

"We're not sure, but it scored well."

"Compared to what? They may have said it scored better than any deodorant spot ever had in Russia, but for all we know, this may be the *only* deodorant commercial in the history of the country."

"We don't know. Listen, they just want us to do this, okay?"

It never ceases to amaze me how brand managers who spend millions of dollars on research can take the most obscure bit of data, or global scuttlebutt, or a hint from a clueless boss, and use it to justify spending close to a million dollars producing an absolutely forgettable piece of shit.

The Russian spot, we were told, was a fairly straightforward, action-packed, high-energy compilation featuring Russian men sweating manly eastern European sweat, doing a variety of manly things. Our task was to come up with simple ways to replace the more overt Russian scenes with more iconic American elements. We had hoped that we could remedy the situation with a quick (cheap, painless) fix with stock footage or maybe inject a couple of fresher, more vibrant stock scenes of well-scrubbed, shirtless Americans playing beach volleyball, or touch football, or Frisbee. Maybe we could give it an audio upgrade with a contemporary American rock track (the Strokes? Lenny Kravitz?), or jump-start it with a stunning graphics package.

We gathered in a screening room—an art director, a producer, an account executive, and I—and braced ourselves as the producer popped the tape into the deck. Two scenes into the spot, we knew we were in trouble. This is before we were subjected to the gloomy images of surly Russian men playing chess, or wrestling in a USSR-era gym, or playing soccer in the shadows of the Kremlin. Then there was the quality of the film itself. "Dark," "grainy," and "amateurish" are three words that came to mind. And "white." Which is understandable, since there aren't a lot of Hispanic or black men in Russia.

We watched it one more time before unanimously deeming the production quality of the spot, even with any number of upgrades, unusable in the States. Swapping out Russian vignettes with new footage would only make the original scenes look even more archaic in contrast.

It didn't matter. We could get Springsteen to score the music and put the hottest graphics house in the world on the case, and it still wouldn't be enough to compensate for the poor quality and unsuitability of the film.

We'd need to reshoot the original, we told the managing partner on the account, and that would be a horrible waste of time and money, since the spot did sort of suck anyway, right?

He didn't think so. "You're telling me that you're saying that none of the Russian footage is usable?"

"Yes, we are."

"Well, then, take another look and come back with some solutions."

At one point, several years before I came to Y&R, I had decided that I didn't want to become the head of an agency, or start my own agency, or even become the creative director of an agency. Not that I was on the verge, or that level of success was necessarily within my grasp. It's just that I'd had a brief taste of the all-consuming life at N. W. Ayer and had quickly rejected it (or, it could be argued, it rejected me). Even if I did have the talent or presence or political savvy to operate at such a level, and that all remained to be seen, the life sacrifice seemed too great. So for years I chose to work success-fully and mostly without incident as a lone-wolf writer, or running my own small creative group within a larger department. The only problem with remaining at that level was that no matter how much experience or insight I brought to a project, there would be times when I had to acquiesce to people of higher rank, less experience, and lesser, let's call it "emotional intelligence." My brother, a New York City firefighter, was dealing with a similar situation on his job. A twenty-year veteran, he chose not to pursue the lieutenant, cap-tain, chief path because regular firefighter hours allowed him to run a masonry business on his days off. But now, after having seen just about everything during his two decades in the Bronx, he found him-self having to answer to people who outranked him, but often had considerably less knowledge about fighting fires. "That's what we get," I told him, "for sticking around so long and doing whatever the hell we wanted." Of course his situation was exponentially different because lives were at stake, while in my position the worst that could happen is the client takes her deodorant business somewhere else.

Ultimately, we brought back several solutions, none of which I could in good conscience recommend. The only choice would be to reshoot the entire spot. And again I said that would be a colossal waste because the commercial was devoid of anything close to an idea. We hoped our costly verdict would convince them to make the whole bizarre assignment go away.

But, of course, it didn't. The spot had tested well somewhere on the planet, and the client, I'm assuming the senior client, was de-termined for some strange reason (demonstrate global synergy to the satellite offices? his father was half-Russian?) to make it work.

Several days later I got a call in my office from the managing partner on the account. The client was willing to commit to a total reshoot, he said, provided it was "in the spirit of the Russian spot." And of course with a much lengthier and more intrusive demo of the deodorant's sweat-destroying Nanoabsorbers™.

That afternoon my flabbergasted producer started making calls to see if we could find a director who would be willing to film this mess. We agreed that we certainly couldn't convince a top-level, A-list shooter. Or a B-lister, for that matter. So we targeted promising up-and-coming directors who wanted to get a foot in the door at a big agency and build a reel. When that failed, we looked at kids fresh out of film school, and then we looked at the reels of old hacks eager to work on anything. We had taken dozens of calls with directors and production companies and had come up empty.

Typically, on these calls I would speak first, explaining the Russian genesis of the spot ("Yes, we're copying a Russian idea") and our goals for the look and feel of the film, and some hypothetical thoughts about what they might want to do to make it feel more "American."

This was usually followed by a prolonged silence.

Sometimes after I described the mandatory eight-second Nanoabsorber™ demo, I could hear the creak and scuffing of chair legs on the other end as directors got up to leave the room.

We prayed that the project would die.

We hoped that something would come along to get us out of this hell. A more important, real assignment. A Ukrainian version of the same spot that tested even better. But nothing.

Meanwhile, my literary agent called. He told me that he was getting ready to send my manuscript out to publishing houses. I crossed my fingers and silently prayed that in the next few weeks he wouldn't quit, die, run off to join the circus, or, worse, pursue a career in advertising.

The good news is the producer and I couldn't find even a half-decent director, not even a hack, to take the job. The truly unsettling news is we found someone brilliant.

The producer knocked on my door and told me that Janusz Kaminski was available and eager to shoot the spot. I looked at her as if she were crazy. Janusz Kaminski is one of the finest cinematographers in the world. He won an Academy Award for *Schindler's List* and was nominated for another for *Saving Private Ryan*. He was cinematographer on *Catch Me If You Can, The Terminal, AI,* and, with Cameron Crowe, *Jerry Maguire*. What the hell did he want with an American remake of a Russian deodorant spot? Had Spielberg blackballed him? Had he recently had a disfiguring eye injury?

"His producer says he likes to shoot," she told me. "And he's got some time on his hands until he starts prepping *Munich* next month."

"He likes to shoot," I said. "Filming a Bar Mitzvah would be more rewarding than this. Is he, you know, crazy?"

She shook her head. That afternoon we took a call with the Oscar-winning cinematographer. When I finished my setup, I checked to see if Janusz was still there. Shockingly, he was. And after the Nanoabsorber™ chat, not only was he still there, but he offered several ideas about how to make the demo more dynamic.

Before we ended the call, I asked Janusz if I could ask one last question.

"Sure."

"You've been behind the camera for some of the finest films of our time, why the . . . why would you want anything to do with a packaged-goods deodorant commercial, a spot without a prevailing idea that's in essence a bunch of familiar vignettes?"

He didn't hesitate. "Because I like to shoot," he said. "And I think this can be anything but familiar."

Now all we had to do was tell the client and the managing partner that we had miraculously stepped in one beautifully composed, 35-millimeter pile of shit.

First we went to the managing partner and told him that, to our great surprise and pleasure, we had found an extraordinary director who actually wanted to work on the spot. "It's a real opportunity to give some juice to an otherwise-forgettable group of vignettes," I said.

"What's he ever done?"

"Ummm, only every major motion picture with the name Spielberg attached to it since 1993."

"For instance?"

I was ready. I held up a bunch of classic and soon-to-be-classic DVDs. "You wanna start with the Academy Award winner?"

"But doesn't he have a commercial reel? And he doesn't sound American to me. And has he done packaged goods before?"

The producer and I looked at each other. I got up to leave.

"Hey," the managing partner called after me. *Maybe he's come to his senses*, I thought. I turned around only to be asked, "How's it going with the shit-shrinking cat food rewrite?"

How did I end up here?

For twenty years I made ads. One led to another. Some took me to other jobs, and some took me to places I'd never been, and some allowed me to meet some of the most interesting people in the world. Sometimes the ads would teach me something I didn't know and fill me with pride and joy. Other times they would frustrate and disappoint me and make me wish that I had chosen a more admirable profession, or that a more admirable profession had chosen me. It was not uncommon back then, near the end of my career, for younger people who had just started in the business to ask how much advertising had changed since I began. Typically, I would roll my eyes and say it had changed a lot. And typically, I believed it.

But more and more I was beginning to realize that maybe I was wrong. As I left the managing partner's office, I realized that it wasn't advertising that had changed so much.

It was me.

Later that afternoon I went back into the managing partner's office and closed the door. I told him that I was extremely disappointed with his reaction to our director. I told him the spot was shit and needed something different, and that by rejecting my recommendation, he was, in effect, rejecting my instincts, my sensibility, my career, and me.

We awarded the job to Janusz Kaminski that night. During the next week we had dozens of meetings and dozens of contentious discussions about the demo and the vignettes and how we were going to make the most American deodorant commercial in the history of television.

One afternoon a junior account person came into my office with a notebook full of questions and suggested changes in the shooting board. She'd been sent by her boss, the managing partner. While we were speaking, the phone rang. It was my literary agent. He'd sent my novel out a few days earlier, and I had been trying my hardest not to think about it. He told me that in the last twenty-four hours, he already had three offers on the table.

I looked at the close-up drawing of a sweat-stained armpit on my desk, then at the account person, who was barely halfway through her punch list. I cupped my hand over the phone's mouthpiece and said to the young woman, "Would you please give me a minute?"

I was dialing before she'd even closed my door. When my wife answered, I told her the news, and we both began to cry.

A week later I was in the Chinatown district of Vancouver, Canada, drinking Irish Breakfast tea and eating a crafts-service burrito made by a Moroccan chef while doing a reshoot of a Russian deodorant commercial with a Polish director who also happened to be prepping for a film set in Germany about a bunch of Israelis and Palestinians.

If that's not the stuff of a quintessentially American ad, my last, I don't know what is.

Part 2

At Large in Adland

Thoughts on Impressions

I saw a subliminal advertising executive, but only for a second.

—Steven Wright

I Was Bombarded by 20,000 Messages (Or Maybe It Was Just 102) While Writing This

The goal of the exercise was to chronicle and occasionally comment upon every ad-like object that I was exposed to in a randomly selected twenty-four hour period.

If I were fifteen years old, marketing people would be extremely interested in something like this. They would fly planners and trend watchers in from all over the country to witness it, to film it, to seek deeper meaning in every click of the mouse, turn of the page, zap of the zapper. They would record my radio presets and count the blinks of my dilated eyes during every second spent watching kids trying to be just like me on the WB network.

Of course, they would pay lavishly for the white paper that would emerge, or to link in to a streaming video of the fifteen-year-old's frenetic, media-saturated day.

Because the marketing person who best understands the relationship between a horny, pimply-faced, disaffected, enigmatic man-child and the culture he consumes more ravenously than any other demographic is the wealthiest person in adland.

But, alas, I am not fifteen years old.

Depending on the source, which ranges from *Consumer Reports* and *Adweek,* to the Center for Interactive Advertising, to the (privately funded) Institute for Concerned People Who Make Up Facts to Scare Us With, to the (corporately funded) Institute That Takes Scary Facts and Finds Ways to Make Us Comfortable with Them, the average American is bombarded by anywhere from 250 to 20,000 advertising impressions every day.

The two ballpark figures that emerge most frequently in links generated by a Google search for "advertising + bombarded" (a nine-impression event in and of itself) were around 250 or 3,500 daily impressions, with not much in between. So this is still quite a disparity. Being exposed to 3,500 advertising impressions a day translates to roughly 2.5 impressions per minute, or one every twenty-four seconds. Being exposed to 250 impressions a day would mean about one every six minutes. When I worked in advertising, I used to see ads in my sleep. Some already existed. Some I was making up for the next day's meeting. But I imagine that most people do not see or create ads in their sleep. So clearly, the impressions-per-minute ratio would rise by more than a third for those human beings who participate in the act of sleeping and whose lives are not consumed by making ads. And since I was a liberal arts major whose last math book included crude drawings of sticks and stones ("If five sticks equals one stone, how many sticks would equal seven stones?" I didn't know ... I was stoned), I won't bother to calculate the impressions-per-minute math for someone supposedly exposed to 20,000 commercial messages in a twenty-four-hour period, but I think we can all agree that it would be an absolute shitload, a disturbing total capable of *A Clockwork Orange*–like ramifications, and that using the phrase "bombarded by" in this context would be justified and accurate, and quite possibly an understatement.

So what is the most accurate measurement of the average American's daily exposure to advertising? Are we being bombarded or massaged or simply pestered by advertising messages? To answer any of these questions, one would first have to determine what exactly constitutes an "average American." What counts as an ad? What's the difference between being exposed to an ad and simply being in the same room or on the same train or highway as one? Do they register peripherally? Subliminally? Telepathically? Cumulatively? Do logos count? How about secondhand ads (when someone tells you about an ad she saw)?

Let's find out.

The Daily Advertising Diary of an Average American Who Happens to Have Worked in Advertising for Twenty Years

October 18, 2007: In the shower from 5:30 to 5:45 a.m., I listened (or didn't, which will probably be the most arbitrary and debatable aspect of this) to sports talk radio, thinking whether I should work out and how I was going to get anything done today with all the stuff going on—school drop-offs, visit Mom in the hospital, a nephew's varsity football game, plus I had to create and build an entire haunted house for a kids' party scheduled to start at 2:00 p.m. tomorrow. Still, I managed to remember this: The twenty-minute scores update was brought to me by Verizon Wireless (1). The traffic by TomTom (2). The weather by your Tristate BMW Dealers (3). Then there was some talk. Two of the hosts are having a diet contest, and one of them is getting his meals sent to him by a diet-food sponsor who happens to run ads on the show. There's no way to con-firm whether this product mention, or live read, is in fact paid for, but my well-tuned bullshit detector says yes, it is (4). However, when the hosts begin talking about the top story of the day, Joe Torre leaving the Yankees after twelve years as manager, I begin to wonder without further prompting about how this might affect Torre's endorsement career—for instance, the Bigelow green tea spots he reads on this station all the time. I conclude that internally prompted messages by the subject and creator of this experiment do not count.

Reaching into my medicine cabinet for my shaving cream, I de-cide on another rule: the labels and logos of random products (shav-ing cream, cereal, small-batch Kentucky bourbon) lying about the house will not count, either. However, labels and logos purposely placed in advertising environments will count.

Here's the difficult part: during my fifteen-minute shower and shave, there were other commercials on the radio, but the thing is, I can't remember any of them. Did I hear them? I guess. Did they register? Not enough for me to so much as remember the brand, let alone the concept, even though I was sort of trying to at that point but hadn't yet bothered to start carrying a notebook and pen. But I imagine on some insidious level they did register.

Anytime you hear or see a message, media planners call this an impression. And the theory goes that even if you say you didn't see or hear a message, you did. And the more times that you're exposed to it, the more it registers. So much so that after several weeks of playing, for instance, a thirty-second TV spot, brands will switch to a less expensive fifteen- or ten-second version of the same spot and get nearly the same level of recall. So let's say there were four other messages in that fifteen-minute radio block. Since I listen to this station at the same time almost every morning, there's a very good chance I've heard them more times than I would like to know. Let's raise the impression total to eight.

Downstairs in the kitchen I turn on the countertop radio, preset for NPR's *Morning Edition.* I listen to the news at the top of the hour while I take care of the dogs, brew some tea, make some lemon-and-honey water for my wife and me, and prepare for the day. National Public Radio: untainted by the stain of commercials, pure, free, and totally not-for-profit. No need for a pen and notebook now. But guess what? Today NPR is having a pledge drive (9). At least the local station I listen to is.

"The last half hour was brought to you by the law offices of . . ." (10).

"Thanks also for contributions by the Chevron Corporation (11), United Technologies (12), . . . and support from listeners like you (?)."

On my way to pick up the *New York Times* at the end of the driveway, I decide that the *Times*'s masthead logo doesn't count but the message for a new hand lotion on the plastic wrapping does (13), as does the sample of the lotion itself that's inside (14). It's a Friday paper. Pretty big. Lots of sections. Usually I read it at the gym while pretending to do cardio on a stationary bike. But today I don't go to the gym. Today I am physically lazy. So today I read it on the run. Sports and Business at the counter while talking to my wife in the other room, who is checking the weather and getting ready to do a televised workout. I poke my head in for Local on the 8's trademark (15) and decide that the Weather Channel logo or bug that's ghosted over the lower-right corner of the screen is a message, too (16). I read the Arts and Travel sections while my three-year-old watches *Curious George* in the other room on PBS. Yes, it's PBS, but they've got sponsors, too, and I can't stop myself from hearing about them.

Not counting "viewers like you" and the Helena Rubinstein Foundation, I count two (18).

Upon Further Review

I try to finish the *Times*'s front section and the Op-Eds in a quiet, tiled place where, in theory, dogs and children are forbidden. My first instinct is to say that I did not look at one single ad (other than the outside wrapper and the free sample inside) from that paper this morning. I am certain that not one ad registered in the least, because I know myself and I know what I look for in a paper. The agate page in the Sports section. The Op-Eds. The book review is almost always on the front page or the back inside page of the Arts section. The ad column is usually near the back of the Business section. I don't wander or linger. So unless a headline grabs me, I get what I need and move on, and I never read the ads. Magazines are another story. I'll look at magazine ads. Maybe it's the glossy stock, the superior production quality, or the fact that because of the lead time associated with magazines (some ads have to be placed months in advance), they're not as obnoxiously retail in nature as newspaper ads.

Yet out of curiosity I decided to take a look at the paper I had just "read" to see if any of the ads rang a bell. Upon further review, I did notice a few. Okay, more than a few. I noticed all kinds of ads. Here's a sampling of the branded messages I vaguely recall skimming over and a sampling of the thoughts that occurred to me as I skimmed.

First Arts Section
Okay, this was a Friday morning, and there were a lot of movie ads.
The Darjeeling Limited. Doesn't seem like such a must-see now, with only a quarter-page ad on a Friday. Post–alleged suicide attempt

Owen Wilson bandaged is still kind of creepy, and I know it's an ad, but what's Jason Schwartzman thinking, riding barefoot on the back of that thing? Tailpipe burn waiting to happen (19).

Elizabeth: The Golden Age. With this pedigree I wonder why so many people are saying this sucks. Too many films about Elizabeth? About queens? Maybe like the Merchant Ivory productions of the 1980s and 1990s, the genre has run its course. Maybe Helen Mirren and Cate Blanchett should have some kind of jousting match to see who the best queen really is (20).

Lars and the Real Girl (21).

Into the Wild (22).

Wristcutters (23).

Dan in Real Life (24).

Rendition (25).

Other movie and theater ads from this section that I absolutely did not notice but upon further review actually may have: sixteen (41).

Second Arts Section

None. Just a bunch of gallery listings that I had no time to consider this morning. Oh yeah, there was this one: the International Fine Art and Antique Dealers Show. Full-page ad. Interesting, but it looks kind of pricey and snooty for our blood. And has anyone ever found a bargain in a Manhattan antiques store (42)?

Escapes (Travel) Section

The Plaza, Costa del Este. Quarter-page ad for a new boutique hotel in Panama City. Wow. Check out the cleavage on this woman . . . Is this for a strip club? In the *Times*? In the Travel section? Oh, it's for a hotel. Check out the tower/phallus jutting into the sky. Must be one of Trump's properties (it's not). It's in Panama? They're making it seem like she comes with the room (43).

The Plaza, Costa del Este. Quarter-page ad for a new boutique hotel in Panama City (reprise). Where's that strip-club ad again? Wow. Oh, yeah. It's not for a strip club; it's for Trump's hotel (it's not). Spectacular. Viva Panama (44)!

Business Section

J. H. Cohn, LLP Accountants, quarter-page ad. This is weird. An ad in the Business section with a big picture of none other than the suddenly unemployed number-one news story of the day: Joe Torre. Strange placement today of all days. And check out the tagline for whatever the hell this company is: "How are you managing?" Well, today, um, we're not managing at all. Right, Joe (45)?

Sports Section

None. I swear. Unless you want to revisit the whole Joe Torre– Bigelow Tea ad by association theory.

Metro Section

67wine.com. Full-page, back of section. Check out this massive list of wines from a company whose name I'm not paying any attention to. Wine is good. Really good wine is really good. Too bad I don't know more about what separates one from the other. Remember when you worked for that asshole at that wine magazine when you got out of college and took the job because you didn't want your in-laws to think you were an unemployed slacker? Too bad you didn't pay any attention to all the free stuff you got to drink. I wonder what that jackass is doing today (46).

Main Section

None. But then again, a lot of them do look familiar, which makes me think I must have noticed at least some of these giant, logo-driven, not entirely unfamiliar billboards for the high-end likes of Movado (47), Gucci (48), Tiffany & Co. (49), Old Navy (50), T-Mobile (51), and Verizon (52).

Escapes (Travel) Section (Again)

The Plaza, Costa del Este. Quarter-page ad for a new boutique hotel in Panama City. Yup, Panama City. I was right. Not affiliated with Trump in any way. Not a strip club at all. Funny how I never considered Panama City a vacation destination yet now feel a strong desire to immerse myself in the culture (53).

Transcript of Phone Call Received at 7:46 a.m.

ME *(after neglecting to check caller ID)*: Hello?

RECORDED VOICE OF DISTURBINGLY CHIPPER WOMAN: Good morning. This is your neighbors Bill and Susan. We're calling to tell you that if elected as your state representative, John Doe will put an end to the shenanigans in . . .

ME *(hanging up, thinking)*: "What's so bad about shenanigans? I can deal with shenanigans as long as they don't involve cold-calling voters, usurping the Constitution, breaking any laws, or initiating any wars without congressional approval" *(then making a note to absolutely not vote for John Fucking Doe or anyone on the anti-shenanigan ticket)* (54).

An Abridged Chronicle of the Online Advertising Experience

The thing about online advertising is it's supposed to be more customized and easy to measure than any other medium. But my experiences have proven otherwise. For instance, there are several ways

to see how many people actually visited my Web site, jamespothmer
.com (shameless plugs don't count), the other day when an online
article I'd written for Forbes.com attached a link to it. The Stat-
Counter for the site said 554, which was an all-time daily high. The
most I'd previously had was somewhere around 300 the day my
novel was reviewed in the daily *New York Times*. An average day sees
somewhere between 10 and 25 visitors, so this was exciting. But the
cool (or depressing) thing about StatCounter is it lets you dig
deeper. StatCounter will tell you where your visitors linked from (almost all from Forbes.com), what country, state, city, and Internet
service provider they came from (in this instance almost every state
in the Union and twelve other countries), as well as which pages on
the site they viewed. Most important, StatCounter also chronicles
how long each visitor spent on the site. And this is where the total
of 554 starts to get significantly less, um, significant. Because a
closer look at 554 people who were connected to my site that day reveals that 335 spent a total of zero seconds there. I don't consider
spending zero seconds anywhere a visit, so these were clearly not
visitors. Why did they even link there to begin with? Did they get
cold feet? Did my site take too long to load (it is sort of slow, but
still)? Between clicking on the hyperlink and pulling back their fingers, did 335 people suddenly become overwhelmed with the feeling that they'd made a horrible, horrible mistake?

The good news is the remaining 219 visitors spent an average of
seven minutes logged on to my site. The shortest was seven seconds
("Oh, it's that asshole"), and the longest was sixteen hours, which
leads me to believe that either someone left his computer on or I'm
in the honeymoon stage of a relationship with my first official
stalker! Forty-one of the 219 visitors actually wrote messages on my
blog. So how would one measure my Web traffic on that particular
day? Would the number be 554, 219, or 41?

The numbers are also open to interpretation at mega-sites, like

Forbes.com, whose numbers are being calculated by companies such as Nielsen/NetRatings and comScore. According to an article in the *New York Times,* the *Forbes* site had 11.6 million visitors the month my piece ran. For the same period Nielsen/NetRatings put that number at 7.5 million, and comScore said 5.8 million. Digital skeptics might say it is all highly subjective and open to interpretation, but the truth is that the online ad experience is the most measurable of all media. Where else can one record time spent on a page, or click-throughs, or times the video trailer was watched or e-mailed to a friend? I suspect that accurately measuring online traffic and the demographic makeup of that traffic will only get better, although it will remain a major point of contention between media companies and advertisers as they negotiate rates for years to come.

Perhaps the best way to measure a site or product's popularity isn't by hits or time spent, but, according to Barbarian Group's Benjamin Palmer, by the number of endorsements that visitors bestow upon it.

A quick note on customized ads. The other day I was participating in my favorite online group, the Fiction Files, talking about Joseph Conrad's classic *Heart of Darkness.* I happened to mention in one of my rambling, weakly substantiated, intellectually challenged comments how odd it was that the Polish-born Conrad preferred to write in English, his third language. Five minutes later, while my fellow Fiction Filers were taking the conversation to a more enlightened cyber place, the sponsored links on my page were displaying, in addition to the usual suspects about self-publishing and sex, a link to a travel agency that specialized in trips to Poland. Some call this prescient and intuitive. I call it frightening and unnerving. Ever meet a bug-eyed total stranger at a party who somehow knows way too much about you? That's how "customized" Web ads (and people who spend sixteen-plus hours on a Web site with three hours' worth of content) make me feel.

A Personal and Mostly Hypothetical Re-Creation of an Intuitive Online Advertising Experience

Hello, James!

Hello, James P. Othmer. We have some great personalized recommendations for you in our bookstore. For instance, we noticed that customers who bought *Extremely Loud and Incredibly Close* by Jonathan Safran Foer also bought trendy, must-read fiction by people much younger, hipper, and more gifted than you, like ZZ Packer, Chuck Palahniuk, Jhumpa Lahiri, and Zadie Smith. Perhaps you'd like to consider some more realistic, age-appropriate recommendations by authors with whom you might actually identify, like Nick Hornby, Richard Ford, John Irving, and the late Saul Bellow.

By the way, we've also noticed that your wife has recently purchased *Woman Power* by Dr. Laura, *All Men Are Jerks Until Proven Otherwise* by Daylle Deanna Schwartz, and (her fourth copy in six years of) *The Peter Pan Syndrome* by Dan Kiley. You might want to know that other husbands of wives who have recently purchased *Woman Power* by Dr. Laura, *All Men Are Jerks Until Proven Otherwise* by Daylle Deanna Schwartz, and (repeatedly) *The Peter Pan Syndrome* by Dan Kiley have taken it upon their adult selves to purchase *Things a Man Should Know About Marriage*, *Fear of Intimacy*, and *How to Romance the Woman You Love—the Way She Wants You To!* and *not* *The Complete Frank Miller Batman* or Chris Ware's graphic novel *Jimmy Corrigan: The Smartest Kid on Earth*.

We've also noticed that you've recently ordered yet another copy (your third in six years) of *On Becoming a Novelist* by John Gardner as well as *The Faith of a Writer* by Joyce Carol Oates, which leads us to believe that you're still trying to write or one day hope to write **the Great American Novel**. May we suggest instead *Moving On* by Larry McMurtry, *Snap Out of It* by Ilene Segalove, or *The Delusional Person* by Salomon Resnick? Or perhaps you should simply stick to your career in advertising.

Also, based on your recent history (notably the **camo cargo pants** and **sleeveless mesh T-shirt** purchases from our **sporting goods shop**), we have some more sartorial recommendations for you in our **designer menswear boutique**, including a stunning new **Armani suit** that has been recommended for you by a friend. We can't tell you this friend's name, but we can tell you that she used to sleep in the same room as you.

What else? We've also noticed from your **customer profile** that yesterday was your birthday and that you spent most of it lurking on **hotsororitywebcam.com** and **Metstraderumors.com**. All of the above, combined with your recent purchases from our **music store** of less than uplifting CDs by the likes of **Tom Waits**, **Trent Reznor**, **Nick Cave**, and **Morrissey**, suggests that you might be **clinically depressed**. And you might be interested to know that previous customers who we thought were **clinically depressed** and who also purchased CDs by the likes of **Tom Waits**, **Trent Reznor**, **Nick Cave**, and **Morrissey** also purchased **discounted psychotropic meds** like **lithium**, **Prozac**, and **Zoloft** direct from our **online pharmacy**. You also might want to know that many of the same **clinically depressed** people who also purchased CDs by the likes of **Tom Waits**, **Trent Reznor**, **Nick Cave**, and **Morrissey** and had also purchased **discounted psychotropic meds** like **lithium**, **Prozac**, and **Zoloft** from our **online pharmacy** had previously tried, without success, self-medicating with **Jack Daniel's whiskey**, **Patrón Reposado tequila**, and *Monkey Business* by the **Black Eyed Peas** (all of which, incidentally, even though they won't help one little bit, can be purchased at our **online liquor** and **music stores**).

If you'd like additional, **more brutally frank recommendations** for every aspect of your life, please click **here.**

If you're not **James P. Othmer**, and that's not necessarily a bad thing, please click **here.**

Online, for Real

Here it is just after 8:00 a.m. and I'm already up to fifty-four impressions. Even though I've only overheard the TV programming of others, I haven't left my house, and I've not yet turned on my computer.

Obviously, online there are exponentially more types of ad experiences than one could ever find in the real world. From simple banner and pop-up ads to sponsored links, to boldfaced words embedded in search engine listings to audio, video, and print ads.

Online you can see almost every print and TV ad in current circulation (as well as tens of thousands from years past) as well as much more interactive, content-driven fare. Online I can find everything from a YouTube link to an AT&T campaign I did almost twenty years ago to a snack-chip site for a contest that will allow the winner to create the next Super Bowl ad. If so inclined, online I could also join a gaming site like World of Warcraft or a site like Second Life, where my avatar could explore an entire new world, replete with paid advertisements. But I'm too busy and old to cultivate an online gaming obsession, and I'm not interested in Second Life, and, based upon the declining numbers of participants and advertisers on the site, not many others are, either. At least for now.

As intimated above, how to calculate it all is nearly impossible and deeply frustrating. And unless you work for Google (thanks for the eighty-six-page media kit!), Yahoo!, Microsoft, or some other company that sees gold in your digital footprints (all of whom are seeking to find a standardized way to gauge legitimate impressions), it's infinitely boring stuff.

I'm actually kind of shocked when my Mozilla Firefox Web browser page opens and I don't see any ads. There's a nice clean page with a few instructions and the ubiquitous Google search box, which technically can be called an ad, but because of its utility in this instance, I won't. A closer look will later reveal a line about telling all your friends about Firefox, but I didn't notice it and don't remember reading it anytime before, so it doesn't count. Time to click through to Yahoo! to check my e-mail. On the Yahoo! landing page there are banners for Finding the Chrysler Dealer Near You (55), Unique Designs for Personal Checks (56), and Yahoo! music (57). To the left are smaller ads for Netflix (58), an online college diploma program (59), and a home-financing broker (60).

But the good news is my in-box has received twenty-two messages overnight! When I worked in advertising, I dreaded the quotidian misery of the onslaught of corporate e-mail, but now, sadly, I get excited when I see a number like 22 in my in-box. Maybe it's film news from Hollywood! Perhaps I finally sold that short story! Maybe it's a new fan! An old friend!

To a corporate executive the never-ending messages of the in-box can exact a painful psychological toll. But for a work-at-home suburban dad freshly pardoned from corporate life, it is a receptacle for possibility, a connection to the outside world left behind.

At least that's how it feels before you start clicking through. One glimpse at the message roster and I feel embarrassed for the part of me that thought I actually had any legitimate messages at all. The relatively civil ones this morning include the Public Theater, mediabistro.com, Quality Paperback Book Club, Sierra Trading Post (twice), Netflix, Buy.com, Papyrus, Marriott, Toys "R" Us, and Telecharge, bringing the total to 71. Annoying, yes, but this is not the worst form of spam, and in truth I am probably responsible for most of it, having done online business with these companies at one time or another and agreeing (or neglecting to say no) to their offer to continue the relationship. *Wired* magazine (via the folks at PodCamp Pittsburgh) has a definition for this form of semi-solicited spam:

> **Bacn** *n*. Spam by request. Bacn (pronounced "bacon") is a byproduct of legitimate email lists and feeds—bulk messages for which the recipient has signed up yet never has time to read.

A *Wired* reader added this to the definition: when you're distantly connected to a friend on a social network via obscure references, it's called Six Degrees of Kevn Bacn.

Things become a lot less civil when I click over to my Jamespothmer.com mailbox, and it has nothing to do with *bacn*. Sixteen messages! However, only two are personal. I'd like to categorize the rest as ads, but messages with subject headings like these give even the lowliest coupon ad a bad name:

Bigger Penis Is Not Just an Illusion
You Won't Believe Your Eyes When You See Your New Penis

For the most part, I don't have a major issue with the intrusive nature of advertising in any form. Of course in my lifetime there have been ads that have irritated me, or offended me, or have appeared in what I considered inappropriate places at inopportune times (see my thoughts on pharma ads later in this section). But spam is another beast entirely. There is nothing to like about spam. Despite filters and blockers, despite my flagging it, deleting it, and chopping it up into a million bytes, spam always seems to come back in some reconstituted, increasingly offensive form. Like the Blob. Or Geraldo.

Seven New Messages from Ladies Waiting for You!

Radio, TV, and print ads are easy to police. If you've had enough, you can shut them off, turn down the volume, fast-forward, zap, look the other way. And if they really offend, you can call the station or publisher. You can boycott the brand, write the company, or damn the advertising agency that had the audacity to create it. But not spam.

Unique Financial Opportunity from Deposed African Prince!

Spam comes from some anonymous, evil destination, not on any map, seemingly untethered to any legitimate corporation, media outlet, nation, or state. Spam seeps into your personal space, your workplace. Don't waste your time, as I have, trying to unsubscribe, or to send nasty replies to spammers, or to track them down. I believe this only served to bring my name to the attention of millions of vengeful search bots, digital vermin whose ability to pester, mislead, and offend makes snake-oil salesmen of the nineteenth century seem quaint and virtuous. The inventor of the search bot had to have been an extremely bright and gifted person. Just as, I imagine, the inventor of a biological weapon is an extremely bright and gifted person. Too bad they didn't apply their gifts elsewhere.

Wundercum for Massive Ejaculations!
All Eyes Will Be on the Monster in Your Shorts.

And so on. Sometimes the subject headings are legit enough to make me click, or at least think I should in case it is a real e-mail from a friend, acquaintance, or someone with a paying job. Lately I've also noticed a disturbing trend regarding the names in the From box. They contain aspects of, or slightly resemble, the names of the people with whom I regularly communicate. A friend in the business says this is also the work of the spam bots crawling around my hard drive, extracting any piece of information that can be used against me.

My wife doesn't think it's the work of bots. She thinks I'm crazy.

Still I wonder, do the spam masters think that after seeing their messages sixteen times a day for 221 consecutive days, I'll finally have some kind of penile epiphany and decide, hey, maybe these people named Abraham R. Exion and (a personal favorite) Viceroy W. Woody are right? Maybe that *is* the root of all my problems. Maybe my life is the way it is because my watch really is crap, I don't help enough deposed African kings, my penis is laughingly sub-gargantuan, and my ejaculations are not nearly as massive and geyser-like as those that a forty-eight-year-old who just celebrated his twenty-fifth wedding anniversary deserves.

Why not just give in and click through and write this person and send him my credit card and secure banking info and get this thing going? One would have to be a fool to get sucked in by their outrageous claims, right? Yet the ads never stop. So someone must be biting.

I barely finished deleting the last spam in my in-box when yet another message appeared to torment me and my beleaguered member.

She Will Bow Before Your Enormous Girth!

It is 8:29 a.m. I've been awake for approximately three hours. The impression tally now reads 87, but I know that a more liberal interpretation of the methodology could bring it closer to 500.

My in-box is flashing again.

For the first time, I'm feeling bombarded.

A Conservative and Extremely Rough Estimate of Online Ad Impressions for the Remainder of the Day

I'll check my e-mail accounts again at lunch, before dinner, and be-fore bed. I'll goof around on the Fiction Files on MySpace for a half hour while not watching a kids' show after dinner. I'll Google myself on Google.de to see if there's any news about *The Futurist,* which was published in Germany this week under the more German-friendly and optimism-repelling title *No Future.* I'll decide that see-ing your own name in the sponsored links doesn't count, and that pop-up ads in German next to reviews of your book that you can't understand don't count, either. Friend requests from strangers pimping self-published books or indie bands do, though. I'll also call up my iTunes page. The landing page for the iTunes Store has six medium-sized ads, eight postage-stamp-sized images of CD cover art, and a list of top new downloads, four of which make it onto my screen. Since I was whacked by thirty-two impressions the first time on the Net this morning, I'll times it by three and add another two dozen from my MySpace and German Google visits.

Of the eighteen impressions on iTunes, let's say that six may have registered in the most subliminal fashion. This is not so bad. However, on a day of shameless procrastination, YouTube surfing, and supposed online research, the number of impressions that flash before my eyes would likely be more than several thousand. Today it's a reasonable 158 online (213 total), most of which I will not re-member, none of which I even considered clicking through to find out more.

Out-of-Home Advertising; Or, the Reclusive Hermit
Briefly Leaves His Cave

Earlier I discussed the folly of the concept of an average day or an average American. Clearly I am not an average American. I am a weirdly idiosyncratic person of many moods and interests. Some days I am a Luddite hermit writing in silence for eight or more hours. Others I am a stressed-out Manhattanite repeatedly sprayed with media bird shot. I estimate that a typical two-way commute to Manhattan—driving or by train—and walking through its neighborhoods, having lunch with friends, attending a few meetings, and shopping would add another thousand impressions. This would include kiosks, signage on the Metro North platform and on the train, billboards on the West Side Highway, messages on the sides of trucks and buildings, sandwich boards, taxi roofs, elevator ads, cup wrappers, and so on—in short, everything in the swirling, constantly evolving diaspora of branding that is the streets of Manhattan.

Add another five hundred impressions for every fifteen minutes you happen to spend in Times Square.

But today I will not be going into Manhattan. Today, I'm in a suburb sixty miles from New York City, with two short errands to run, so this should be easy. The first is picking up my three-year-old son from preschool. This is a six-mile round-trip on back roads, briefly intersecting the town's main artery, Route 6. At the end of my driveway I see a Century 21 sign on my neighbor's lawn (219). Stuck in the ground next to that is a sign urging me to elect someone for town judge. I decide roadside political signs should count (220), even though I am now dreading the remaining 5.9 miles of my midday journey. I'm all for political activism, but really, do these crudely designed, generic pieces of cardboard and plywood have any impact on voter turnout? Could the Reelect Joe Schmo sign you saw this morning possibly be the deciding factor once the curtain closes on your voting booth? Some lawns have more than one sign. Others have five-by-seven-foot billboards. At every piece of public land that happens to be near an intersection, every square inch is claimed by political signage. The main intersection of the road I'm on and Route 6 alone has twenty-two ads for eleven different candidates. An independent tally of my journey tabulated by my nine-year-old daughter at a later date reveals sixty-three political signs (282).

Plus, I have the radio on an all-news station (291).

Then there's the father in the parking lot wearing a T-shirt touting his construction company (292).

When I meet my son, he hands me a pumpkin mask that could only have been made by a child of extraordinary gifts and a promotional flyer for the Scholastic Book Club (293). I keep the radio off on the way home, preferring to talk with my son about pumpkin-mask-making technique and the problem with girls, specifically the Julias. One Julia would have been bad enough, but in his small playgroup there are two, and lately they've been tormenting his days, nights, and nap times. I'm able to convince him that girls, and maybe even the Julias, are not that bad. After all, there's even a girl Power Ranger! But I'm still unable to do anything about those political signs (356). And why didn't I know our neighbor's house was for sale (repeat viewings count: 357)?

Two thoughts occur to me as I sort through the just-delivered mail (377) while making my way back into the house. First: Every single ad I have seen and heard to this point has absolutely sucked. Nothing memorable or catchy. Nothing conceptual. Nothing beautiful, even in a patently gratuitous way. Not one of the 377 impressions to which I have thus far been subjected has made me laugh, or think, or do, or buy, or consider buying, or want to tell someone about it.

The second thought is that more than 99 percent of these impressions were almost certainly not created by a major advertising agency, or for a large, recognizable brand. So far, it's just been a noisy, ugly mess haphazardly put together and malevolently thrown in my face—our faces—by amateurs and hacks. Unless, I wonder, is it possible that the really good ads are the ones you don't consciously remember?

A four-hour, mildly productive, advertising-free siesta interrupted only by the phone call of a friend who tells me I must tune in to the Joe Torre farewell interview on WFAN. Which, of course, is sponsored by Bigelow Tea (378).

Only the Very Old and the Very Sick Watch the Evening News

Or maybe the evening news just makes people feel very old and very sick. Either way, whether you're a fan of Katie, Charlie, or Brian, the 6:30 to 7:00 p.m. national network news is all about pharma advertising, all about our myriad physical and psychological ailments.

If I had a dime every time I heard the words "Ask your doctor" or saw a crude clip of phallic imagery during a commercial break from the network news, or was forced to contemplate a stomach-turning side effect, I'd almost be able to afford my own health care.

According to a 2008 report released by York University, "The Cost of Pushing Pills: A New Estimate of Pharmaceutical Promotion in the United States," in 2004 in the United States alone, pharmaceutical companies spent twice as much on advertising and promotion as on research and development. And the study claims that its estimate of $57.5 billion spent on pharma advertising and promotion (versus $28 billion on R&D) is conservative because it doesn't take into consideration efforts like off-label promotion, ghostwriting, and seeding trials, not to mention over-the-counter brand-name meds. The study concludes that the pharmaceutical industry in the United States, which accounts for 43 percent of all global pharma sales and promotional expenditures, is indeed market driven, and not the research-driven, lifesaving industry it professes to be.

Which makes one wonder how a major network could ever do an exposé of the big drug companies without fearing it would be left without a sponsor. Or how a physician who benefits from the numerous promotional vacation boondoggles, I mean conferences, paid for by pharmaceutical companies can give you a straight answer when you do, as the voice-over announcer repeatedly instructs you to, ask your doctor.

I've had only limited experience on the, um, creative side of pharmaceutical advertising. Once, near the end of my run as a creative go-to guy, I was asked to join a brainstorming session for a pitch about a new drug that apparently was for people who had allergies but didn't know it. We had to come up with ways to convince consumers who thought they were allergy free that they really may have something wrong, as well as a name for the pill and the condition it was to treat. We were told by a moderator that anything that can be easily abbreviated or that ends with the word "syndrome" seems to work well, I'd guess because "syndrome" sounds like something fleeting, beyond your control. Put "syndrome" on the end of any horrible human behavior, and for some reason it sounds less threatening, less your fault, and not such a bad thing to have. Feel like punching a stranger in the face on the side of the road? Chalk it up to traffic-related anger syndrome (TRAS), which can be treated by the green (means go) pill Flolane. Suffering from TRAS sounds much better than simply being a raving fucking lunatic.

Hinting at but never saying the supposed benefit in the name of the medication helps, too. I imagine that spam bots would be great at naming syndromes and their respective meds.

After helping myself to the fine buffet spread put out by the account team and watching a short film about the "opportunity" at hand, I realized that I would rather risk being laid off (a distinct possibility during an especially lean agency time) than do this. So I told them I suddenly remembered that I had to go to another meeting, but in retrospect I should have chalked it up to SACS, selective awakened conscience syndrome.

Once, I briefly worked on an over-the-counter pain-reliever account. In a few short weeks I learned about the difference between ibuprofen and acetaminophen, and acquired the equivalent of a master's in semantics. It could be argued that in no other environment (scholarly, poetic, political) does a single word get the amount of critical attention that it does in a pharma ad. It is not uncommon for dozens of people gathered around a conference table to be discussing, for an hour, the merits and faults of an adverb.

For instance, one day, while I was presenting some print ads to the creative director, his phone rang. It was the agent for a recently retired baseball pitcher, a future Hall of Famer. The agent said that after giving it some thought, his client, our client's high-priced spokesperson, was willing to say that the occasional slight lower-back pain he experienced was arthritis.

I briefly worked on one other pharmaceutical account when I was asked to cover for a recently fired creative director on a campaign for a drug that treated something called deep vein thrombosis syndrome, or DVT. The best I could tell, DVT was a real and deadly problem. People who sat in planes or on couches for extended periods without moving were particularly at risk. At the time I was fairly sure I was also about to be referred to as recently fired. My anchor account, KFC, was gone, and we had yet another chief creative officer who had said he wanted to energize the agency with hot young talent, so me and my senior vice president's salary and billable-hours-free time sheet were feeling particularly vulnerable. And even though I wasn't completely morally opposed to working on the DVT med business, I knew it was a risk for my reputation and standing within the agency ranks. This is because, although pharma business is incredibly lucrative for agencies, it is mostly considered an unimaginative and unrewarding quagmire—a creative ghetto.

Generally, pharma work at a mainstream agency (there are many solid agencies that specialize in pharmaceutical ads) is often given to a creative team that is willing to take a lot of shit and probably is not considered "hot" or terribly creative at the time. More often than not, they're older, without an account to bill their hours against, and near the end of the line. So I spent a week working with an art director and seventy-five lawyers trying to settle on legally acceptable copy to accompany the visual of a digital ball of flame coursing heart-bound through the veins of unsuspecting, recumbent humans. On couches. In airplane seats. On park benches. At one point I suggested an electric chair but was told with a straight face by a junior account person half my age that this would be too distracting. It would take attention away from the solution.

Thankfully, something happened beyond my control (FDA intervention? a new strategy? or perhaps they realized I was completely incapable of taking this seriously), and my tour of duty on the pharma front came to an end.

In short order, during this evening's *NBC Nightly News with Brian Williams,* there are ads for ED (erectile dysfunction [X 3 = 382]), arthritis (383), depression (X 2 = 385), allergies (386), and (prostate-related) weak urine stream syndrome (WUSS! [387]).

Several times in the past few years I made the mistake of asking my daughter to watch the evening news with me. I thought it would enlighten and educate her, but usually it just embarrassed me. I'm no prude, but do I really need to hear endless talk about boner pills, genital herpes, clinical depression, birth control, and leakage of the bladder, anus, and other orifices at 6:30 p.m., with an eight-year-old?

They tell us during graphic portions of the news that we may want to look away, or have the children leave the room, but they should really be telling children—no, all of us—to leave the room when the civics lesson ends and the more-information-than-anyone-needs-to-know biology lessons begin. Relying on network news pharma ads as her teacher, my daughter would think that when we are young, our legs can't stop moving, we menstruate four times a year, we are ravaged by genital herpes despite taking great measures to not get pregnant, and we are extremely depressed; when we are middle-aged, we desperately want to get pregnant but can't, perhaps because most men can't achieve an erection (yet others are afflicted with interminable boners), and we are also bald, overweight, and extremely depressed; and when we're older, we are arthritic, forgetful, still depressed, riddled with cancer, and either can't pee at all or pee so much we have to wear diapers.

Lately, whenever my daughter approaches when the news is on, I encourage her to go to another room to watch something less offensive, like *South Park.*

What about this as a side effect of watching too many pharmaceutical ads: you tune in to a show feeling great and leave convinced that forces beyond your control are conspiring against you, physiological time bombs are rampaging through your veins, and you have no fewer than seven potential syndromes pillaging your body? And if you happen to be a person of a certain psychological ilk, with Munchausen's syndrome, for instance, the nightly network news is nothing less than must-see TV, a program filled with a constant stream of new and FDA-approved syndromes and conditions to cherry-pick for your own pleasure/misery.

Consider my all-time favorite, Mirapex, which treats something called RLS (restless legs syndrome), a condition whose degree of absurdity is topped only by its potential side effects: "Tell your doctor if you experience increased gambling, sexual, or other urges."

Kind of makes one wonder how many evenings that began in front of the TV with a little bit of cappuccino-induced leg bouncing—something as innocent as, say, keeping time to the Mirapex jingle—ended in a Vegas hotel room with a bankrupt RLS sufferer snorting coke off a transsexual stripper's breasts. "Well, I lost every cent of my 401(k) nest egg, and my marriage, and I caught a rare strain of syphilis. But at least I no longer have that irritating leg-bounce-up-and-down thingy."

The Side-Effect Channel

In only two developed countries, the United States (which expanded and legalized drug advertising in 1997) and, for some reason, New Zealand, is it legal to broadcast this kind of unabashed, deceptive, dangerous bullshit.

I recently shared some of my opinions on pharma marketing with an acquaintance who worked at an agency that specializes in it. She agreed that much of it was intrusive and over-the-top and occasionally entered a gray ethical space. But, she countered, without pharma companies, who would fund the research grants and facilities, the scholarships, the university libraries? Without pharma ads, thousands of people might live with an undiagnosed, untreated illness. Plus, she said, most of this stuff actually works, saving and improving millions of lives.

Cancer drugs, yes. Restless legs? Please.

After my brief foray into pharmaceutical advertising, I came to the conclusion that it (the ads, not the drugs) should be banned. If you don't feel well, ask your doctor. Don't wait for a commercial to tell you that you don't feel well and then ask your doctor, who may or may not have recently returned from a junket to a Costa Rican eco-lodge paid for by the very makers of the commercial that brought you to him in the first place.

And if pharmaceutical ads aren't banned, how about this: ads paid for by a co-op that basically and only says, "If you don't feel well, see your doctor"?

Or this, which I thought of during my stint on the DVT account: the Side-Effect Channel. The Side-Effect Channel is based on the premise that the small type and fast legal talk that deliver the harmful, disgusting, and potential side effects are hardly proportionate to the exorbitantly produced manner in which we are exposed to the benefits. On the Side-Effect Channel pharmaceutical companies would be obligated to match their benefit-driven ads with commercials of the same length, production value, and conceptual quality that dramatize, not just list, the side effects.

Like this, for instance:

Open on a tennis court at an upscale retirement community. A sixtyish man and woman in white tennis togs, Steve and Rita, greet a sixtyish single man, Brad.

STEVE: Hey, Brad, where's your better half?
BRAD (*frowning*): Well, she's not holding up so well.
RITA: Is Mary's sporadically twitching pinkie toe syndrome acting up again?

BRAD (*shakes his head, sadly*): No. Thanks to Rigorto, her STPTS is under control, and believe me, that was on the verge of becoming a slight nuisance. But the funny thing is, also thanks to Rigorto, her anus has been leaking like a sieve.

STEVE: Ouch. But my doctor said that there's only a slight chance of anal leakage with Rigorto.

BRAD (*laughs*): Tell that to our white four-hundred-thread-count cotton Indian sheets. And the white leather passenger seat of my antique Aston Martin.

Cut to Mary in her room, quietly weeping, staring out the window at her friends and husband in their dry brilliant white shorts. Cut to her non-twitching pinkie toe, then pull back to reveal that she is wearing a giant diaper with the Rigorto logo on the back.

ANNOUNCER/V-O: That's right. While Rigorto can occasionally remedy an otherwise-innocuous and non-life-threatening condition, it can also make a real mess of your gastrointestinal tract, your social life, and your wardrobe.

Cut to a mandatory negative-reinforcement demo: dark coffee poured upon a piece of white muslin cloth that browns from the middle out.

SUPER/TYPE: Dramatization, actual and leakage may be significantly more explosive.

Cut to the tennis court, where Steve and Rita are crushing Brad, running him ragged. After a brutal point, Rita looks at the entrance of their building.

Cut to Mary, stepping outside.

Cut back to

STEVE: Well, it looks like we may finally have a game after all!

Mary takes a few more tentative steps toward them, but stops as a look of horror comes over her face. She clutches the back of her shorts, turns, and runs.

A/V-O: Rigorto. Anal leakage is a distinct possibility.

Including the drug ads, I was exposed to fourteen commercials (392) during the nightly news.

Whither Prime Time?

When I was a boy in the late 1960s and early 1970s, one of the only things that helped alleviate the anxiety of the end of summer and the return to school was the well-publicized and highly anticipated return of the network-TV season.

But now the concepts of a fall TV season and prime time in general are bordering on obsolete. The problem isn't that people hate the programs. Indeed, many shows are being seen by more people than ever. The problem is how and when people are watching them, which is basically whenever the hell they want. And often without commercial interruption.

The reasons why—including the emergence of cable, video games, the zapper, podcasts, cell phones, YouTube, the Internet, the DVR, On Demand, and countless other entertainment options vying for consumer eyeballs—have been well documented. Also well documented is the extent to which networks are going to try to retain viewership and, more important, the advertising dollars without which their shows would not exist.

At the 2007 Network Upfront Week in New York City, network spokespeople went to great lengths not just to tout their new shows but to reassure advertisers that they were doing everything possible to keep viewers watching, especially during the dreaded traditional commercial breaks. Among the concepts showcased and eventually employed was Fox's introduction of an animated cabdriver whose job was to link ads and programming, or the CW Television Network's "content wraps," which mixed sponsors' products into programming snippets. In addition to original programming, CBS has original "Innertube" content on its Web site, and in the past year some of *Saturday Night Live*'s most popular skits were viewed by more people on YouTube, the NBC site, and other viral outlets than when they originally aired. For AMC's popular *Mad Men* drama about Madison Avenue admen of the early 1960s, the network cut a deal in which Jack Daniel's whiskey is integrated into the lives of the booze-loving characters as well as into commercial breaks. For the 2008 season MTV Networks is wooing advertisers with a series of "Podbusting" short films that resemble content but are actually commercials, as well as a screen-within-screen technique that will allow viewers to stay tuned to shows like its popular *TRL* broadcast.

Fine ideas all, but not the game changers that the industry needs. In fact, much of the networks' added-value promotional efforts to date feel more like one-off, desperate gimmicks than like a new economic model that will save the networks and the advertisers that sponsor them.

Some people will tell you that TV is dead and the future is digital, but really, what does that mean? Saying today that the future of TV entertainment and advertising will be digital is the equivalent of saying in 1907 that the future of entertainment will be all about electricity.

What genre of digital? Based on what creative and economic model? Who will make it, who will pay for it, and who will reap the benefits?

Despite the preponderance of emerging entertainment options, people still really like to watch television (to the tune of 8.7 hours a day in the average household, up from the previous year, according to August 2007 Nielsen numbers), but given a choice, they do not like ads with their television (DVR ownership is doubling every six months). And every day it is becoming far easier for people to avoid having to watch ads on TV.

———

Because of and despite all of the above, it has become increasingly fashionable to talk about the death of the thirty-second spot. Sure, audience numbers are continuing to go down, and online media are getting an increasing share of advertising budgets.

But dead?

The Death of the Thirty-Second Spot
(A Media-Neutral Dream)

This is how I imagine it will go down. Just before dawn they will kick open the door to Thirty-Second Spot's subterranean Madison Avenue holding cell and jerk him to his feet. "And now a final word from our sponsors," one of his executioners—let's say it's TiVo—will mock. And then another—the Nielsen Box? the Webisode?—will sneer, "Let's go, old-timer: it's time to make the donuts."

Then they will shackle Thirty-Second Spot's once-lavish production values, put a black hood over his mandatory product shot, and lead him by his call to action out into the silent canyon of Madison Avenue. As they hustle the media legend toward a carriage drawn by the Budweiser Clydesdales, high above the street iconic advertising creations will press their maudlin caricatures against the dusty windows of the great agencies that Thirty-Second Spot made famous. "Don't cry, Mr. Whipple." "Chins up, Keebler Elves." "Jumping won't solve anything, Crash Test Dummies."

They finally tracked him down on the day after the Super Bowl, unshaven and disheveled in the large-screen-TV section of Circuit City, repeatedly humming the once-ubiquitous Alka-Seltzer jingle, "Plop, Plop, Fizz, Fizz," waiting for a commercial break that would never come. Technically, he had been on the run since an unconvincing Upfront Week with the networks in May, followed by an absolutely miserable showing in the November sweeps that not even commercials embedded in storylines, a show inspired by, of all things, cavemen from an insurance company commercial, or a humiliating series of teasers that directed viewers to "the good stuff on the Web" could help.

Of course, industry leaders and shepherds of the world's leading brands will come forward to make a final, halfhearted round of appeals. "Thirty-Second Spot is still a unique and viable marketing force," they will say, again. And, "It's an American institution that can do things on a scale that can never be replicated on small screens."

Touching, yes. But we've heard all this before. And the numbers, declining for decades, do not lie.

After a ceremonial lap along the length of Madison Avenue, the carriage will cross the Queensboro Bridge, and the Clydesdales will stop outside a commercial soundstage in Queens. There, a matching pair of Viagra pop-up ads will lead Thirty-Second Spot inside to his final resting place, in front of a giant green screen.

The audience will be filled with Hall of Famers. Mean Joe Greene and the Coke kid. The Maytag Repairman. Bartles & Jaymes. The Go Daddy chick. Madge. Mikey. The frogs. The penguins. The pasty figures in the pin-striped suits silently weeping in the corner: those are the ghosts of Mr. Blandings, the red-haired dude from *Thirtysomething,* and Darrin Stephens.

After the California Raisins perform "What a Wonderful Life" a cappella, there won't be a dry eye in the house.

So this is how it will end. First someone will impatiently shout, *"Wassup?"*, which leads to a viral-video-enhanced chant of *"Just Do It!"* And then twelve hooded figures will appear and form a firing-squad line. They'll be hooded, but these still-thriving digital versions of soon-to-be-former TV icons will hardly be anonymous. After all, it's difficult to cover up a swish, a gecko tale, a uniquely shaped cola bottle, or the giant red shoes of a certain hamburger clown. One of the hoods will even be adorned with a mustache of milk.

Ready . . .

In a final indignity the execution of Thirty-Second Spot will not be televised.

Aim . . .

And yet it will be watched by more people than ever watched a network television show. It will be watched streaming live on the Internet. It will be posted on scores of viral-video sites and shared and replayed and commented on by millions for weeks—no, decades—to come. Millions more will watch it on their cell phones, their favorite tiny gadget, and they will forward it to everyone they know, who will do the same. On our favorite tiny gadget. Inevitably, based on its popularity, someone will create a Death of Thirty-Second Spot alternate-reality game, and finally a TV show that people can watch wherever and whenever they want.

The show, of course, will be saturated with commercials, some as long as a minute.

Last Impression

If this evening's viewing behavior is any sort of indicator, and if my wife and I happened to be part of the demographic about which they give a damn, things don't look good for the networks.

We watched a show on demand. Ironically, it was a commercial-free rebroadcast of last week's episode of *Mad Men*. While we were ordering, there was a video trailer in a small frame in the corner of the screen for another movie (393). When it was over, another trailer (394) played while we scrolled for another on-demand show about some lady who speaks to dead people on the Lifetime network. My wife likes shows where people speak with dead people. This was interesting because before and after each twenty-two-minute episode, and we watched two, there was a legitimate ad. I think it was for Dove. Definitely a cosmetic company (398). Can't be sure, because I was actually looking at my laptop while the show was on; I'm not a big fan of the supernatural.

There was more spam waiting for me online, but this time I was quick to delete anything remotely unfamiliar. At the end of the day, when I am less interested in the promise of the unknown and more interested in eliminating distractions, I am impervious to *bacn* and spam bots.

Later, after the kids had their baths and were in their pajamas, I went to their bedroom to read them a story. It looked like my day would end with just under four hundred impressions. Quite a number, but I'd thought it would be considerably more. Other than the spam incident and the proliferation of roadside campaign signs, I never felt particularly bombarded, or irritated, or offended. Nor did I once find myself sitting up and taking notice, thinking that this advertiser, or this product, was speaking to me. Thinking, "This is well-done. An ad I would have been proud to make."

Plus, again, I'm forty-eight. I'd like to think of myself as a young, media-savvy forty-eight, but the fact is I didn't grow up with video games and the Internet. I don't text, don't have a BlackBerry-like device, and rarely use my cell phone. I opened up *Dinotopia: Journey to Chandara,* but my son spoke before I could begin.

There was a toy he desperately wanted to get for his birthday next month. Some new piece of Power Rangers gear. He saw it on a commercial that afternoon on Nickelodeon. As I began to read, I decided that secondhand commercial messages should indeed count (399).

When I was still making ads, the assignments would stick in my head long after I left the office. As much as I'd try to decompress, I'd still think of them on the train, while making a fire in the woodstove, while watching TV. Sometimes I'd get up from the dinner table and scramble for a pen and paper. In my car I would call myself on my cell phone and leave a message: an insight, a headline, the hint of a tagline, the premise for a campaign.

Sometimes I dreamed about the ads I had to make.

Sometimes I dreamed about making ads I didn't have to make, for products that didn't exist.

Often, while consumed by an assignment, I would get up from a deep sleep in the middle of the night and madly write out an entire TV commercial, replete with stage directions, and sell it the next day.

However, more often than not, the thoughts made no sense, sucking at best and at worst revealing aspects of my dream mind that should never have seen the light of reality.

Thankfully, I don't dream about ads anymore. But if I did, I wonder, would they count?

Maybe I should ask my doctor.

The Opposite of Subliminal

The more the data banks record about each one of us, the less we exist.

—*Marshall McLuhan*

What you call love was invented by guys like me to sell nylons.
—*Don Draper, character on the AMC series* Mad Men

This Episode of the Apocalypse Is Made Possible by the Men and Women of the American Advertising Industry, and Viewers Like You

I'm embarrassed to admit that the first time I'd heard of *The Hidden Persuaders,* Vance Packard's seminal 1957 book about the insidious ways in which advertising "depth researchers" used manipulative psychological methods to corrupt our minds and empty our wallets, was in Mark Greif's smart 2007 essay in the *New York Times Book Review.* The essay, which was written to commemorate the fiftieth anniversary of the book's publication, alternately fascinated, intrigued, and shamed me.

According to Greif's essay, "Packard had tried to warn Americans of a new mutation in advertising. Powerful admen [in the

1950s] were working to tap the irrational in the consumer mind, using the applied psychology and sociology supported by the government in World War II."

The Hidden Persuaders topped the *New York Times* best-seller list in August 1957 and remained a best seller for more than a year. By 1975 there were more than three million copies in print, and with the subsequent publication of two other best-selling books, *The Status Seekers* (1959) and *The Waste Makers* (1960), Packard had become the very thing that he seemingly held in such contempt: a household brand name.

How come I'd never heard of *The Hidden Persuaders*? How come I'd never heard of a best-selling book about my industry that, among other things, contended that "the most serious offense many of the depth manipulators commit . . . is that they try to invade the privacy of our minds. It is this right to privacy in our minds—privacy to be either rational or irrational—that I believe we must strive to protect."

I'd certainly heard of and read David Ogilvy's *Confessions of an Advertising Man* (1963), which apparently was an answer to Packard's indictment, and *Ogilvy on Advertising* (1983) and a number of other supposedly inspiring books about the craft and legends of advertising. Why not this? Did the Man take measures to suppress it? Had Packard's hypotheses on consumerism been debunked or exposed as faulty or dated?

Not according to Greif's essay, which concluded with these words: "Whatever its flaws, I'll keep recommending *The Hidden Persuaders*. For me, it's the original inoculation against manipulation, and every once in a while—perhaps especially in this political season—one needs to go back for a booster."

Because I happened to be writing a book about advertising, and since part of that book was to include a section on strategic planning and focus groups, and since I was about to take a trip to Chicago to spend a day at Leo Burnett Worldwide with members of one of the largest and most sophisticated strategic planning and research divisions in the world, I thought it might be a good idea to first take a look at *The Hidden Persuaders.*

My copy arrived the day before my flight. The best trips are often the ones in which you set out with one itinerary and end up in places you'd never imagined. The minute I began reading Mark Crispin Miller's introduction to the new edition of *The Hidden Persuaders,* I realized my visit to Leo Burnett, which I had originally planned to help provide a basic overview of a day in the life of strategic planners, wasn't going to be as straightforward as I'd imagined.

"A nation built for shopping cannot possibly endure as a democracy," Miller wrote. And, "For our toxic air and water, our tasteless crops and doubtful meats, our ever-rising cancer rates, the 'obesity epidemic' striking down our children, the poisoned imports sent to us from China and, of course, for global warming, we can now belatedly thank Earnest Elmo Calkins, Rosser Reeves, David Ogilvy and all the other geniuses of advertising, and especially, the corporations that retained them."

Well, now. I'd already felt conflicted enough about my tour of duty in advertising, and now I was realizing that everything in the world that I'd always worried about and railed against was actually my fault. Right down to the doubtful meats.

My initial instinct was to dismiss Greif and Packard and Miller.

Surely I'd never witnessed anyone from Packard's "hidden world of motivational research" propose the employment of proprietary psychological techniques to "probe our minds in order to control our actions as consumers." I hadn't seen any "powerful mutations" in the business. Sure, when immersed in an assignment, we would often rely on focus groups and research, and mine our everyday lives for some sort of clue or insight that might form the basis of a creative idea. But it never felt as formal or insidious as Greif, Packard, and now Miller contended. We were usually overworked and shooting from the hip, doing the best we could with limited resources, and often retrofitting our supposed research findings to fit a creative idea, not meeting with manipulators.

Plus, some of the language Packard used to make his case, even fifty years later, seemed intentionally alarmist and hell-bent on doing some persuading of its own, via shock and fear. He repeatedly called the researchers "probers" who were "probing sample humans in an attempt to find how to identify, and beam messages to, people of high anxiety, body consciousness, hostility, passiveness, and so on." Today language like this comes off as more bizarre and kind of funny than shocking, but obviously in 1957, in the middle of the Cold War, it resonated. So yeah, my first inclination was to dismiss him, just as Ogilvy and the powers that be in advertising had dismissed Packard a half century ago.

But the book was fascinating. Reading it spurred me to question not just a fifty-year-old marketing practice but its lasting effects, and the way in which its descendants shape our lives today. Did advertising driven by motivational research turn America into a society grounded in consumerism (in which personal happiness is equated with the purchase and consumption of material possessions)? Are advertisers and researchers appealing to our basest, often most destructive behaviors and desires, or are they creating them?

And even if the answers to all of the above were yes, I thought, what could possibly be the solution? To more stringently regulate or outright ban advertising—First Amendment freedoms be damned? Should the government institute policies limiting consumer purchases? Or programs that would make us feel ashamed for our excessive consumerist lifestyle—capitalism and market economy be damned? Weren't most attacks on advertising in effect attacks on capitalism?

Would the logical outcome of anti-consumerism be, as the University of Florida professor James Twitchell has written, "a return to the sumptuary laws of ancient Rome and medieval times," where the upper-class leaders of government regulated the habits of consumption, often to keep a rising lower class in check?

Then there's the libertarian view of anti-consumerism, which basically is: Who the fuck is anyone to claim the right to decide for me what good or service is necessary, or what is wasteful, or even offensive?

Then again, historically, the behavior of many advertisers has been reprehensible. Packard's book made me recall the 2001 PBS documentary *The Merchants of Cool,* which chronicled marketers' attempts to capitalize on the all-powerful, all-consuming teen market, often by appealing to adolescents' lowest desires, glorifying, for instance, violence, sex, and antisocial behavior. *The Hidden Persuaders* also made me recall in a new light a meeting I once had with my yogurt clients in which I was told that they were going to make a shift in the target for their drinkable children's product. For years they had focused their message toward moms, playing up the yogurt's appeal as a nutritious snack that would help their kids grow big and strong. But in the meeting they told me now they wanted to target the kids, to focus on taste and fun, and to have animated characters disseminate their message. The reason? Research had unearthed something called "the nag factor" where, if kids see messages for something they desire often enough, they will nag Mom into consumer submission. And that was an easier behavior to trigger than having a rational conversation with busy moms. Surely it wasn't illegal, but was it unethical? And if so, why hadn't I called them on it?

I read most of the book the night before I left for Chicago and finished the rest in flight. I was supposed to be prepping for my meetings at Leo Burnett, but my thoughts were with Packard. In fact, the more I thought about his book as I rode the Blue Line train from O'Hare to State and Lake, the more I believed that even more sophisticated versions of the methods described in *The Hidden Persuaders* are still being employed today. But today, nobody seems to care.

The first question I wrote in my notebook was, why?

> *I am the center of the culture. I am genesis, herald, harbinger. The absolute germinal zero point—that's me. I am the sun around which all the American else orbits. In fact, I am America, I exist more than other Americans. America is the center of the world, and I am the center of America. I am fifteen, white, middle class and male. Middle-aged men and women scurry for my attention. What Internet sites I visit. What I buy. What my desires are. What movies I watch. What and who I want; when and how I want it. People get paid a lot of money to think of how to get to me and mine. Everything is geared to me. When you see those herky-jerky close-ups in action movies, where the camera jumps and chops its way in rather hyperly to the close-up of the hero, that is not for anyone but me . . . Don't worry if you don't get it—that's the point. You are excluded.*
>
> —*Dana Spiotta*, Eat the Document

What Makes the People Tick Whose Job Is to Figure Out What Makes You Tick?

In 1935 Leo Burnett did what ambitious ad folks have done since the industry began: he jumped ship from his current job and started his own agency. His first client, which had left his former agency with him, was the Minnesota Valley Canning Company.

His first campaign for the canning company? The Jolly Green Giant.

Perhaps based on this formula, Burnett went on to create some of the most iconic and bizarre brand characters in advertising history, some of which haunt my dreams to this day: Morris the Cat, Charlie the Tuna, the Maytag Repairman, the Pillsbury Doughboy, Tony the Tiger, and the Marlboro Man. To many, even to this day, Burnett is synonymous with simple, if not hokey, campaigns, known originally as the "Midwest style."

But despite his being more than a thousand miles from the hucksters of Madison Avenue, there was nothing simple or hokey about the way in which Leo Burnett went about his business. Famous for his campaigns and his work ethic and for making agencies more socially responsible, he was also one of the first to have his agency use motivational research in the making of ads. Prior to the 1930s, most agencies limited their research to statistical analysis. For instance, Arthur Nielsen employed statistical science to measure advertising effectiveness in magazines starting in the 1920s, and the father of professional polling, George Gallup, left his job at Northwestern University in 1932 and for sixteen years headed up the research division at Young & Rubicam Advertising on Madison Avenue. Although he was often skeptical of an overdependence on research, Burnett was at the forefront of a group of admen who took research beyond the realm of statistics and into the subconscious. Through many quotations attributed to him, including some of his speeches (of particular note is his retirement speech, "When to Take My Name off the Door," viewable online), Burnett can come across as an incredibly dedicated, motivating, and righteous leader. There's nothing unscrupulous in nuggets like:

"Steep yourself in your subject, work like hell, and love, honor and obey your hunches."

Or, "Anyone who thinks that people can be fooled or pushed around has an inaccurate and pretty low estimation of people—and won't do very well in advertising."

And, "Regardless of the moral issue, dishonesty in advertising has proved very unprofitable."

Sound bites like these get you into the Advertising Hall of Fame and your signature etched on the walls outside the worldwide headquarters. Yet what's subject to debate with Burnett, indeed with anyone who has ever worked in advertising, and, I imagine, with us all, is what exactly constitutes "dishonesty." Consider some of these other notable Leo-isms:

"Good advertising doesn't just circulate information. It penetrates the public mind with desires and beliefs."

Or, via the "thought force of symbols, we absorb [ads] through our pores, without knowing we do so. By osmosis."

And later, "Television is the strongest drug we've ever had to dish out."

Perhaps Burnett thought that if something was true, it couldn't be dishonest. Sneaky and irresponsible, yes. And in some instances (the legendary success of the Marlboro Man campaign) potentially fatal, but not dishonest. So was it wrong to, as Burnett did, purposely incorporate symbols into ads that would register subliminally? Is there an ethical difference between "stimulating basic desires and beliefs" and exploiting fears and playing off the weaknesses and anxieties of the public?

Still in the Shadow of the Jolly Green Giant, but Not Yet in the Door, and Further Proof That Advertising Is a $670-Billion-a-Year Enigma

Because I was more than an hour early for my first meeting at Leo Burnett, I called a Chicago-based writer whom I'd "met" in an online literary salon/book group. I know this sounds like a good way to get murdered, meeting a virtual stranger in a far-off city, but we'd been corresponding for almost a year, and he worked just around the corner from Leo's offices at 35 West Wacker.

After some book talk, my friend asked me about advertising, and my progress with this book. I kept it short. After all, he was a literary man—indeed online he was scholarly, well-read, funny, and erudite—and he was probably just being polite. Presently, he pointed out the window of the coffee shop. "I guess you heard what happened here just the other day," he said.

I shook my head.

He told me: a guy at DDB Chicago, a big creative executive, forty years old, married father of two girls, jumped off the upper floor of the Fairmont Chicago Hotel.

I looked out the window. From where we sat, I couldn't see the hotel, which left just enough to the imagination to make the incident seem more tragic. For some reason, whenever I am in Chicago, at least once I get the distinct feeling that I am living in the 1920s, in a Theodore Dreiser novel.

"Why?"

"I'm not sure. But it's a big thing beyond Chicago because a lot of people are blaming the advertising blogs. One was especially harsh, tearing him up over an internal memo he'd written."*

I shook my head. There I was, a supposed expert writing a book about advertising, and I needed the moderator of the Fyodor Dos-

---

* The blog, Agency Spy, had criticized a leaked, internal, cliché-ridden inspirational memo that the creative director had written. The post and the anonymous comments that followed, as is often the case with ad blogs, were brutal and personal. Then a few days later, with the news of the man's death, the posts took on a different tone. Some contended that the blogger and the blog's cowardly, anonymous hecklers were responsible for driving the man to jump. Others blamed the stress of the industry. Then one notable post made an allegation that the *Chicago Tribune* and *Chicago Sun-Times* chose not to run: the presence of another woman in the hotel, which set off an entirely different ethical discussion about privacy and the ramifications of too much transparency in the blogosphere.

toyevsky *The Idiot* thread from the Fiction Files to tell me the latest ad industry news. I wondered what type of person would kill himself over advertising, let alone a badly reviewed memo? Also, I was curious as to why a subject like this was on my friend's finely tuned cultural radar. "So, do you read advertising blogs?"

"Sometimes," he said. That's interesting. I'd deduced from our e-mails that he was some kind of consultant, or a professor. Way too cultured to wallow in the muck of advertising. Before I could reply, he reached into his pocket and pulled out a nicely designed business card. It was for an advertising agency. He was the president.

Leoland

When great pitchmen die, animation makes them immortal.

When I worked on the Kentucky Fried Chicken business, some years after the death of its founder and corporate face, Colonel Harland Sanders (whom my boss once repeatedly called "the Captain" while setting up a disastrous presentation before dozens of horrified franchisees), much debate was dedicated (and, I imagine, is to this day) to how to deal with the image of the man in the white suit. A significant amount of money was spent on a series of branding explorations, which seemed to resurface whenever sales were down. Should the Colonel's image be drawn realistically, or cartoony, or with an Andy Warhol silk-screen effect? And regarding TV, was simply showing his animated face on the bucket enough? Or should his animated, disembodied head be a graphic "bug," a constant presence in the lower-right corner of the screen? Or should he be fully animated, featured skipping through live action in the spots, his voice provided by an actor like, say, Randy Quaid? Or finally, should we just cease using his likeness altogether because, really, who wants to think of a dead guy when they're munching out?

My agency tried each of these approaches at one time or another. I imagine the agency that had the Wendy's account after the
owner and pitchman, Dave Thomas, died struggled with similar
brand-legacy concerns. And the people doing Orville Redenbacher's
current popcorn commercials have chosen to sign off with a grainy
black-and-white film clip of what I couldn't help but see as the old
man's ghost. It didn't make me think about hot buttered popcorn. It
made me think about death, and a recently disturbed grave site.

Stepping out of the Chicago chill and inside Leo Burnett Worldwide, I wondered if the master brand-character maker Burnett, who
died in 1971, had a say in how his own brand legacy would be managed. My guess, as a visitor escort took me up a special guest elevator, was yes, judging by the preponderance of his signature on the
walls, the legendary apple baskets on the lobby tables (carrying on
the mandatory creation myth*), and Leo's words and likenesses
everywhere, as ubiquitous as mouse ears in Orlando (not surprising,
since Disney is a Burnett client).

The cumulative effect a visitor feels after just a few minutes inside is that the agency was founded not by a man but (like Disney)
by a mythological figure. Or at the very least by someone who tacitly
understood Middle America's love affair with dreams and symbols.

Regardless, today Leo Burnett Worldwide, which is now owned
by the French communications consortium Publicis Groupe, has
ninety-seven offices in eighty-four countries with more than eight
thousand employees, including more than a thousand in Chicago,
and has annual billings in excess of $10 billion. Leo's current clients

---

* Leo legend has it that when the agency opened in the midst of the Great Depression in 1935, a Chicago newspaper columnist predicted that Burnett would be
out in the street selling apples within months. Burnett vowed to give them away instead, and in an agency built upon symbols, the fittingly loaded symbol of apples in
the lobby, beckoning clients and visitors alike to indulge, has prevailed for more
than seventy years.

include some of the world's most recognized and, not coincidentally, research-intensive brands: McDonald's, Coca-Cola, the Walt Disney Company, Kellogg's, and the U.S. Army.

A Road Map Called Desire

Several years ago, a creative team at a large agency beginning a new assignment would typically get a one-page brief from a strategic planner. For more important, higher-billing assignments, the brief would be the end product of a period of concept testing, or behavioral research geared to glean a salient insight about the target, combined with common sense.

For instance, on the AT&T consumer business, while formulating a brief, a planner would speak to current customers or the competition and determine what they liked and disliked most about their phone service, and about AT&T in particular. Sometimes this would lead to a straightforward rational target insight such as customers want a simpler bill, or a headier nugget about their desire for "anytime, anywhere communication," or, in an age where individuals feel increasingly marginalized and alienated, a greater desire to have a voice or be part of a community. For the client, however, the business opportunity (read: obstacle to overcome) would be framed differently. For instance, "Establish leadership in this new era of communications by empowering users via our network capabilities, or become obsolete." Or, "Increase minutes on the network."

For AT&T's business clients, planners discovered that on a functional level, reliability was the most coveted attribute, but on a more behavioral level time was the thing they valued most in their lives. It was the planners' job to take this information, distill it down to a brief, and share it with us. Sometimes our eyes would light up with the opportunity to work against a compelling behavioral insight or desire; other times our eyes would simply roll because, while the better insights often lead to legitimate trends, the more pedestrian observations sink to the level of cliché.

In basic terms, there have always been two reasons to conduct advertising research: to discover what your consumers want or feel in relation to a product or service; and to confirm if a campaign will work or is working.

I was always a big fan of up-front research. To make great work, I found it helped to know as much as possible about the target, the product, and the relation between the two. But the latter, testing that critiqued storyboards or finished spots, I saw as nothing more than a way to kill good and especially breakthrough work, rather than give it life. In fact, many of the best ads I was ever a part of suffered brutal, torturous deaths in focus groups, often while I sat on the other side of a one-way mirror, apoplectically gorging M&M's and berating the twelve men from Teaneck who held my fate in their hands. For a while I even put a video clip of a focus group participant's response to my work at the front of my commercial show reel: after watching a video storyboard for a proposed commercial for AT&T's innovative products that I loved, and which, until that moment, the client loved, too, a thirty-five-year-old homemaker said, "What kind of drugs was the guy who wrote this taking?"

For the record, the spot, to the best of my knowledge a drug-free idea, was a surreal tale of a futuristic traveling bubble-wrap salesman who, after tucking in his children by teleport, liked to say things such as "Living in the future is sweet, baby!"

If you think this is sour grapes on my part (which it is), there's a telling video on YouTube that brilliantly demonstrates the way in which even a classic commercial can be nibbled to death by the ducks of a focus group. In the video, created by Arnold Communications in Boston, a focus group is exposed to an exact storyboard version of Chiat\Day's "1984" Super Bowl spot for Apple Computer, arguably the most provocative and powerful commercial of all time. After the commercial finished, the people gathered around the table wasted no time in tearing it to pieces, with comments ranging from "I like happy and this isn't happy" to the suggestion that the actors should "maybe wear T-shirts bearing the Apple logo" or "break out into a dance routine. Like Michael Jackson." Their final, near-unanimous recommendation was that the client, Apple, "definitely should not move forward with this commercial."

Some of the most innovative approaches in marketing and planning and research have originated at Leo Burnett. And year after year, it is as close to a lock as one can get to win more Effie Awards than any other agency in the world.

Yes, but Has Anyone Ever Seen Ice Cubes While Looking at Sex?

Ben Kline doesn't much look like a persuader, hidden or otherwise. Instead, the chief strategy officer for Leo Burnett Worldwide/Arc looks and, more important, acts like a listener. Which makes sense, since his job, as well as that of most of the people who report to him, isn't to convince or persuade but to observe, gather, and interpret as much information as possible before distilling it down to a blueprint for creatives. So, in a perfect world, before a creative team floats the first feather of an idea into the air for any ad on any Leo account, Kline's team has provided them with a concise plan that is a fusion of many disciplines.

"Ideally, we want the research group to guide the behavioral discovery. What is the behavior that is defining a business? This takes some time and some digging. We also want to know, how do people react to an experience? What do they want? What bothers or surprises them? An extra development in the modern age, because we have so many additional media components and potential canvases to create with than we used to, is that we now have experience planners. As much as possible they will observe consumers in their natural environments engaged in the behavior related to our brand, rather than a bad or sanitized focus group facility.

"For instance, for certain goods, we'll do ethnographies in someone's home, engaging in extended conversations and interviews, trying to understand what makes them comfortable and why. But for our Miller Brewing client, we're much better off in a bar, observing and talking."

In addition to chronicling consumer behaviors and desires in their natural settings, environmental planners at Leo take on some of the additional responsibilities of media planner. The task of the media planner used to be relatively simple: allocate print, TV, and outdoor spending in a way that would deliver the biggest bang (most impressions) for the budget. But now there are myriad new elements, seemingly every day: viral video and guerrilla marketing, YouTube and Webisodes, Facebook and other forms of social media, all customizable on a micro level. "Especially because of the digital component today," Kline told me, "it's important that we map out the context of the media, to determine where a message will have the most impact and meaning. So at this point we can determine: here's the behavior, here's the experience, and here's the points that matter most where this person can come into contact with this brand."

Finally, all of this information falls into the lap of the planner, and, according to Kline, "the art of planning is to drive the most relevant behavior into a powerful insight that creatives can work with. Basically, the planner says what she expects this work can do, what behavior it can change, and what the desired outcome is."

It's almost unheard of for an agency or client to cite real-world, in-progress examples of the planning process, especially at an agency this big, where mega-clients guard the management of their brands like state secrets, a strategic nuance has the potential to change a category, and the annual billings for most brands exceed the gross national product of many nations. But this abridged case history for a recent McDonald's commercial has been given the Leo Burnett PR stamp of approval and demonstrates how various planning disciplines come together: researchers and experiential planners noticed that more and more dads had been bringing home takeout as a treat for family dinner (behavioral/experiential insight). However, broader studies of men revealed that certain types of men were feeling confused about their patriarchal role, unappreciated by their families, and less than heroic in general (emotional insight).

Working with this information, creatives then conceived of an execution that portrayed an everyday dad as less than sitcom-dad goofy for a change, and even a tad heroic. The result: a spot called "Dad's Making Dinner," which shows children around the world frantically announcing this fact to their siblings, not in horror, but with excitement, because Dad is bringing home big bags of food adorned with Golden Arches. Then, because experience planners noticed that these same dads spend a lot of time not only watching sports (no surprise here) but also online, perhaps playing violent real-time video games to act out their unfulfilled aggressions, we might see online teasers in addition to traditional, full-up TV ads on the expected sporting events.

Other than the fact that a lot of people (me included) are spending an inordinate amount of time thinking about hamburgers, the above scenario doesn't seem particularly evil to me. I know, fast food makes us fat and lazy, and it's filled with preservatives and cholesterol and hormones that make us addicted to programs like *The Jerry Springer Show*. But it's not crack. And we do live in a market economy. And the way in which the agency went about forming its strategy and executing its creative product didn't seem particularly insidious. A simple, human truth was unearthed, needs and markets were identified, and a message was created and revealed in places and media where it would resonate most.

To a morally conflicted ex-adman it kind of made sense. In fact, the more I spoke with Kline, a veteran of premier creative shops, including Fallon and Wieden+Kennedy (where he oversaw Nike's global brand), the more I was reminded of a section in *The Hidden Persuaders* where Packard actually admitted that "a great many advertising men . . . in fact, numerically a majority, still do a straightforward job and accept us as rational citizens (whether we are or not)." Not only that, these admen, Packard continued, "fill an important and constructive role in our society. Advertising, for example, not only plays a vital role in our economic growth but is a colorful, diverting aspect of American life; and many of the creations of ad men are tasteful, honest works or artistry."

Kline was hardly the supreme commander of the evil probers; he was a smart guy linking products with desires, as are most people in advertising (other than the smart part).

But Packard's critique still lingered in my mind, if not in the very walls of Burnett's offices. Fiftysome years ago Packard had spent a lot of time doing research in Chicago, and "the depth boys" at Leo Burnett had figured prominently in his book as unabashed persuaders.

In fact, a highlight of *The Hidden Persuaders* is the case history of how, with the introduction of masculine, western imagery and new packaging, Burnett transformed the image of Marlboro from a feminine, filter-tipped brand to the smoke of the rugged horseback-riding cowboy, capturing a huge portion of the male market share while still retaining the bulk of the brand's female smokers.

The story of the Marlboro Man is the stuff of advertising/branding legend. But that was before the rise of consumerism. Before the surgeon general. I asked Kline if he'd ever considered whether the research findings his department unearthed might be used for less than ethical purposes. For instance, to manipulate or corrupt rather than provoke and inform?

I expected a dismissive laugh, or a quick call to security for two men in Jolly Green Giant suits to escort me from the building, but Kline smiled and shook his head. "There's too much at stake for the brands we're working with. We're basically trying to figure out what people want and connect them to it in the most meaningful way."

"What about this book I just read?" I continued, holding up my dog-eared copy of *The Hidden Persuaders*. "It claimed that back in the '50s our thoughts and feelings were being manipulated by research people in ad agencies. Fifty years later, is there some kind of modern version of this?"

"What?" Kline laughed. "Like sex in the ice cubes?"

Actually, I thought, that's *Subliminal Seduction,* another book that tried to expose the insidious evil that admen sneak into our lives (like airbrushing the word "sex" into the ice cubes of a liquor ad, or phallic imagery in all kinds of ads), and which I hadn't read in some time. So, feeling like a jerk, I laughed, too. Ha! What was I thinking? Evil persuaders and manipulators, trying to probe our minds. Preposterous!

Then Ben Kline leaned forward and told me this: "You know what you should really check out?"

"What's that?"

"The UCLA Brain Mapping Center."

I swallowed hard and nodded.

"You'd get a big kick out of it because the science there has advanced so much in the last few years. It's a pretty sexy thing; as a testing source, it eliminates the tendency we all have to either lie or not interpret what we're feeling into words. What you're literally seeing is the brain firing in regions where stuff gets coded and there is no room for error—it's true or not. You can take the vagaries of human response out of the equation, so you know whether your message is having an effect."

To someone whose life has been built upon the vagaries of human response, this sounded both compelling and troubling. "You," I began. "You've seen it?"

"Yeah. It's fascinating."

"And . . . and you think there's an advertising application for it? For brain mapping?"

"Right now, it's probably good only as a way to do post-testing. To determine whether someone liked a spot or not. But in the future . . . and this is my opinion because others in our group—I call the twenty-fifth floor the best intellectual bar fight in the business because we have so many passionate brains walking its halls—they will dismiss it totally."

"In the future?"

Kline shrugged. "Who knows?"

Advertising people who ignore research are as dangerous as generals who ignore decodes of enemy signals.

—*David Ogilvy*

Pay No Attention to the Worldwide Man Expert's Breasts and Vagina

The first time I met Rose Cameron we were in the back of a town car leaving Madison Avenue for an afternoon client meeting with AT&T in New Jersey. Because I'd been too busy scrambling to prepare for the meeting to bother with lunch, I was tossing down a turkey sandwich, a protein shake, and a blond brownie while she briefed me on our latest plan of attack. She was new to my account, and I was not. We had reached the stage where every meeting with this client might be our last, and I had reached the stage where, because of the circumstances on this and every account I'd ever worked on, I had become desensitized to fear and resigned to whatever fate awaited us at their offices in Basking Ridge.

While listening to Rose, who had previously worked on the IBM business at Ogilvy & Mather, rattle off a string of profanity-laced telecom, B2B (business to business), IT (information technology), and human insights, each a nugget of truth and prescience about the work and home lives of our target (mostly male IT people and C-suite executives), I realized that she was not your average planner. She was force-of-nature smart, uninhibited, and funny. And she wasn't afraid to tell her creative counterpart, in her thick Scottish accent, that he had honey mustard on his cheek, and jacket, and jeans. "You're such a guy," she said. "And no, I don't want a piece of your bloody fucking blondie."

I knew then that we would get along famously, and for the brief time we worked together, under less than ideal circumstances, we did. Today, Rose Cameron is a senior vice president and planning director at Burnett, working on brands such as Coca-Cola, McDonald's, and Pontiac. She is also one of the agency's resident "single-subject experts." More specifically and not at all surprising, her single subject of expertise is no less than half of the planet's adult population.

The last time I'd spoken with Rose was when I interviewed her for an article I was writing about male trends for a nudity-free men's magazine. This is when she told me about her alternate title, and the global study of men she had overseen for Burnett. Our conversation ranged from a discussion of the Darwinian utility of the shape of the head of the penis (something to do with making sure one's sperm stays in while the sperm of the previous baboon/caveman/warthog is scooped out—an anecdote that, to the best of my knowledge, did not make it into the study) to the specific findings of her research, which has been widely quoted and regularly updated since it premiered to great industry fanfare at the 2005 Cannes Lions International Advertising Festival.

Among the findings: "This is a confusing time for guys. With the world trending increasingly feminine, more and more of the social constructs that men have taken for granted are teetering." And, "What all [men around the world] have in common is a desire to want to know how to win respect and admiration as a man."

According to Cameron, this confused, feminine-trending male is the by-product of a number of factors. As societies transitioned from industrial to technological, workplaces became less physically demanding and more sexually integrated. This left an increasing number of men, many of whom reported to women, confused, with fewer outlets to demonstrate physical prowess, blow off steam, and temper anxiety. Which is why it's no coincidence that the man study found that more and more men worldwide have been turning to violent, uncensored, highly competitive, and totally anonymous online gaming to behave however the hell they want to, without consequence. Feeling emasculated, frustrated, and confused in the workplace? Go online and become, for instance, Remhto (Othmer, backward), god of sex without small talk and senseless, intergalactic violence, and you'll feel a whole lot better.

Some of this worldwide male confusion, according to the study, also suggests that modern men are lacking in role models to guide them, primarily because their fathers haven't exactly set the most shining examples.

I couldn't resist giving the phenomenon a name.

The Hasselhoff Effect

So, according to the man study, the definition of what it means to be a responsible man is being rewritten by men who seem anything but responsible. According to Cameron, who surveyed thousands of men in fifteen countries, the much-maligned bachelor is getting older, and he just may have a better handle on responsible, twenty-first-century masculinity than anyone thought.

According to the study, in 1970 more than half of American men in their mid-twenties were married. Today it's less than one in five. Apparently, a generation of men—men raised in divorce, or who have glimpsed their bitter, unfulfilled dads silently weeping in the garage, or who have been subjected to the YouTube video of David Hassel-hoff slobbering drunk in front of his daughter—are giving marriage, fatherhood, and the concept of masculinity a bit of a rethink.

"Because of the environment in which they were raised, men in their mid-twenties today are far more sensitive to the repercussions of their actions and the ramifications of 'responsibility,'" said Cameron. "They've seen that their fathers' concept of masculinity didn't work out so well."

To hedge their bets, Cameron said, "they want to ensure that they've explored every avenue and figure out what it means to be a fulfilled modern man before they commit to a marriage." This includes anything from extreme tourism to pursuing vocations because they want to rather than ought to, to experiencing every aspect of a relationship with a woman short of the matching gold bands.

Cameron called this process "self-actualization." Your father would probably call it fucking off.

So we have reached a point where being noncommittal might be the most responsible thing a man can do. Cameron said that if this trend plays out, because men aren't following the same old man path anymore, the divorce rate will actually keep dropping. "This is potentially because more actualized men are beginning to create married lives that truly reflect their needs."

The Johns Hopkins sociologist Andrew Cherlin recently wrote, "Marriage used to be the first step in adulthood; now it's the last." Which would seem to mean that at some point, that twenty-seven-year-old single dude whose life is the envy of married men and the bane of single women will declare himself self-actualized enough to tie the knot.

Then he can start making a whole new set of Hasselhoffian mistakes that an entirely new generation of children can blame him for.

As an intellectually curious person, I love this stuff. This type of information reveals yet another aspect of who we are and what we value and desire without passing judgment. But as an advertising veteran, I also realize that information such as the man study can be abused. Because, as Spider-Man's uncle Ben said, "With great power comes great responsibility."

Which makes one wonder where brain mapping might fit in. Or hypnosis.*

In addition to leveraging its man study to make a big promotional splash in the ad world, Leo Burnett was making another, more im-

---

* It's true. According to a recent *Adweek* article ("Marketers Use Hypnosis to Mine Deep Thoughts"), many brands and agencies are putting focus group participants under. For instance, wide-awake participants said that the name of the carmaker Volvo equals safety. Yet when asked the same question while hypnotized, they revealed a less flattering truth: Volvo also equals being middle-aged. The participants were then given the suggestion that as soon as they woke up, they were to rush out and purchase a new, fully loaded Volvo (only kidding, I think).

portant announcement: there was a shitload of money to be made off modern man based on the study's findings. Indeed, with up to 80 percent of men surveyed around the world saying that the images they saw in contemporary advertising were out of touch with reality, Burnett saw a great opportunity to help brands get it right. One way was to better define and differentiate the typical male archetypes.

"In recent years," Cameron said, "marketers were too preoccupied with metrosexuals [for example, the well-coifed soccer star David Beckham] and retrosexuals [the Vince Vaughn character in *Old School,* who refuses to adapt]. It's been overhyped, and we found the distinctions to be far more complex." Globally, the study found that 24 percent of men fall into the metrosexual category, with 16 percent clinging to retro ways. This information led to a more nuanced dissection of the male psyche, especially for the 60 percent of men who had previously defied categorization. This led to new, additional labels like patriarchs (good family men) and power seekers (greedy, egotistical bastards). The study goes to great lengths to chronicle the struggles of men trying to balance their desires to be both. Hence the previously mentioned McDonald's "Dad's Making Dinner" spot.

Bombs Versus Burgers

Since Rose and I had previously spoken at length about the man study, I settled for a brief update (the upshot of which is, three years later, we males are still confused, misunderstood, and complex beings). Over a late-afternoon beer in her office, Rose did a riff about the classic archetypes of businesses. I'd heard a lot of this before while working at Y&R. Kind of like Joseph Campbell meets Campbell's soup, but Rose's explanation of it was still interesting. McDonald's, for instance, had been the dreamer. Now it is the innocent. She said its recent commercial with the young African American kid who brings his boom box to the family table and eats his Happy Meal to "Cha-Cha Slide" is a perfect example of the innocent archetype.

Finally, I asked Rose if she had ever considered the ethical implications of her job. If there were times when she felt that she was the proponent of an evil industry. Before she could answer, I told her about *The Hidden Persuaders* and my talk with Ben Kline and his tip about brain mapping and my father being a hardworking bricklayer who never had to think about things like this and the state of my tortured and conflicted soul.

Maybe I wasn't trending feminine, but I was a million miles from being the Marlboro Man. "Are you done, Othmer?"

I nodded.

"I just got back from a trip to Washington," Rose said, "where I was speaking on behalf of the pro bono group the Council for Opportunity in Education [coenet.us], which is all about helping get disadvantaged kids access to higher education and university degrees. I was there and they were listening to me because I am a senior vice president and planning director at one of the world's largest advertising agencies. I know the difference between right and wrong, and wherever I can, I try to make things better, to get my clients to do better. I have the power to influence positive changes.

"Do you know that a few years ago, at the funeral of one of my grandparents, I was standing beside my father, and when the ceremony was over, he looked at me and said, 'So, Rose, when are you going to do something worthwhile with your life?' "

This was the same man who sent the worldwide man expert to a boarding school in Scotland when she was four years old and who, as a scientist for the U.S. military, had helped to develop the Stinger missile. "You mean worthwhile, like inventing a bomb?" she told him. "A missile that could kill and devastate entire populations?"

After I finished my beer and said good-bye, I got onto the down elevator, this time unescorted, and thought about the state of man, Marlboro and otherwise, and the Stinger missile. I wondered if it was ever actually marketed and, if so, whether the message had been supported by research.

> *Advertising is not the noblest creation of man's mind, as so many of its advocates would like the public to think. It does not, single-handedly, sustain the whole structure of capitalism and democracy in the Free World. It is just as nonsensical to suggest that we are superhuman as to accept the indictment that we are subhuman. We are merely human, trying to do a necessary human job with dignity, with decency and with competence.*
>
> *—Leo Burnett*

Zapping the Zeitgeist

Half the money I spend on advertising is wasted; the trouble is, I don't know which half.

—John Wanamaker

The Super Bowl of Super Bowl Ad Reviews

This wouldn't be a proper book about advertising without a consideration of its biggest day. I wish I could wax obnoxious about my storied Super Bowl advertising past, but the sad truth is I came close to airing a Super Bowl spot only once, in 1997, and the reason it didn't air wasn't my fault. It was the Denver Broncos' fault.

That's because my agency's new Denver-headquartered telecommunications client had said that if the highly regarded Broncos, who had a 13-3 regular season record and were led by the future Hall of Fame quarterback John Elway, made it to that year's Super Bowl, they would run at least one of the spots we were in the process of shooting. That all fell apart as I sat in a Seattle bar with my production crew on January 4 and watched a lowly wild-card team, the upstart Jacksonville Jaguars, overcome a twelve-point deficit and score on six consecutive possessions to upset the heavily favored Broncos.

I tried to pretend that I didn't care, that I didn't mind missing out on having my spot watched by some ninety million viewers, including the industry trades and every creative director in North America. I tried to forget that if it was well reviewed, it very well could have changed my life. But my bar tab said otherwise.

So when I finally sat down to watch Super Bowl XXXI in 1997, it wasn't to watch my telecommunications spot; it was once again to watch the brilliance of others, and to hear my father-in-law, after watching the latest Bud, FedEx, or Pepsi spot, say what he has said during every Super Bowl for the last twenty-five years: "Why don't you ever do something like that?"

Today, for younger creative people who work across a number of new-media channels, Super Bowl ads don't seem to have the glamour or appeal they once did. But still, the Super Bowl remains the most visible and powerful advertising medium in the world, truly capable of changing the careers and fortunes of the people who create its most memorable commercials.

One Day of Passion Versus 364 of Abstinence

In late 2007, more than two months before the kickoff of Super Bowl XLII, all but two of Fox's sixty-three in-game commercial units had been sold, and for record rates. This was a dramatic departure from the previous few Super Bowl broadcasts, when networks were peddling unsold, discounted inventory right until the moment when the performer du jour was carted out to bastardize the national anthem.

The quick sales weren't because the spots were selling at bargain rates: indeed, to the pleasure of Rupert Murdoch, Fox Sports, and the NFL, brands were spending up to $2.7 million for a thirty-second spot on the February 3 broadcast,* with discounts available to repeat advertisers (if you can call $80,000, as opposed to $90,000, a second a discount).

According to Lou D'Ermilio, senior vice president of media relations at Fox Sports, selling out a Super Bowl at unprecedented prices, while the leaves were still on the trees in Manhattan, was, well, unprecedented. Even taking global warming into account, I thought that this autumnal windfall had to be good news for big-time, big-brand, TV-heavy advertising, which needs all the good news it can get, right?

But then I began to wonder, why? Why, this year in particular, were the mega-brands so quick to commit to spending more money on a half minute of network airtime than it costs to produce most full-length features being screened at Sundance?

They sure weren't splurging (as they had in prewar, pre–Janet Jackson Nipplegate, dot-com-infatuated 2000) because of a robust economy. Or, one would hope, to jump on the Tom Petty halftime show bandwagon.

No, I realized, Super Bowl advertisers weren't going for broke because they were flush with fourth-quarter profits, or bullish on the future, or because Fox has a special tie-in program with MySpace.

They were going for broke because they were desperate.

At first glance, it didn't make a lot of sense. After all, this was advertising's biggest day of the year, and if the NFL matchup gods cooperated, it had the potential to become its biggest day ever. There wasn't anything particularly desperate about that.

After all, what was there not to like about having ninety-three

---

* For the 2009 Super Bowl, despite the worsening economy, NBC Universal got close to $3 million per thirty-second spot, or $100,000 per second.

million captive, engaged viewers, a third of them women, in more than 63 percent of American homes—all not just watching but anticipating, embracing (to the tune of 99.6 percent audience commercial retention), and critiquing your message? And if they did happen to reach for the dreaded DVR, it would be not to fast-forward past your ad but to stop the live action on the field, the so-called content, so they can play it—your ad!—again and again.

The reason for the desperation had less to do with what was happening in adland on Super Bowl Sunday than with the state of network-TV advertising the other 364 days of the year. Because on those days that don't feature a Super Bowl, the dynamic is almost completely inverted.

On those days, commercials are not embraced by consumers; they are something to be avoided at all costs. Zapped, TiVoed, and DVRed into oblivion. On those 364 days, many TV programs aren't watched live. They're watched whenever the viewer gets around to it, sometimes on a screen smaller than a Post-it note.

So on Super Bowl Sunday, network TV was poised to set an all-time one-day viewership record. But on the following Monday and on every day until the next Super Bowl, it would revert to a ratings tailspin that continues to drop to historic lows. Throw in the 2007 writers' strike, which just about killed the new network season as well, and it becomes glaringly obvious why brands with a big, timely story to tell gobbled up that Super Bowl time much earlier than usual. They had no choice.

I tried my hypothesis on Tom McGovern, U.S. director of sports media, Optimum Sports, who buys time for the Super Bowl perennial PepsiCo, and he didn't laugh. "With the uncertainty in prime time, there's definitely been a trend to advertise with live sports and mega-events. Major brands need major outlets with mass reach to launch new products and campaigns. The Super Bowl is the best and one of the last places to make that kind of splash."

The promise of a rare large, captive audience is also why there would be more movie trailers (twelve) during the 2007 game than ever before on a Super Bowl broadcast. While trailers aren't exactly the kinds of commercials that will be passionately discussed the next day around watercoolers or in the blogosphere, they were being so prominently featured this year because of three letters: DVR.

"If you're a movie opening on a fixed date, you can't wait seven days for people to look at your trailer," explained D'Ermilio at Fox Sports, before repeating his hard-to-contest company line: "The Super Bowl is 100 percent DVR-proof."

Reflection of the Culture or Accidental Zeitgeist?

It is a widely held belief that a consideration of the Super Bowl ads of a given year will accurately reflect the buzz of pop culture if not the zeitgeist of the day. Consider some of the usual suspects: Budweiser's "Lizards" (1997) taking the piss out of the concept of corporate spokespeople (the frogs) by trying to kill them; or Apple's Orwellian Ridley Scott–directed classic "1984"; or the White House Office of National Drug Control Policy's series of 2002 spots that ominously linked smoking marijuana to, among other things, terrorism; or perhaps the spot that most accurately reflected the American economic zeitgeist at any given time, the 1999 E*Trade "Dancing Monkey" spot that captured the unbridled enthusiasm of the dot-com era when it proclaimed, "We just wasted $2 million. What are you doing with your money?" A statement that, according to my former colleague Corey Rakowsky, an associate creative director at Young & Rubicam Advertising, "made us feel for the first and perhaps last time ever that money isn't so serious."

For the record, money started becoming serious again several weeks after the following year's Super Bowl, a game in which seventeen dot-com companies advertised, when the Nasdaq began its historic crash.

"Year after year, clients demand that we be as edgy as the Apple '1984' commercial, forgetting that the context of 1984 was much less competitive and demanding of attention," says Jeff Goodby, co-chairman of Goodby, Silverstein & Partners in San Francisco. "Super Bowl commercials are an anomaly of communication, and, I must say, I usually discourage clients from attempting them, even though we've had a pretty good track record of success [including the Bud lizards and the E*Trade monkey]. If '1984' ran now, it would be a good spot. In 1984 it changed everyone's approach to advertising on the game, forever."

Brian McDermott, a creative director at McCann Erickson, said that Super Bowl ads absolutely are a reflection of the zeitgeist: "For starters, advertising is a fashion industry. The type of humor used in a commercial . . . the type of film, the casting, music, wardrobe, settings, and of course the subject matter all reflect what agencies think will resonate best at a particular moment."

Ernie Schenck, cofounder of Pagano, Schenck & Kay and a columnist and contributing editor for *Communications Arts* magazine, agrees that spots like "1984," "Lizards," and "Dancing Monkey" reflected the tenor of the times, but he feels that in recent years "they've gotten more stupid. More sophomoric. It's weird that the work in recent years has been so uninspiring because it costs so damned much money, especially at a time when TV as an advertising medium is under such heavy fire from the Web."

Ted Cohn, another former colleague still working in the industry and the author of the astute and funny arts, politics, and pop culture blog Teddy Vegas, is inclined to say that Super Sunday's ad offering is *not* a reflection of the national zeitgeist. "Each year a handful of creative teams at the same three or four agencies spend a few weeks sowing their creative seeds in the soil of entertainment possibility. To the extent that I see any trends, I'd say the ads overall have tended to rely more and more on the tried-and-true conventions of talking animals, talking babies, and sexual innuendo. And they have more and more wholeheartedly embraced the sheer gratuitousness of advertising as a medium."

Another former colleague who would prefer to remain anonymous had a different take on the zeitgeist hypothesis: "The last few times I watched the Super Bowl, with its lavish halftime shows and multimillion-dollar thirty-second commercials and its sheer, unabashed celebration of excess, I couldn't help imagining someone thinking of it as a three-hour-long recruitment film for Al-Qaeda."

This led me to wonder what kind of impact the Tom Petty halftime show might have on Al-Qaeda recruitment.

The Phenomenon of the Almost

Rather than looking for deep cultural meaning in the dozen or so beer commercials (all based on the premise of the extent to which a man will go to protect his twelve ounces of hops, barley, and malt or to steal the beer of another), perhaps we can glean more revealing truths from sampling a relatively new phenomenon: the ads that *didn't* make it onto the Super Bowl yet found audiences of millions nonetheless.

At the Super Bowl ad factory DDB Chicago (which has done scores of Super Bowl commercials for clients like Bud, Bud Light, and Cars.com) and at most Super Bowl agencies, it is not uncommon for hundreds of concepts to be pitched internally for every spot that eventually makes it on the air. Depending on the account, up to several dozen of the best are then storyboarded to take to the client, for one or more rounds of meetings. Then the work that survives the client (and the franchisees, and the board, and the CEO's mistress) goes on to several stages of testing to make sure that it hits all the right brand-differentiating notes, isn't overly offensive (minorly offensive seems to be okay), and has the creative juice to break through as a Super Bowl spot. But if the trend of previous years continues, you will see more and more spots that were deemed unsuitable for TV finding new fame online.

Not long ago, those spots that were rejected by a client, that failed in consumer testing, or that were finally banned by the network or the NFL would be stuck in a closet never to be seen again. But now "banned" doesn't necessarily mean "killed." Now "banned" merely means "forbidden," and if YouTube, iFilm, and a number of other viral-video sites that run Super Bowl Almosts are an indicator, "forbidden" means "watch me again and again and again."

Besides being the master of the on-air Super Bowl commercial, repeatedly dominating USA Today's much ballyhooed Super Bowl Ad Meter, Bud Light has also claimed the crown as the king of the banned online spot. Consider, for instance, its banned 2007 "Skinny Dipping" and "Bottle Opener" executions, which have been viewed more than a million times each on YouTube. Or its banned "Wardrobe Malfunction" spot that almost aired the year after the Janet Jackson debacle before the network nixed it. The 2007 Bud Light "Swear Jar" commercial never made it onto the game, but millions have seen its extended-play version online. (A cautionary note about trolling for notorious ads online: on certain sites you may experience the curious phenomenon of having to watch a commercial you don't want to watch before viewing the one you do want to watch—ads sponsoring ads.)

Some marketers seem to create risqué ads knowing full well that they will be rejected by the powers that be and thereby eligible to be stamped with the golden "Banned Super Bowl Ad" label that will make them viral cult classics. Is there such a thing as a premeditated banned spot? Consider the 2005 "Sauna" spot for the immune-system-bolstering product Airborne. The network rejected it because at one point the star of the spot, Mickey Rooney, drops his towel. Granted, Mickey Rooney is adorable, but did Airborne really think any censor in her right mind was going to subject ninety-three million people to seeing his bare, octogenarian ass?

Online, any commercial tagged "Banned or Uncensored Super Bowl Commercial" will do exponentially better than those that actually made it on the air. The most glaring exception to this rule is Britney Spears's 2002 Super Bowl extravaganza for Pepsi. In the last year more than three million people have viewed it on YouTube. One would think that three million views for a seven-year-old spot is a good thing for a brand. But someone at Pepsi has got to be wondering if, based on Britney's continuing exploits (propensity for shaving her head, fleeing rehab, and making regular appearances on PerezHilton.com), it should be the first company to ban its own ad from the Internet. What does the online proliferation of enormously popular banned Super Bowl Almosts say about us? That we want to see that which has been kept from us, for starters. And that, in their current state, TV commercials, even the highly anticipated Super Bowl extravaganzas, do not go far enough. We want more. Especially the rejects from the medium we're rejecting.

Finally, do the sixty-plus ads we watch every Super Bowl Sunday in any way reflect the zeitgeist or the economy—or merely the superegos of a cabal of mostly white young male admen working for a handful of huge corporations with multimillion-dollar production budgets? Do overproduced, overpriced messages featuring furry animals, scruffy-faced men who say "dude" a lot, an abundance of scatological humor, and cloying nods to the green movement truly represent the hearts and minds of America? How about the fact that it's okay for a pharmaceutical company to use a product to sell gratuitous sex but using gratuitous sex to sell a product is a Super Bowl no-no? What does that say about us?

How 238 People with Nothing Better to Do on Super Sunday Control the Future of Advertising

On any given Super Bowl Sunday, approximately 238 people in auditoriums in McLean, Virginia, and cities such as Houston and Chicago, being paid all of $50 apiece, will be the most influential people in all of advertising. In theory, all that they'll be doing is gorging on salty snacks, watching football, and rating commercials for *USA Today*'s Ad Meter poll. But in practice, the opinions of the otherwise-normal 238 have incredible, often disastrous influence, impacting the fate of careers, brands, and agencies.

Just ask the principals at Chicago's Cramer-Krasselt agency, which in 2007 created several spots for its $60-million-a-year client, CareerBuilder.com. After none of CareerBuilder's three spots managed to crack *USA Today*'s Ad Meter top ten, despite having one spot rank as high as sixteenth, the agency was told that after its five years of working with CareerBuilder, the account was being put up for review. "To our amazement, to our total astonishment, all that astounding business success was less important than one poll," wrote Cramer-Krasselt's president, Peter Krivkovich, in an internal memo that found its way to *Adweek*. "It's so ludicrous and they are so serious about that poll it's almost funny."

Understandably, Cramer-Krasselt's take on the Ad Meter is different from that of the folks at DDB Chicago, whose work for Budweiser and Bud Light has established it as something of an Ad Meter dynasty. The DDB Group's creative director, Mark Gross, takes obvious pride while rolling off stats about his agency's success with the meter, and he admits that it takes a certain type of spot to crack the code. "Visually driven comedy, based upon a simple story line, with a surprise that leaves you smiling." It also helps to have a seemingly limitless budget that allows Bud Light to sometimes shoot several dozen spots and do thorough pretesting. Gross said spots that score highest in a pretesting environment that, incidentally, is not unlike the Ad Meter methodology are the ones most likely to make it on the air. For instance, prior to the 2008 game, Anheuser-Busch claimed that its Clydesdale "Rocky" entry for the mother brand scored higher in pretesting than any previous A-B spot, and the game-night meter results would prove it right.

"Whether you're shooting for it or not, the meter is a reality," said Jill Nykoliation, president of the Toronto ad boutique Juniper Park, whose Frito Lay client is a regular Super Bowl advertiser. "There's nothing we'd do differently as far as tapping into the essence of the brand or the psyche of the public, but because it's a Super Bowl spot, we might ultimately choose to produce the spot different."

One would think that a polling device as important as the Ad Meter would be incredibly sophisticated and the methodology intricate and complex. But according to *USA Today*'s polling editor, Jim Norman, the only difference between this current Ad Meter and the one used when it was introduced twenty-one years ago is that this year's gadget is wireless.

"On a device a little bigger than an iPod, the audience rates a spot on a scale of 1 to 7 (later prorated to a 1-to-10 scale)," Norman explained. "The score from each device reflects the highest point reached during a spot, usually the punch line of a joke [or the point at which a woman's breasts are most seductively presented]. The final score for each spot reflects an average of the highest grades given by each individual."

The recruitment process is equally straightforward. Norman says that in an attempt to reflect the makeup of the ninety-three-million-plus watching the game, they recruit about 60 percent men and 40 percent women of various ages, economic backgrounds, and races. None of whom, apparently, have anything better to do on the de facto national holiday that is Super Sunday.

Why test in McLean? Because *USA Today* has its offices there. And is the second location based on a desire to reflect regional diversity? Not according to Norman. Usually it reflects a desire on *USA Today's* part to go to someplace fun, affordable, and convenient.

Anyway, according to Norman, the spot that recorded the highest score ever is the 1995 Pepsi commercial that featured a boy sucking so hard to get the last drop that he sucked himself right into the bottle. The score was 9.66.

By comparison, 2007's top spot was Bud Light's "Crabs Worshipping Ice Chest," which scored 8.56; the lowest, at 4.05, was for Salesgenie.com's lone spot. Apparently inspired in some strange, self-destructive way by his results, Vinod Gupta, the chairman and CEO of Salesgenie's parent company, infoUSA, vowed to do even worse in 2008, the results of which are discussed below.

Of course the Ad Meter, despite its influence, has been subjected to the wrath of many agency and brand executives over the years. It has been called everything from irrelevant to fascist. Does Norman agree? "It is," the veteran pollster said, "what the numbers say it is."

As I prepared to watch the 2008 game, I wondered what the principals at Portland's acclaimed Wieden+Kennedy agency thought of all this hoopla over a simple poll. If at the end of the day the people who brought us, among many others, the classic "Just Do It!" Nike campaign think that the opinions of 238 people in a controlled environment really matter.

I wondered because at that very moment Wieden creatives were finishing up postproduction on the latest round of CareerBuilder's Super Bowl ads, not to mention a new spot for Coca-Cola.

Charlie Brown and the Giants Pull Upsets for the Ages

Going into Super Bowl XLII, the Giants had about as good a chance of defeating the undefeated New England Patriots as Charlie Brown had of winning at, well, anything. Yet by game's end both underdogs had won.

The Giants had sent the Pats' QB Tom Brady and their head coach, Bill Belichick, back to the drawing board for perfection, and Charlie Brown—thanks to a simple, playful, visually brilliant piece of branding magic for Coke created by Wieden+Kennedy—literally rose high above the competition in the year's clash of ad titans.

The sixty-second Coke spot chronicled an aerial battle royal at a Thanksgiving Day Parade between cartoon-character balloons over a giant inflatable bottle of Coke. At first the war is between the precocious demon-child Stewie of Fox's *Family Guy* and the animated 1960s icon Underdog. The commercial had me transfixed, a clash between goofy 1960s values and contemporary postmodern snark played out on a grand scale, high above and sometimes smashing into the skyscrapers of Manhattan. When the Charlie Brown balloon finally swoops in out of nowhere and claims the Coke bottle (not long before David Tyree snatched Eli Manning's miracle fourth-quarter pass out of the air), the spot ratcheted up several notches in my eyes, from memorable to the hallowed level of former Coke classics "Hilltop" and "Happiness Factory."

Why? Perhaps it's because by this stage of the game I had grown tired of and a little embarrassed for the men in the many formulaic sitcom-ish skits making asses of themselves for the tenth year in a row in order to sneak—oh my goodness!—a bottle of beer! Or maybe it was because I was still disturbed by the image of the hideous woman rubbing, um, nuts—a.k.a. the supposedly tasty product—on her person on behalf of the good yet misguided folks at Planters.

Or maybe it was the fact that this year's game featured derivative, contrived ads featuring geckos and cavemen, but not for the brand that put them on the cultural map, Geico. (Note to creative directors and chief marketing officers: Cavemen, lizards, frogs, and Clydesdales have sort of already been claimed. Please e-mail me for a complete list of available critters.)

Budweiser's Clydesdale "Rocky" commercial was charming and on brand, but its funniest spot of the game was Will Ferrell in character from his forthcoming *Semi-Pro* movie, extolling the benefits of Bud Light, riffing lines such as "Bud Light: it refreshes the palate, *and* the loins."

Strange how the best beer spot of the game was one that made fun of beer spots.

The rest was pretty standard, lavishly produced, pushing the bounds of tasteless Super Bowl fare. Sure, there were laughs to be had—FedEx's "Giant Pigeons" and Tide's "Talking Stain" were solidly entertaining—but nothing broke new ground or made much of an impression on me.

Yet if this is the case, how can I explain my reaction to a commercial that was based on the clamping of jumper cables onto a young man's nipples? How can I explain the fact that I laughed when I saw this disturbingly shocking ad for yet another wonder drink, AMP? And it wasn't just me. The people watching the game with me that night—aged ten to seventy-two—laughed, too, even though the spot featured all the things that we claim to despise in TV ads. It was crude, gratuitously unsettling, and semi-disgusting, which, one would think, were not on the brief for something that supposedly tastes good. But it happened. When the cables locked onto nipples and the Salt 'n' Pepa music kicked in to make the simple point that AMP gives you crazy mad energy, I laughed.

Only later was I ashamed of the fact that I laughed. Like so many other Super Bowl commercials, it was a one-off, another quick hitter from the school of shock. It didn't build meaningful brand equity, or make me feel smarter or better about the world.

It certainly didn't tap into or even hint at whatever the zeitgeist may be these days.

But Charlie Brown did. Charlie Brown beat Stewie and Underdog and finally won. And unless a giant Lucy is lurking around the next corner, waiting for the sequel, Coke won, too.

Part 3

The Merchants of What's Next

In Search of Advertising's Future in Cannes

> Historians and archaeologists will one day discover that the ads of our time are the richest and most faithful reflections that any society ever made of its entire range of activities.
>
> —*Marshall McLuhan*

End of Days or Just a Really Long Night?

The future of advertising is hunched over in the center of Boulevard de la Croisette outside a tiny yet unthinkably crowded café on the French Riviera at 4:18 a.m., hands on tanned yet wobbly knees, uncertain whether she will succumb to the excesses her industry has bestowed upon her and puke, call it a night, and stumble back to her overpriced, mega-agency-sponsored hotel room or gather her wits, her stomach, and her constitution and rally to take her skills to another, more exciting place where the party is just getting started.

This was my first night, a Sunday, at the 55th Cannes Lions International Advertising Festival. Every June, thousands of industry insiders congregate in Cannes for a chance to schmooze, drink, postulate, speculate, celebrate, copulate, pilfer clients, and ride the celebrity coattails of the renowned film festival that preceded it. But this year many of the record ten thousand delegates have come to

Cannes in search of something more. They've come to figure out whether the young woman in the street is a metaphor for the state of advertising or simply someone who has had one too many Cosmos at Cannes's infamous Gutter Bar (a.k.a. 72 Croisette).

Depending on whom you speak with in Cannes, which seminars you take in (Rupert Murdoch or Tony Bennett?), which parties or galas you attend and on which side of the Croisette—with the big-agency muckety-mucks on the veranda at the Carlton InterContinental or bumping and bumping (there wasn't enough room for grinding) to music spun by a U.K.-imported deejay at a digital production company beach bash across the street, where the average age is considerably younger—advertising is either at the end of its days or on the threshold of a creative revolution not seen since Bill Bernbach transformed the business in the 1960s.

Most of the anxiety in the $670-billion-a-year global industry, of course, revolves around the emergence of digital advertising and the corresponding audience erosion in the so-called traditional media of TV, print, and radio. Is advertising as we know it about to be hijacked by a coterie of Google/Microsoft/Yahoo!/AOL-controlled algorithms? According to the Yankee Group, 25 percent of all current media consumption is online, and by 2011 annual online media spending in the United States alone will double to more than $50.3 billion. This has advertisers and agencies seriously rethinking the mega-agency model and questioning the very future of the thirty-second television spot that has been the foundation of branding since the days of Milton Berle.

At one time America created the most entertaining and effective advertising, and its stars were the arbiters of branded cool. But now, at least for one week every year, Cannes has become the center of the advertising universe. With delegates representing more than eighty-five countries, Cannes most accurately reflects what has truly become a global industry. It also doesn't hurt that Cannes has recently provided a media platform for superstar talent from beyond the world of advertising. Like Al Gore, who gave a keynote speech on sustainability here in 2007, months before he won a Nobel Peace Prize. Or this year's top speaker, News Corp.'s Rupert Murdoch. But the truth is that, on account of the above, Cannes matters more than ever because of the quality and diversity of ideas it attracts.

"Advertising is so clearly an international pursuit now," said Jamie Barrett, senior vice president and creative director at one of America's most consistently creative agencies, Goodby, Silverstein & Partners in San Francisco. "It feels almost provincial to be talking about work in a regional or even national sense. To have any real context as a creative person, or any real inspiration, you need to know what's going on around the world. And to get that sense, the best place to go is Cannes."

Perhaps this is why this year more people from more countries than ever have come to Cannes. They want to find out if branding yet to come is indeed all about interactive, where seemingly only the whim of public opinion can make the difference between a branded cultural phenomenon watched and shared and commented on by millions and just another piece of orphaned video in the YouTube ghetto. They want to know who or what will rise up and save the industry and justify their expense reports and find the brightest, shiniest new way to sell a world of goods to our globalized, brand-obsessed, logo-saturated planet. They want to know what we all want to know, always: What's next?

I was tempted to ask our unsettled friend in the street. But I'd come to Cannes to find out for myself.

Plus, it's only Sunday. Make that Monday.

The Future of Advertising, Apparently, Will Have Nothing to Do with Advertising

Consider these early prizewinners at the festival: the first involves a minute-and-a-half video featuring either a very talented gorilla or a human in an incredibly convincing gorilla suit playing drums to a classic Phil Collins song ("In the Air Tonight") and ends with a picture of a Cadbury milk chocolate bar and the tagline "A glass and a half full of joy." The gorilla "ad," created by Fallon London, began innocently and traditionally enough as a 2007 British TV spot, but it took on an entirely new life online. According to the Cadbury gorilla's very own Wikipedia entry, it received more than 500,000 views in the first week it was posted. Current online view totals are estimated at more than 10 million. In addition, hundreds of parody videos, many also viewed more than a million times, began to appear online. So, in essence, a piece of viral online branding claimed a Grand Prix in a category that was historically the domain of the best television commercial in the world.

The drum-playing, Grand Prix–winning ape was only the beginning for a festival that would become, after years of so much bullshit, skepticism, and hype, online/360/viral/interactive advertising's coming-out party. For instance, another Grand Prix winner, for McCann Erickson's campaign for the Halo 3 video game, revolved around a series of mind-bending, imagined documentaries about the futuristic Halo 3 universe, as well as one about the making of a twelve-hundred-square-foot battle diorama, a monument "created in the year 2607" and dedicated to those who died "in the greatest battle in human history." Oh yeah. There were TV ads for the Halo 3 launch, but none won anything at Cannes.

Yet another Grand Prix went to an Orwellian interactive mystery that included scavenger hunts, cryptic clues on T-shirts, and planted USB drives in concert arena bathrooms for, of all things, a new album titled *Year Zero* by the industrial rock band Nine Inch Nails. The combination of the Cadbury, Halo 3, and *Year Zero* wins had made a definitive statement: the age of inflicted media (traditional TV, print, radio, and pop-up ads that bombard consumers) has given way to an era where the consumer controls the interaction with a brand. And if the message is not compelling, immersive, and (besides "I," this was the word of the festival) "engaging" enough, the brand is screwed.

With inflicted media the consumer had no choice. With immersion he has all the power.

Also interesting isn't just that the winning creative seems light-years away from anything we used to consider advertising, it's also the types of places that are creating it.

No one, it seems, wants to make ads or work at an advertising agency anymore.

During the past eighteen months, much of which was spent on the road visiting what I had thought were advertising agencies, I couldn't help but notice how many companies have increasingly taken to defining themselves by articulating not what they are but what they are *not*. And more and more, what they do not want to be called is advertising agencies.

For instance, I saw the following quotation, attributed to Lee Clow, chairman and chief creative officer of TBWA\Worldwide, on a poster taped to the office door of Kristi Vandenbosch, president of TBWA's digital shop, Tequila\, in Playa del Rey: "Who wants to be a fucking ad agency?"

And this: the first words one sees on the agency philosophy section of the Web site for the San Francisco digital marketer EVB are "We're not an ad agency." And on the Web site for the heralded New

York–based creative boutique Droga5 (owned by the global advertising holding company Publicis) is this subversive tease: "We believe that all agency rhetoric (including ours) blows."

Why do so many advertising agencies, once one of our biggest codifiers and manufacturers of cool, seem to be saying: Old, evil, out-of-touch people work at advertising agencies, making (yawn) TV commercials with (ugh) product demos and benefits, and jingles and unique selling propositions. Probably in black and white, with 800 numbers and a voice-over that says things such as "Act now," and "That's not all," and "Results may vary."

The answer, of course, is that advertising agencies are brands, too. And the sexiest selling point an agency can demonstrate for a prospective client right now isn't a big-budget TV show reel. It's the capability to do everything else. The great TV reel is cost of entry (not to mention still the top revenue generator at most agencies). The other stuff, though, is where the heat is.

Would you rather work for or with a company that makes traditional print and television ads or one that sparks, as David Droga of Droga5 likes to say, "cultural movements for brands"? Would you rather tell the hot-in-a-quirky-way person you've just met at a party at the hotel Majestic that you work for or with (a) an advertising agency, (b) a media-neutral agent of change, or, my favorite, (c) an idea factory?

Why work at an advertising agency owned by a soulless global holding company, a place with the names and/or initials of humans on its door, when you can work at a place (often, by the way, still owned by a soulless holding company) called Mother or Strawberry-Frog, Toy or Tequila, or Naked?

Of course this rejection of the advertising label isn't all about image and vanity. It's also a reflection of the changing of the guard from traditional (TV, print, radio, and outdoor) to the new frontier (digital, interactive, viral, 360, integrated branding—whatever you want to call it). Hence so many shops branding themselves as entertainment marketers or idea factories or whatever else implies the transcendence of the old and the embracing of the new.

Frankly, it had all begun to feel like so much digital bullshit. But, just when all the industry buzz had reached unprecedented levels of tedium, I started to see some tangible proof in Cannes. Maybe there was something to it. With almost every conversation I had, every seminar I attended, and every award given, it was becoming clear: after years of hype and unfulfilled promise, a new advertising paradigm was finally coming of age.

Consider the fact that the work that captured what has become the most prestigious prize at Cannes, the Titanium Grand Prix (for branding that transcends media categorization and, in this instance, description), was for a quirky 24/7 fusion of dance, sound, viral-video platform, and product catalog for the Japanese clothing retailer Uniqlo (the jumping-off point for which can be found at uniqlo.jp/uniqlock).

Created by another non-agency, the production company Projector Tokyo, and without a thirty-second television spot to be found, "the Uniqlo work is viral-branded utility," said the Titanium jury panelist Jean-Remy von Matt, founder and member of the board. "It's so simple, smart, and beautiful. All over the world people have it on their desktops, giving them a brand presence in countries where their products don't even exist."

At the same press conference, Mark Tutssel, chief creative officer of Leo Burnett Worldwide and jury judge of the Titanium and Integrated Lions, explained why, more than the film award, the Titanium Grand Prix has become the top honor in the industry. "It's a glimpse into the future of what we do, the most prestigious and the new standard for what everyone should work for."

As I left the press conference, I thought that if I were to write about much of the winning work this year at Cannes in a way that reflected the work, I would simply be providing clues, or provocative links to even more provocative clues, in chat rooms and phone books, on magic tickets, and I wouldn't be the one writing it.

You would.

Story is king as never before in adland, being told in entirely new ways that would make William Gibson proud.

The Future of Advertising Only Comes Out After Midnight

If the future of the mega-agency is on its last legs, how do we account for big-agency triumphs like McCann Erickson's breathtakingly imaginative, much-heralded work for Microsoft's Halo 3 launch? Or BBDO's genre-bending, Grand Prix–winning "Voyeur" campaign, not to mention Network of the Year honors at Cannes? Or why, night after night, the beach side of the Croisette was lined with agency-sponsored, no-expense-barred galas?

If times are so tough at agencies, why was Leo Burnett throwing a late-night beach extravaganza replete with a video wall, laser show, and Leo-branded, Disneyesque tram to shuttle guests to and from their hotels? If we're entering the age of small and nimble "unvertising," why did it seem as if a contingent from Y&R had co-opted no fewer than three tables per night on the ten-euro-a-Heineken veranda at the Carlton InterContinental? Why were my JFK-to-Nice flights filled with boldfaced-type mega-agency principals much better dressed and with much more interesting luggage than me?

Maybe no one wants to work at advertising agencies anymore, but we sure do like their parties.

In Cannes, nothing is subliminal. The seminars and workshops have titles such as "Tapping the Influencers" and "The Beauty of Big." In Cannes, agendas are in-your-face, the mission statements of the sponsors are ubiquitous, and someone or something is being sold every second of the day. Brand attributes. Production company credentials. New-and-improved visions from eighty-three-year-old ad titans. Here are thousands of talented professionals from every corner of the capitalistic world who have chosen as their vocation the science of knowing what makes us tick, what makes us lean in, what we think we need, and what we don't know we want. More than music, Hollywood, politics, or art: nothing influences, shapes, and reflects the state of the global psyche more than advertising. And nothing reflects the state of advertising at this particular nanosecond more than Cannes.

What's fascinating is that in Cannes, the masters of the branded universe are more than happy to reveal all of it, all of their wisdom and secrets and heretofore proprietary insights. Especially after midnight. Especially when holding a glass of champagne.

Don't believe me? Pick a night, any night.

Okay, on this particular night I followed up a one-on-one afternoon interview and intimate early-evening concert with Tony Bennett at the Majestic with a solitary walk along the Croisette.

There were no fewer than five agency-sponsored galas in action on the beach side of the street. I'd been to half a dozen similar parties during the week, and with each one, no matter how lavish and spectacular, I was becoming increasingly disinterested. I'd been away from advertising for more than two years. At some of these parties I knew a lot of people, at others maybe one or two acquaintances. I'd been partying with strangers until all hours for four straight nights, and there were three nights to go. I told myself I should go back to my hotel and get some rest, seemingly as I was handing my VIP invite to a security guard in a tuxedo and making my way through the velvet rope.

The invitation to this event said black tie, but at this point in the week I knew better than to be concerned about my clothing choices.

People were wearing shorts, AC/DC T-shirts, Thom Jones ankle-hugger suit pants. Some guy was wearing a kilt. I bypassed the endless tables of gourmet food and went straight to the champagne bar.

My eye was immediately drawn to a young executive from an Argentinean agency being followed by her personal film crew as she mimicked socializing, sipping champagne, mingling with strangers, and admiring the high-powered spectacle that she is obviously (fictionally) such an important part of. But then there was a glitch with the camera, at which time she shifted out of one character to reveal her true self, who proceeded to yell at her producer for two minutes before putting the fake smile back on her face and flawlessly repeating the take. It all made her appear shallow and foolish here, at least to the only loser shallow and foolish enough to continue paying attention to her. But it will probably make her look like a star in the slickly edited corporate video yet to come back home.

In Cannes, the people who make the ads are brands unto themselves, and when you walk or work among them, it is difficult not to consider everything part of a focus group, or a series of ad impressions that ladder up to a brand. The disturbingly cheeky way the flight attendant recited the emergency evacuation instructions on the tarmac before leaving JFK. Did that trend start with Southwest? Is there a JetBlue effect? Is that young woman looking at an ad on her iPhone? Rather than hit me up for a ten-euro charge for an electrical adapter for my laptop, a smart network or brand ought to provide it free.

It can't be helped.

Minutes before I left the party, an American creative director from Dallas complained to me about an anti-American bias among the judges at Cannes (even though the United States was winning more than its share of awards). "They give a few token awards to a few big agencies and screw us on the rest."

My cue to move on was when concert smoke began to swirl

across a huge stage in the center of the gala and the deejay asked us to put our hands together for a group of young women singers who emerged from the man-made cloud "all the way from the U.K.!" in flimsy white cocktail dresses. Canned music, part Wagner, part Freddie Mercury—a rock-opera, New Age, Andrew Lloyd Webber–esque audio clusterfuck—filled the air, and the women began to sing, or chant, or whatever. I've tried to remember the name of their band—Sensura? Bravura?—but it eludes me to this day. "Operatic pole dancers" is how an Australian woman with a star tattooed on her bare shoulder described them, but a Google search on that exact phrase came up empty.

I walked across the street to my hotel and, before going to bed, determined to make a quick pass through the veranda of the Carlton. Which is where I found my friend and former colleague Dante Piacenza, who had an extra necklace invitation for the Leo Burnett party down the Croisette at Le Palm Beach. Dante is the former head of broadcast production at Young & Rubicam and was presently working as an executive producer at Elias Arts.

On the Leo Burnett–co-opted, Disneyesque tram filled with partygoers that we hopped on outside Hotel Martinez, I met two young creative partners from the U.K. agency Rainey Kelly. The two have known each other since they were thirteen and have crashed Cannes on their own dime and are subsisting thanks to the generosity of others, namely via invitations to parties with plenty of free food and drink such as this. Soon after reaching the party, Freddy, tall and lean with a bicycle cap whose turned-up bill says "Just Do It" (an homage, ironic statement, or just a hat?), procured a full bottle of champagne and was happy to share, happy to be alive. "I wouldn't miss this for anything," he told me while managing to simultaneously pour, dance, and signal to his partner to scam another bottle. To thousands of young agency and production company creative people such as Freddy, who didn't shell out thousands on a delegate pass to the festival, Cannes is spring break for people who like to kern type, Mardi Gras for those who dissect YouTube hits as if they were Bergman films. What was I thinking, wanting to go back to my room?

Around 2:00 a.m., waiting for the tram back to my hotel that will never come, I struck up a conversation with a creative team from Saatchi & Saatchi New York, who told me they had a TV spot short-listed in the film category. I asked them if they agreed with what the creative director from Dallas had contended earlier, about the anti-American bias. The art director, a woman in black leather pants, told me that it would be ironic if this was the case because, although they worked at a U.S. shop, she is from Austria and her partner is from the Netherlands.

At 3:00 a.m., walking back toward my hotel with Dante, determined not to stop again at the Gutter Bar, I passed four men drinking and dancing on the roof of a van sponsored by the Shoot Argentina Film Commission. A few steps beyond the van I recognized a Russian ad exec whose seminar on the history of Russian advertising I'd left earlier in the day when he began to read the body copy of a *second* nineteenth-century print ad about smallpox prevention. A young woman from Australia staggered in the other direction with a Gold Lion in one hand and a bottle of wine in the other.

Of course we stopped at the Gutter Bar, which was again overflowing into the street with thousands of people. Bottles broke on the pavement. Some groups were sitting on blow-up mattresses and couches. Music blared from myriad car speakers. During the entire week in Cannes, I never saw a police officer. There must have been some kind of agreement: unless there's a murder, or a serious copyright infringement, the rich ad people have diplomatic immunity.

Still later, I wandered across the street to the Hotel Martinez, where a half-dozen Japanese ad people were jumping fully clothed into the outdoor pool. Almost anywhere else, at any time of day, this sort of behavior would stop conversations. But at 4:00 a.m. in Cannes it wasn't enough to make anyone in the crowd pay more than passing attention. If it happened on YouTube, scored to music and sponsored by, say, a sports drink, we'd probably all watch.

But live, it just felt fake.

I was contemplating a canary yellow car smaller than a golf cart parked on Rue d'Antibes outside the Gutter Bar when Dante somehow reappeared. On top of the car's tiny roof were more than twenty-five speakers, the quality of which didn't impress the English-speaking homeless man whom I'd seen at various times during the previous four days. I tried to explain to the homeless man that the quality of the speakers was beside the point, that the car was the promotional gimmick of a jingle house, and the fact that several thousand advertising zealots were staring at it was pretty cool. But he remained unimpressed. As Dante led me away, a matching yellow speaker car pulled up to the curb.

We were very close to my hotel again when a large drunken blond woman stumbled alongside us and asked where we were going. "To bed," I said, for the third time that evening.

"You cannot go to bed," she said. "You must first witness the Norwegian experience."

"Can't do that," I said. "I'm a married man. Almost twenty-five years."

"Me too," said Dante.

"It is not like that. Follow me."

Ten minutes later, sometime after 5:00 a.m., we were ordering beer and pizza at a bar alongside several hundred of Norway's finest ad folks. At some point a Norwegian creative director asked how we ended up there. I pointed at the drunken woman, who had moved on to other projects.

"Oh," he said. "She is one of our finest copywriters. Today, she won a Lion."

I made it back to the hotel as the sun began to rise. In one corner of the lobby a creative team from the United States was having a client call. In another, more than twenty Brazilians were gathered around a Mac G4, waiting for a soccer game to begin streaming live. Presently, a Polish gentleman wandered over to ask the Brazilians if he could watch.

A few moments later I did the same.

The Future of Advertising Is a Seven-Year-Old Girl in Shanxi Province Skimming Her Fingers over the Keys of a Mobile Phone

If the night at Cannes belonged to the young and the stupid, the day was all about getting smart. In seven days I attended several dozen workshops and seminars. If one topic or theme stood out because in many ways it transcends advertising, it was a series of presentations dedicated to contemporary China.

Since pundits from just about every aspect of business and culture agree that we are living in the Chinese century, and since the festival took place on the eve of China's Summer Olympics, it should come as no surprise that there was an unprecedented focus at Cannes this year on the world's third-largest ($60 billion annually) and fastest-growing advertising market. Because advertising in China was re-legalized only in 1978, soon after the end of Mao's Cultural Revolution, the presumptive opinion of many is that Chinese advertising is woefully behind the times and that marketers in China are playing catch-up. But according to a study of more than six hundred Chinese advertisers and agencies undertaken by R3/Grupo Consultores and revealed in Cannes for the first time, because China has no burdensome legacy advertising processes in place and its markets are growing with such velocity, China is actually playing leapfrog, bounding past conventional global marketers, and the world will soon be playing catch-up when it comes to integrated branding.

Should we be scared, impressed, or merely skeptical?

After their presentation, I met with the principals behind the study, ShuFen Goh and César Vacchiano de la Concepción. While their talk was filled with insights and misconceptions about how to market to China's 6.2 billion people, I wanted to know more about their findings regarding advertising and mobile phones.

Goh told me, "The first button a child pushes in China today isn't the television, radio, or computer, it's the mobile. And in China mobile is king." And because the Chinese depend so heavily on mobile content—from financial news to farm forecasts to mainstream entertainment—Goh said the biggest advertising driver and integrated opportunity for China, and soon everywhere, is the mobile phone. Indeed, with 530 million subscribers and adding as many subscribers per month as there are people in Portugal, China Mobile is by far the leading mobile carrier in the world.

"In China the clients know that for a brand to be successful, you have to communicate this way [with mobile as part of an integrated effort] with every job," Goh said.

So is China leapfrogging the rest of the world in integrated advertising as well?

"Absolutely. You saw the mobile figures. With some projects—for instance, with Coke's pre-Olympic spot in China—we were activating messaging [text messaging, video trailers, access to additional online content] in a hundred cities of more than one million people for whom the mobile phone is their primary source of information. These are numbers you cannot ignore."

When I asked if there might be a letdown in Chinese advertising after the hoopla (and concurrent controversies) of the Olympics, Vacchiano shook his head. "The Chinese don't see the Olympics as the culmination of their efforts. They see it as the starting point for something much larger."

Later that day at a cocktail party I tried to get the creative leader of a major U.S. agency to drink the Chinese Mobile Is the Future Kool-Aid, but he waved me off. "No one wants to look at those little screens," he said. But all around us, poolside, table-side, inside the lounge, even while they were pretending to have face-to-face conversations, people were.

The Future of Advertising Is in the Hands of a Young Man Doing a Product Demo for Shampoo in a Rural Market in India

While China dominated the stage at the seminars, India (the fastest-growing free-market democracy in the world) had a breakthrough year at the awards ceremonies. With twenty-three Lions (its previous best was twelve in 2006), including a Grand Prix for its moving "Lead India" campaign, India served notice to the ad world that it was, in the words of the festival's CEO, Philip Thomas, "an awakening giant of creativity."

Considering that India is home to some 1.13 billion human beings, this shouldn't come as much of a surprise. But multinational marketers looking to crack the code in India should note that turning a profit there, despite its size, is considerably more complex and difficult than it seems. Why? Start with sixteen languages, 432 dialects, limited broadband, and a 40 percent illiteracy rate. Then, after taking into account a 70 percent rural population who live in remote, difficult-to-reach villages that some are calling "the great rural mall," retailers may want to rethink their traditional media approach and partner with an Indian agency before proceeding.

Or at least wait until next year, when Goh and Vacchiano of

Grupo Consultores will follow up their report on China with a massive survey on advertisers in India.

The Future of Advertising Is Already Five Minutes Old

After seven eighteen-hour days in Cannes, dozens of parties and seminars, and on-the-record conversations with more than a hundred people, I reckon I still missed more than two-thirds of the events, each of which no doubt staked its own proprietary claim to the Vision for Advertising Yet to Come.

One thing is strikingly clear: there truly is a creative revolution under way in advertising. But to say that advertising's future is all about digital would be as misleading as to say it will have nothing to do with television. Sure, digital will figure prominently, but the future also must include a comprehensive reimagining of myriad other media and elements that will complement and combine *with* digital. The most futuristic platforms will be remixed and served up alongside the most archaic, analog huckster media. The fusion of viral video and social networking with scavenger hunts, sandwich boards, and, yes, public-bathroom drops is only the beginning.

Skeptics who feel the digital/creative revolution won't work with or doesn't apply to packaged goods need only consider the recent history of the world's largest and most scientifically astute advertiser. Five years ago Procter & Gamble, a company whose advertising (including an $8 billion annual spend in the United States) was hardly synonymous with awards shows, sent a delegation to Cannes to learn about creativity. Then they went back to Cincinnati and broke creativity down as only P&G can to see how improved creativity could be leveraged against its global brands. Specifics of what they learned—other than, one presumes, that creativity sells—are unclear. But last year, P&G won fourteen Lions at Cannes. This year it was named Cannes Advertiser of the Year, as the company that best inspires innovative marketing and creativity among its agencies. Which tells us something.

Staid, venerable, focus-group-driven P&G had seen the future of advertising. And if the company's actions are any indication, whether it's called immersive, viral, digital, or interactive, that future better be damned entertaining.

So this is the future I managed to glimpse in seven concentrated days through the eyes of a specific past.

Soon, no doubt, it will all change. It will evolve and morph. As you read this, the most astute advertisers are already attempting to glean fresh truths from our most recent behavioral tics and devising entirely new ways to surprise and seduce, exploit, enrage, and engage us.

The most innovative and effective of it will likely make its way to Cannes next year. Whether it becomes the stuff of a revolution, a trend, or a perishable anecdote is up to the work.

And of course us.

Because sometimes the future of advertising is nothing more than the gathering of the quotidian facts of our most recent pasts and using them against us.

Idea Factories

Lousy Agencies Have Foosball Tables, Too

The challenge of chronicling anything that is new and allegedly innovative, especially in the emerging subgenre of *un*vertising boutiques (ad agencies in denial), is that by the time you read this, the hot new shop may already have cooled down, grown too fast, become a casualty of a global economic downturn, closed its stunningly designed doors, dismantled its indoor skate park, or fired the in-house barista.

Or, it may have morphed into something else.

Or, if it's really hot, and especially successful, the founding partners who had touted themselves to the editors of *Creativity* and *Fast Company* as progressive, beyond-advertising-establishment rebels may already have done the unthinkable and sold a majority share of Crying Clown Inc. to one of the big-three global holding companies.

If any of the above is the case with the profiles of idea factories woven into the pages that follow, what can I tell you? Read them as cautionary tales, think of them as creative sorbets, or the contents of a time capsule labeled "One Jackass's Take on Innovative Ad Shops, Circa 2009."

Of the dozens of agencies I visited and the dozens of campaigns I pursued, the ones that captivated me most weren't the most successful or recognizable or the biggest, but the most progressive, smart, and innovative.

What most interests me is ideas.

Compelling commercial ideas, and the different ways and reasons why people enjoy making them.

The Soundtrack to a Movie That Doesn't Exist
42 Entertainment

Somehow I can't imagine that Leo Burnett or David Ogilvy or Ray Rubicam—even twenty-first-century reincarnations of the legendary admen—would think that placing an object next to a public urinal in a rock concert arena would constitute anything close to the proverbial big idea upon which successful ad campaigns are built.

But if you happened to be taking a leak during a Nine Inch Nails (NIN) rock concert in Barcelona or Lisbon in 2007, there is a chance that you'd not only stumble (or urinate) upon a big idea, you'd become an integral part of it. How? As part of a marketing campaign/alternate-reality game (ARG)/performance-art spectacle on behalf of a forthcoming NIN album called *Year Zero,* the band's leader, Trent Reznor, and the marketing boutique 42 Entertainment went to unprecedented extremes.

It began with a series of highlighted letters on a 2007 NIN concert T-shirt that spelled out the message "I am trying to believe." Curious fans who had the wherewithal (and nothing-else-better-to-do-withal) to do a search on the phrase were then led to a series of 42 Entertainment–created Web sites about a fictional "Year Zero" that depicted a dystopian world where the government has taken complete control of society and imposed a Christian Fundamentalist theocracy that, among other things, drugs the public water supply and has an Orwellian "Bureau of Morality." The Web sites and the blogs they spun off claimed to be the work of freedom-fighting rebels who were sending messages from the future (2022) to warn people in the year 2007 about the horrors to come.

Then, in addition to the above, came the infamous urinal drops. Specifically, USB (Zip) drives were left in bathrooms at NIN concerts. Along with further clues and warnings about the world of "Year Zero," the drives contained unreleased tracks from NIN's soon-to-come album, some in garage-band format, which would allow fans to remix and repurpose the music.

This is all brilliant for a number of reasons, especially since, in 2007, the release of a new Nine Inch Nails album was hardly a cause for mass celebration. Reznor's audience, while substantial in Long Tail terms, had reached the point where it could most accurately be categorized as niche. But as it turns out, it was a rabidly devoted niche, willing to go to great lengths to find out more about the album, and the 42 Entertainment effort took full advantage of this fact. Also, the sensibility and overt antiauthoritarian politics of the album and the ARG campaign were a perfect ideological match for NIN's industrial-rock fandom as well as for Reznor himself. *Year Zero* was to be his last release for a major label and a distribution model about which he'd become increasingly critical. And Reznor went out of his way to say that the buzz surrounding the album, which he called "the soundtrack to a movie that doesn't exist," was anything but advertising. "It's not some kind of gimmick to get you to buy a record," he told *Rolling Stone.* "It IS the art form."

The art form, apparently, worked. Not only did *Year Zero* reach No. 2 on the *Billboard* chart after its release, it won a Grand Prix at the International Advertising Festival at Cannes.

I didn't know a lot about Nine Inch Nails or Trent Reznor, but I had been following the "Year Zero" campaign for some time before its big win at Cannes. But what interested me most wasn't simply the novel delivery mechanisms it employed; it was the ways in which it used long-form narrative storytelling techniques to brand or (sorry, Trent) sell a product. This was notable in an industry that had by necessity placed a premium on brevity and overt calls to action, but what transfixed me is the fact that the "Year Zero" narrative form itself, long or not, was unlike anything I'd encountered in advertising or storytelling.

I met with Susan Bonds and Alex Lieu of 42 Entertainment on the veranda at the Carlton InterContinental in Cannes the morning after their big win. Bonds is president and CEO and Lieu is chief creative officer of the small Pasadena-based marketing and entertainment (anything but advertising) firm. Between half a dozen interruptions from well-wishers ranging from tech geeks in AC/DC concert T-shirts to Hollywood studio types to agency CEOs, they described how two people who never spent a day working at an ad agency ended up at the epicenter of adland.

"We're an entertainment company that does original content that brings people together through storytelling. The fact that we both spent time at Disney helped us a lot in that regard," Bonds explained. "Because at Disney, the audience experience always comes first."

Instead of the traditional copywriter/art-director dynamic employed by most ad agencies, 42 Entertainment (which is also the company behind the campaign for the highly successful launch of the box-office-record-breaking Batman film *The Dark Knight*) typically relies on its alternate-reality-game background and involves everyone from sci-fi authors and sitcom writers to video game developers to create a storytelling experience that they say is exponentially more engaging and immersive than any traditional TV commercial.

Their creative process is different from the traditional advertising approach, said Lieu. "We always start by observing what people are doing new on the Web, and then we take that and think of how to build a compelling connection through stories."

"Rather than tell a linear story in a classic arc," explained Bonds, "we write the spine of a great story and then create the evidence as if it happened. Then the player collects that evidence and builds the story. Which is what we did with *Year Zero*."

"And," Lieu added, "unlike most agencies, we work very closely with the content creators, like Trent Reznor and [the *Dark Knight* director] Christopher Nolan.

"The industry is moving beyond sticking a message to content," Lieu continued. "When the audience pieces a story together, the depth of engagement is phenomenal. We build the audience *into* the content. They own it."

"We call it distributive storytelling or narrative," Bonds explained.

So, rather than repeatedly shoving a commercial message down consumers' throats, distributive narrative creates a thoroughly modern universe built upon the pillars of classic storytelling that not only engages consumers/players with a brand for *hours* (and, in the case of *Year Zero*, *months*) but also creates, click by click, a movement of brand believers that makes the participants feel as if they are part of—McLuhan-ites take note—a larger cultural movement.

I mentioned that in Cannes, there seemed to be a blurring of categories. YouTube hits were winning in the traditional film category. Cyber and viral and integrated each had its own category, but in truth it seemed that most work could have won in any category.

"All interactive marketing is supposed to be viral," said Lieu. "For instance, we're also entered in the Titanium Lions category. Even after fifteen years, the landscape of cyberspace marketing is changing so fast that people have a hard time benchmarking and finding value in it." Bonds added, "They're still trying to fit it into conventional advertising categories and media buys."

All of which sounds perfectly believable when you're promoting a summer blockbuster or a long-awaited album by a notoriously progressive artist to an already rabid audience. What about a campaign for something considerably less sexy? Does a person really want to have a "totally immersive audience experience" that revolves around toilet paper, or pudding? What about a packaged good with a product demo, or the lowly retail ad? How does this process fare with more traditional clients?

"Fine," Bonds said. "We just did something for Toyota Camry [iflookscouldkill.com] that is far from traditional but is for a traditional category. Whatever we do is a holistic approach to connecting with consumers through storytelling."

At the time of our conversation in late June, 42 Entertainment was already fully engaged in the covert guerrilla campaign for the upcoming Batman film, *The Dark Knight*. I'd heard stories of secret cards being placed in hard-core comic book hangouts and the release of other cryptic online clues. I asked if, since they'd already bragged about having worked so closely with Christopher Nolan, they could tell me more about the campaign.

Lieu sat back and folded his arms. "Oh, we can't talk about something that's still in play."

Bonds shook her head. "Got to respect the fourth wall."

Elf Yourself
Toy New York

The Grand Lodge of the Royal Order of Masons is located at the end of the same Flatiron district street as the small specialist/generalist agency Toy New York. For those unfamiliar with the ways of the Freemason, according to *American Heritage* it is, among other things (depending on the location of the lodge and the political climate), an organization based on "spontaneous fellowship and sympathy among a number of people."

I know this because I looked up the definition electronically while standing on the sidewalk between the two buildings, fifteen minutes early for my first visit to Toy, a company whose nontraditional approach to advertising seems to be based on a similar faith in the power of spontaneous fellowship and sympathy among a number of people—but in Toy's case, the fellowship does not exclude women, and the number of people came primarily via the Internet.

I was visiting Toy's new loftlike digs on West Twenty-third Street after lots of people told me they were worth checking out because of the pedigree of the founding principals as well as the breakthrough online holiday campaign they had done for the OfficeMax chain, particularly a strange, corny, yet enormously successful Web site called Elf Yourself.

My memory of my first Elf encounter from the previous holiday season is foggy. I vaguely remember having been invited to "Elf Myself" by a friend who also worked in advertising, for a digital agency. I vaguely remember the dancing elves and something to do with downloading a photo of myself onto an elf's face. However, I distinctly remember abandoning the project midway through the download, urging my then-nine-year-old daughter to take over. Which she did, pasting our faces on myriad dancing elves and sending them out into our digital community for, I'm thinking, hours.

I thought it was cute, and cool in a quirky way. What I didn't know at the time is that we were taking part in a seminal online-marketing phenomenon, and the first digital effort to infiltrate pop culture since, well, the Subservient Chicken. Because if the chicken was the Jackie Robinson of digital advertising efforts, the talented and brave pioneer breaking down barriers and erasing stereotypes, the elves were Willie Mays and Hank Aaron, taking it to a whole other level.

One thing about having a loft as a company office space is that the layout doesn't work particularly well with the traditional lobby format. With lofts, where many of the idea factories I visited are situated, there is no soothing, receptionist-guarded barrier haven between the elevator banks and the chaos happening just around the corner. With lofts, when the elevator doors open, you're immediately released into the workplace, which in a way reinforces the "we're not an advertising agency" vibe and, more important, says "transparency." We have nothing to hide here, and we have no desire to impress you with a gilded atrium or a mahogany-paneled conference room. We're all about the work.

So I simply got off the elevator at Toy and started to wander around. Fortunately, the first person I stumbled upon was Anne Bologna, a founding partner and the president of Toy. Bologna did her best to make me feel welcome, even though the small staff was obviously busy. She introduced me to the other founding partners: David Dabill, the chief financial officer; and Ari Merkin, the creative director who was in the middle of writing a manifesto for a new business pitch for a fast-food chain.

Bologna led me to the open conference space toward the back of the loft. There was a large-screen TV on a freestanding shelf and another set of shelves filled with Elf-related booty—plaques and trophies from the spring awards-show season.

Bologna sat across from me and began to dispense with the list of "not's" that are a requisite part of every idea factory's creation story:

We are not big.
We are not fancy.
We are not an advertising agency.
We are not a TV-making factory.
We are not exclusively a digital agency.

We are not beholden to a big holding company.

We are not inherently evil.

And we are not, despite the author's prior insinuations,
Freemasons.

Part of the reason for my interest in shops such as 42 Entertainment, Toy, and other idea factories is that I never worked in a
creative boutique, let alone an agency bold enough to have a subversive manifesto. I worked at huge, venerable agencies with global
networks, hundreds of employees, shareholders to report to, and, in
theory, financial stability. Creative shops were usually the opposite:
small start-ups dependent on one account, run by an entrepreneurial creative team and account person. Creative shops were sexy,
provocative, and swashbuckling. It took guts to open one and even
more to work at one.

At least a half-dozen times over the years I entertained the idea
of breaking off with a partner and doing my own thing. And every
time, I chickened out. The challenge of running my own agency was
always intriguing, but the financial risks and the life commitment always proved too daunting. Usually my plan was dependent on a
client who liked me and my work but was unhappy with the agency
I worked for. Starting a shop with a nationally known brand would
certainly make things easier, but the flip side is that your entire
livelihood, at least until you attracted additional clients, would be
dependent on the emotional whims and career trajectory of one person. Plus, despite being competitive and intrigued by a challenge, I
was never entirely convinced that I wanted to go all out, that I
wanted advertising to dominate my life.

Bologna continued to explain why it was so important to em-
phasize what Toy is not.

"It's because it is extremely important that clients understand
that we are operating under an entirely new model. That, in many

respects, the old model is incredibly flawed. By saying we're not a TV-making factory, we are saying that there are many, many ways to get your product noticed other than an expensive TV campaign. That is the structure they [big, old, evil ad agencies] sell to the client. They have legacy drag and holding company issues. There are beasts to feed, and this dramatically affects their ability to take risks. We believe in the new model. We believe in taking risks and being smart and nimble. So much so that we all jumped out of very comfortable jobs to prove it."

Oh yeah. Reason number seven why I never started my own shop: jumping out of the comfortable job.

The comfortable jobs that Bologna, Dabill, and Merkin left were at Fallon New York, where Bologna was president and Merkin was creative director. Prior to his gig at Fallon, Merkin worked at the rapidly ascending and now flat-out big Miami shop Crispin Porter + Bogusky, where he won numerous awards for his groundbreaking work for Mini Cooper, Truth Anti-Tobacco, and Ikea, for whom his "Lamp" commercial garnered a Grand Prix at Cannes.

"We all got along really well," Bologna continued, "and we all began to realize that there was a better way to do things, and that being attached to a legacy agency wasn't the answer. So, we're financially independent, we get to choose our clients and say no to them if it's a bad fit. It's our philosophy that under those conditions, creativity can flourish."

The abridged, PowerPoint-free version of "Elf Yourself, Part 1" is as follows.

In 2006, Bob Thacker, OfficeMax's senior vice president of marketing and advertising, contacted Bologna with a seemingly modest assignment. He wanted to seed the idea to consumers that Office-Max, the number-three office supply chain behind Staples and Office Depot, was a viable holiday gift option. The only catch was that the production budget for the effort was less than the cost of the average thirty-second TV commercial (around $300,000).

So rather than creating one more commercial to throw into the network holiday din, Toy enlisted some of the best digital production companies around to produce twenty separate holiday Web sites that featured hours of OfficeMax-branded online content.

Nineteen of the mini-sites enjoyed modest success, but nothing like the level of action that came out of the Elf Yourself site. Created by Merkin and Jason Zada of the digital marketing firm EVB, Elf Yourself not only transcended the online genre; it transcended advertising and became the kind of cultural event that marketers dream of. Hosts of *The Today Show* and *Good Morning America* elfed themselves. The *New York Times,* CNN, and many others featured the site. And not only were millions of people elfing and forwarding greetings of themselves, but hundreds were uploading Elf Yourself videos onto YouTube. Bologna ran through some of the numbers for me. Half a billion hits and thirty-one million visitors in less than five weeks. When most Web marketers measure how long visitors spend on their site, they speak in terms of minutes. For Elf Yourself, Toy measured it in *years.* Bologna and company slipped this factoid into its OfficeMax case history: the total time spent online by Elf Yourself visitors was more than six hundred years.

From a creative standpoint, the aesthetic of the site was crude and basic, and the act of elfing was painfully simple. Plus, there was no overt brand message burned into the process. Yet people of every age embraced it. Most likely because, unlike so many online-marketing experiences, Elf was such a simple, joyful experience that people felt compelled to pass it along and share.

Just as was the case with Burger King's Subservient Chicken, everyone wanted to know if all the online hype translated to an increase in holiday traffic. Online tracking services said that Office-

Max's brand awareness absolutely went up as a result. Thacker told *Ad Age,* "We were looking to build the brand, warm up our image. We weren't looking for sales . . . [but were] trying to differentiate ourselves through humor and humanization."

In addition to the OfficeMax account, Toy was doing work for the Oxygen network, including a promotion for the *Janice Dickinson Modeling Agency* program that included a faux downtown New York City modeling agency storefront, replete with a window poster that read: "Now hiring beautiful people." They've also helped launch the wireless reading device the Amazon Kindle and recently landed the *BusinessWeek* magazine account. Bologna also mentioned a top secret project with YouTube (which I found intriguing, if only because I was curious what the future of advertising needed an agency for*) and a recent meeting about an online-content project with Ashton Kutcher.

Rather than expending so much energy saying that they aren't an ad agency, I thought, they just needed to say, "We created the Elf, we did branding for the world's largest viral-video network, and we broke bread with Demi Moore's boy toy," and people would fill in the blanks.

The primary reason I came to Toy was to find out how Merkin and Bologna were going to follow up the radical success of Elf Yourself. The first year the assignment was very much under the radar, and there had been minimal expectations. But this year there were colossal expectations, from the CEO of OfficeMax, who had now decided to become more intimately involved in the process; from the OfficeMax employees who had proudly claimed ownership of and promoted the first round of work; and from the trade press. Plus,

---

*It turns out that YouTube wanted help helping advertisers make the most of their channel. Toy produced a "Tubetorial" for ad folks on its brand channel that's, in essence, a really smart YouTube video.

one year earlier, that type of online campaign was fairly novel. By the time the holiday season of 2007 rolled around, everyone was playing in the viral realm, many doing shamelessly derivative knockoffs of the Elf Yourself site.

Toy's answer to the pressure wasn't to do more, bigger, and/or better. First, it decided to do not twenty sites but one. And that one, again cocreated with EVB, was a slightly modified version of Elf Yourself. To some that may seem like the definition of playing it safe, but I thought it was ballsy, a rare demonstration of restraint in the excess-driven, egomaniacal world of advertising. The most significant change to the site seemed to be the introduction of additional elves.

In March 2008, I went back to Toy for an early-morning update, and to discuss the results of Elf Yourself year two. When I got off the elevator, there still wasn't a lobby, or a receptionist. Window washers were climbing over desks on the Twenty-third Street side of the space, to gain better position to squeegee more light into the idea factory. Dabill was joking with one of the squeegee men, and nearby Merkin had his head down and was writing feverishly.

Toy, an agency founded on the premise that a great toy is one that inspires you and compels you to share it with others, and that brands need to engage your imagination and be as exciting as a new toy, was now two years old. Bologna came out of the kitchen area and waved for me to join her at the conference table. I asked how business was, and she said the phone doesn't stop ringing. Then I thought about our first conversation and her thoughts about large agencies bound to selling TV and answering to shareholders and having beasts to feed.

"What if you get so popular you start to become the type of place that you used to work at, you know, numbers to meet, people to keep busy?"

She looked around, shook her head, and said, "That's not gonna happen."

Then we got down to talking Elf stats.

According to Nielsen Online Strategic Services, nearly one in ten Americans visited the OfficeMax Elf Yourself site, up nearly tenfold from its first year in existence. Blog pass-along posts, according to Nielsen, were also huge, and of the twenty most common search terms in the four weeks of December, six included the word "OfficeMax."

According to OfficeMax, 193 million people visited elfyourself .com in year two, creating more than 122 million elves while spending more than a total of twenty-six hundred years on the site. For those still wondering what holiday elves have to do with office supplies, OfficeMax also reported that more than 47 percent of customers surveyed linked the "Elf Yourself" campaign to the store.

In addition to having to top those numbers every holiday season until the entire world has repeatedly elfed itself, Toy may find that its biggest challenge is to leverage the success of the elves while not becoming beholden to them. In other words, it needs to do something equally amazing for someone else.

On my way out I shook hands with Bologna and waved good-bye to Merkin, who still may or may not have noticed me, and to Dabill, who was still talking to the squeegee guy. Back on the street, in front of the Grand Lodge of the Royal Order of Masons (where, incidentally, I was about to take an interesting tour), I decided while scribbling notes that Bologna, Merkin, and Dabill were right: Toy absolutely was not an advertising agency.

Because at a real agency, a founding partner would never have spoken with the squeegee guy.

Bankable

BBDO

Judging from the companies profiled on the preceding pages, one would think only small, quirky shops that renounce the word "advertising" can qualify as idea factories. Of course, this is hardly the case. Just about every working agency today qualifies, and some of the best—including the well-chronicled, paradigm-busting large agencies Wieden+Kennedy, the Martin Agency, and Crispin Porter + Bogusky—continue to create and innovate as well as or better than the smartest, nimblest idea factories. Google them or check out their Web sites and you'll see.

But for tangible, debauchery-free proof that rumors of the death of the mega-agency are greatly exaggerated, consider the role that BBDO Worldwide, one of America's largest and oldest agencies, enjoyed at Cannes. Long celebrated and eventually denigrated for its lavish, celebrity-dependent, Super Bowl-or-bust TV extravaganzas for A-list clients like Pepsi (Britney, Madonna, Michael Jackson), Visa (Derek Jeter, Michael Phelps), GE, and FedEx, BBDO has undergone a transformation under its chief creative officer of three years, David Lubars.

On the afternoon that we met at an outside table at the Hotel Majestic, Lubars was feeling particularly satisfied. His home office in New York had just won the Agency of the Year Lion as the most-awarded single agency at the festival, and BBDO Worldwide, the most-awarded network of agencies, was named Network of the Year. Winning awards was nothing new for BBDO. But winning them on the coattails of one dominant campaign that didn't involve a single thirty-second television commercial was significant for the onetime TV factory.

The campaign, for BBDO's longtime HBO client, was an integrated effort called "Voyeur." The mission of "Voyeur," which won ten Lions at Cannes (and was created with a significant yet not entirely substantiated assist from the digital production company Big Spaceship), was to position the cable network as the home of the greatest storytellers in the world.

Brands like to "own" things, and marketers are more than happy to accommodate. A case can be made that Target owns a certain Pantone of red. A coffee maker wants to "own" morning's first pleasure. Once I worked for a fast-food client who wanted to "own" happiness. BBDO helped HBO lay claim to storytelling with a series of compelling, brilliantly synchronized short films directed by Jake Scott and set in eight apartments in a fictional Manhattan building. Each apartment has its own plot that builds to a common finale involving, within four minutes, tales of love, hate, birth, and murder. In 2A, for example, a couple discovers that their upstairs neighbor in 3A has a deadly secret. In 4A a strip-poker party takes an unexpected turn. For the premiere, the films were simultaneously projected on the side of an actual Manhattan apartment building before more than three thousand voyeurs on the corner of Ludlow and Broome, giving the illusion that its exterior wall had been stripped away.

But that was only one aspect of the campaign. More than 1.2 million viewers visited the HBO Voyeur micro-site, seeking additional background clues and story lines about the tenants, and hundreds of thousands more downloaded the stories from the Web and Video On Demand. Without a celebrity endorsement in sight.

"We used to fill boxes with creative," said Lubars, whose 2003 short films for BMW, directed by Guy Ritchie, John Woo, and others, are still looked upon as the pioneers and standard-bearers for nontraditional, product-focused, branded entertainment. "TV used to be the sun, and all other mediums were merely satellites around it. It's still the only place where you can get seventy million eyeballs on an ad, but now if your message is engaging enough, you can get people to voluntarily spend ten, twenty, thirty minutes totally engaged with a brand."

Soon Lubars's co–chief creative officer, Bill Bruce, the chief architect of the Mountain Dew brand's extreme persona, joined us and chose a non-extreme seat in the shade. Because the success of an interactive campaign depends so much, if not completely, on the confluence of creative excellence and the public's embracing of the idea, I asked them how they could guarantee this to a major client like HBO.

"Trust," said Lubars. "We've been working with HBO for a long time. And track record, which is predicated on the level of talent at a particular company. And more and more, rather than have a client commit all of its money to network upfronts [typically in May, when the major television networks showcase their new schedules to prospective advertisers], we encourage them to put money aside in a skunk-works fund, for when we hit upon something extraordinary like 'Voyeur.' "

Later I asked Courteney Monroe, HBO's executive vice president of consumer marketing, if, beyond the advertising bling and the online numbers, she considered the campaign a success. "Absolutely," she said. "Everybody's chasing after buzz. The pressure on marketers to break through is enormous. Our brief to BBDO was to create an experience for consumers to engage in a unique way across multiple platforms."

Of course, HBO is a content provider, and the "Voyeur" campaign was essentially content itself. Monroe would not provide specific campaign or media costs, but because there was no paid network media involved, she said it was "far more cost-effective than a traditional campaign effort." She also agreed that it helps to have your very own network (part of Time Warner, no less) as a media platform, and that selling entertaining content is easier than selling the benefits of a deodorant stick. But, she said, all marketers will eventually have to find a way to make their brand story more entertaining. "You can't just put up an 800 number and a call to action anymore. Experiential branding is critical for everyone."

Storytelling and engagement were clearly the most prevalent themes at the festival. I told Lubars and Bruce that earlier in the day I had heard the legendary commercial director Joe Pytka (who has won a Hank Aaron–esque 110 Cannes Lions as the shooter of everything from Pepsi's Ray Charles "Uh-Huh!" spot, to "This Is Your Brain on Drugs," to the Larry Bird and Michael Jordan "Nothing but Net" McDonald's classic, and whose sailboat was docked within walking distance of the Palais), say, "No focus group in the history of advertising has ever written a good story."

When asked if they felt as if they were creating a new kind of experiential branding that transcends advertising, if the future of advertising is all about creating moments that shape the collective culture, Lubars shrugged. Bruce sat back and folded his arms across his white T-shirt. "Oh, I don't know," he said. "We just try to come up with great ideas."

Lubars looked at me as if I should know better. "Shape the culture? I don't know and I don't care. Let the academics figure that one out."

Return on Attention
Time Warner's Global Media Group

For many of the large pitches and meetings I'd been a part of, when it came time for the media portion of the presentation—when client and agency discussed where, how frequently, and in which media they would run their ads—people had a gift for suddenly finding more important things to do. Agency presidents would briefly "step out" to take a call. Senior clients would have to catch a limo, or a flight. And creatives, they would simply get up and walk away from the table. To mathematically challenged writers and art directors, watching the endless parade of charts and graphs of a media presentation was akin to watching, um, an endless parade of charts and graphs.

Back then, media got no respect.

After all, the choices were limited (TV, out of home, radio), and it didn't seem as if it took a genius to target a TV spot to a demographically appropriate program, with a measurable audience. As Bill Bruce, the co–creative chairman of BBDO, told me, "Until recently, we were using a model and measurements that had been around since the days of Milton Berle." But of course all that has changed, and continues to change.

Today an argument could be made that there is no more important aspect of the advertising process than media strategy. Today, any creative person worth her salt is keenly aware of the myriad possibilities of the new media landscape, and the most successful agency media people proactively share with the creative folks fresh, brand-relevant ideas and insights about the very same, ever-changing landscape. Today, it's more likely that a creative person helped put together the media presentation than it is that she will get up and leave it.

At the advertising festival in Cannes, I ran into Mark D'Arcy and John Partilla of Time Warner's Global Media Group at a midnight lawn party at Le Grand Hotel. Former agency veterans and for a short while colleagues of mine, D'Arcy (chief creative officer) and Partilla (president) clearly think that media is, if not the future of advertising, at the very least where the money is.

To my understanding, Time Warner was simply a media conglomerate, the owner of a large and ubiquitous "family of brands," including Time Inc. (*Sports Illustrated, People, Entertainment Weekly,* and more than a hundred others), AOL, TBS, HBO, and Warner Bros. To me, it was simply a repository of well-known content providers where agencies placed ads. Through the sheer economy of numbers, advertisers could realize savings by purchasing media bundles. I asked D'Arcy what the hell a creative guy was doing in a corporate media empire. And even if media was where the money is, wasn't it, you know, boring?

D'Arcy said if he had to pick a moment, the genesis of the idea for their group came several years earlier when he and Partilla were working on the agency side for a major electronics client. "We came up with a spectacular and original media idea," he said. "The client loved it. Then we presented it to the cable network that would partner on the project, and they loved it. The only thing is, when the meeting was over, as the agency of record, the only way in which we stood to benefit is that our client was pleased and we got to keep the account for a little bit longer. The cable network not only took over control of the project; it made millions of dollars off our idea. In our eyes, it was clearly a flawed model."

Partilla agreed that taking control of a project whose creation it had in effect financed was the network's prerogative. It also prompted him to strongly consider the evolving and growing importance of media. "We'd spent our careers at ad agencies. And looking forward, every job in that world seemed like a variation on the same theme. With 90 percent of most ad budgets dedicated to the media spend, we saw an opportunity for a new, idea-led model where we'd come up with additional creative ways to amplify the effectiveness of the creative spend."

D'Arcy agreed. "Before, the focus at Time Warner and most media companies was on sales. But now we're in an era where media has become everything and the relationship between media and consumers has changed from intrusion to engagement, ads have to be more relevant and entertaining than ever."

"How do you bill for your creative services?"

"We don't," D'Arcy said. "We work exclusively with top-thirty brands, several of whom have entered into long-term agreements with us. If we succeed, it's reflected in a larger media purchase for Time Warner. Sometimes we'll make more on a single project than we'd make in a year on an entire account at an agency."

D'Arcy took me to a screening room to show me some examples. For a project for Johnson & Johnson his group created a series of additional creative venues to complement an existing ad campaign geared toward mothers. This included a short film that complemented a campaign initiated by J&J's agency Lowe & Partners, as well as customized print executions with *Sports Illustrated, Entertainment Weekly,* and *People.* For the prime-time comedy period on the Time Warner–owned TBS network, they came up with a novel way of framing how ads would run. To appear during the selected "Very Funny" sitcoms, the commercial had to be deemed (and branded) "Very Funny Advertising." The TBS Web site even includes a link for the "Department of Humor Analysis."

TBS's goal was to keep viewers watching during breaks by attempting to make the commercials as entertaining as the program. The consumer benefits by not having to watch as many ads that suck. In this instance, it worked. According to D'Arcy, commercials that ran during those periods had 81 percent higher recall and likability than those that randomly ran. "It's getting to the point where viewers have such an expectation of excellence that every moment has got to be quality or they will tune out. We call it ROA: Return on Attention."

But still, I said, most ads do truly suck. "Maybe, but a day won't be far off where a media company can have the ability to tell a brand, 'I have data that says your ad lost us a million viewers during such and such a program, so why should I run it?' "

I asked if mainstream ad agencies should consider their creative enterprise a threat. "Not at all," said D'Arcy.

"No one is going to replace AORs [agencies of record]," added Partilla. "But to succeed moving forward, media companies are going to have to act more like ad agencies, and ad agencies are going to have to act more like media companies."

"And," D'Arcy continued, "they're going to have to accept that to a certain degree, they're going to have to be polygamous. Agencies historically have been monogamous, but now that so much is open source, there is no way a single advertising entity can or should do everything for a brand."

But who controls the DNA profile of what a brand stands for if there are so many players creating messages on its behalf? The chief marketing officer (CMO)?

"Exactly," D'Arcy said. "The most important brand shepherd used to be the chief creative officer at an agency, but now it's the CMO who has to maintain consistency and integrity among the many voices working against the brand."

I told them about a panel I'd watched in Cannes in which the moderator, Sir Martin Sorrell, head of the WPP holding company, asked marketing leaders from Yahoo!, AOL, Microsoft, and Google if they intended to make creative inroads on the traditional agency model. While the online panelists all said no, Partilla was skeptical. "They'd be crazy not to," he said.

D'Arcy walked me to the elevator. I asked, "So, you like this?"

"Absolutely. At an agency we gave our ideas away. Here we're compensated for them as long as they're relevant and successful."

A tone rang, and the door opened on a full elevator. As I squeezed on, D'Arcy was still talking. "Imagine the money Leo Burnett would have made if, instead of giving his ideas away, he would have told his client, 'I'm going to *lease* you the monthly rights to the likeness of the Jolly Green Giant.' "

When the door closed, someone standing behind me said, "A shitload."

The Boiling Point of Wow
Fahrenheit 212

From the outside, the epicenter of what's next doesn't look particularly futuristic or innovative. Especially on a humid Tuesday morning in Lower Manhattan when the skies were far from visionary blue and the Broadway traffic crept past its nondescript, street-level entrance at an unenlightened, sub-medieval pace.

It doesn't help that the epicenter of what's next, the home of Fahrenheit 212—part ad agency, part consulting firm, part product design laboratory—is above a discount sneaker shop in a hundred-year-old office building.

But once I'm on the inside of Fahrenheit 212, a company barely two years removed from gaining its independence from the global ad giant Saatchi & Saatchi, a strange phenomenon occurred. I forgot about the foul weather, the god-awful traffic, and the world's slowest elevator, and I began to grasp why companies like Samsung, Warner Music, Hershey's, NBC, and Gucci had been tapping the eclectic band of entrepreneurial mercenaries of F-212 to generate disruptive ideas and invent products and services that can impact their brands with the force of defibrillator paddles.

And the reason wasn't F-212's all-white decor, state-of-the-art AV toys, or Amy Winehouse's unconvincing take on rehab seemingly looped on the sound system. It's because—and this became apparent even before I met the designer, who had a proclivity for tattoo-ing samples of his favorite projects onto his body—there's something Wonka-ish about the place.

As a result, the more time I spent there, the more I found my-self getting excited about some of the weirdest shit, from the grandiose to the seemingly quotidian. The bottled water in my hand? Geoff Vuleta, the CEO, wasted no time in describing some of the killer innovations they have in the works for a client in that category. The cup of coffee I just declined? Get ready for an impassioned nar-rative about the worldwide coffee market, the preferences of the Japanese and female demographics, and how F-212 is sitting on a line of products that will forever change our relationship with a cup of joe.

Even the piece I'm thinking of writing about them, they had some thoughts about this, too. From basic art direction and sidebar suggestions to a radical new take on nothing less than the entire eye-to-paper reading experience. Some might call this type of visionary pathos bold, or obnoxious, but what it really is, is inspired. And bold. And obnoxious. Because when it comes to ideas, the eighteen-person staff at F-212 can't help themselves.

At F-212 everything is an idea. Or at least one waiting to happen.

Vuleta's tales are peppered with prefab pearls of bizdom like "identification of transformational vectors" or the observation, pro-nounced with less than convincing spontaneity, that 212 degrees Fahrenheit (water's boiling point, for those not in science class that day) is also "the point at which one degree of change can make a profound difference." But as he walked me through one top secret project after another (an unfortunate thing about capitalism is that everything's confidential until it's in your shopping cart), I saw that there is substance behind the stratspeak, and they have identified some pretty damned impressive vectors.

This is why Craig Kallman, CEO of Atlantic Records, had no reservations about enlisting F-212 to help solve Atlantic's—and by association the entire music industry's—seemingly insurmountable strategic problems, most notably how an industry that for generations made its money on records, tapes, and CDs can thrive in a download world. "They had such an obvious grasp of strategy, the proven ability to execute an idea and at the same time be wildly creative and innovative," Kallman told me. "We're fighting wars on so many fronts it made sense to step outside and get the perspective of someone who can force us to look at things differently and see what's possible. So we basically said, 'Here's how we do things. Get under our hood, look inside, and go get creative.'"

Vuleta wasn't particularly keen on discussing F-212's ad agency roots or biting at my numerous suggestions that a lot of what they are doing for clients now is what agencies used to do for clients in the 1950s and 1960s. Back then, clients and agencies were marketing partners in every sense. It wasn't uncommon then for agencies to suggest the introduction of a line extension for a product, or a new revenue opportunity, or an entirely new category to play in. But somewhere along the way, that all changed, and the average client-agency relationship became shorter, more tenuous, and, as a result, more distrustful.

Today agencies primarily focus on advertising the hand (products) they are dealt, while extensions and innovations are left to the overburdened brand stewards. This is where Vuleta and company saw an opportunity.

"Some consulting companies do strategy well," Vuleta explained. "Some don't do strategy but do consumer experience well. We do both."

F-212 is typically brought in to radically rethink a brand or category and create a completely new set of what its president, Mark Payne, calls "big, fast, and doable" consumer experiences. And while the concept of innovation outsourcing is not entirely new, just about every aspect of the high-velocity, unconventional way F-212 goes about it is.

For instance, they don't pitch clients. They wait for clients to come to them, which is pretty brave in an industry where dog and pony shows are the norm. Then there's the five-month turnaround schedule (billable hours be damned) from initial contact to final presentation. And finally, they employ a virtually unheard-of (and some might say insane) compensation model in which up to two-thirds of the total is based on the realization of success.

In other words, for F-212 to make serious money, its ideas have to be market ready and damned successful once they get there.

Like any company trying to differentiate itself from the pack, F-212 is big on process, if only because having a trademarked, proprietary methodology is mandatory these days for entrée into the C-suites of the world. But its greatest asset is clearly the assortment of big and nimble minds it brings to a brainstorming session. Here's how "big, fast, and doable" works. When a client enlists them, all eighteen employees, each with his or her own unique superhero powers, get on board with the project: creative directors (including one who worked in robotics for NASA and designed rides for Disney), financial experts, designers, business directors (including one with a psychology and philosophy master's from Oxford), a strategic analyst with degrees in sociology and international affairs, and an office manager who was an off-Broadway actor.

There are also plenty of people with ad agency experience at F-212, but as is the case at many of the anti-agencies, it is the unconventional career trajectories that are emphasized the most and, perhaps, the most important.

After an initial new-business chat around, the employees spend about five months spinning ideas, trying to turn the status quo on its head. When they settle on a core of about five big ideas, they don't stop with a nifty PowerPoint presentation. They actually make the new products they dream up, presenting them to the client in ready-to-sell form. Often what's presented is the last thing a client expects but precisely what it needs.

For example, Diageo hired Fahrenheit 212 to jump-start its moribund Smirnoff Ice brand. The firm's response, in essence, was to recommend abandoning the brand it was hired to fix. Instead, F-212 wheeled out a selection of all-new, fully designed, and ready-to-drink Smirnoff flavors, including raw tea and a product that simply combined spring water and alcohol. Versions of both are already in market, a fact that makes F-212's compensation model seem slightly less insane.

Besides being immersed in solving the future of music and beverages, F-212 is usually engaged in no fewer than five other live projects, ranging from the development of disruptive applications for flat-screen video monitors to rethinking the taste profile of chocolate.

When asked if his people ever had reservations about having to master and quickly develop a portfolio of ideas in such a broad range of categories, Vuleta replied that speed was actually on their side. "We work at such velocity that we never really have time to doubt or question ourselves, or get scared. Sometimes fear, as well as knowing too much, can make things worse.

"Sometimes we'll show a client ideas on Tuesday, expose it to consumers on Wednesday, and by Thursday we'll have a strong sense of where the heat is."

In addition to the tattoo guy (still no word if the client, Gucci, bought the work) and the NASA guy and the rest of the in-house staff, F-212 is hyperlinked to an equally eclectic stable of outside experts. Like the prolific George in Bulgaria, a 3-D-rendering artist who furiously churns out beautifully realized, broadcast-quality presentation designs for a price that does not portend good things for the future of American 3-D-rendering shops. And Dr. Abdul-Munem Mohammed Daoud Al-Shakarchi, an Iraqi expat scientist with no fewer than five degrees, including a PhD in microbial chemistry, who has some revolutionary thoughts about, of all things, deodorant.

Here's how that went down: a phone call from Al-Shakarchi's agent, who claimed that his client had invented what he called the world's first truly all-natural deodorant. Vuleta took a meeting, then took home a sample of the unscented prototype, which used base carrier oils instead of aluminum for astringent, antibacterial purposes. Vuleta was digging the fact that it was all natural, but after three or four days of using the product, he became acutely aware of the sensation he felt after applying it. Which got him thinking about the relationship between sweat and emotion. Which led to the sort of eureka moment that he generally does not believe in: a tipping point in the history of sweat.

"In the middle of the night I rang up a friend who was a scientist at Procter & Gamble and asked if she thought that, because we sweat for an emotional reason, it would be possible to marry essential, mood-enhancing oils to our base natural product to interact with the sweat, and she said yes." This led to an aromatherapy study, to the development of a patent for the world's first all-natural, mood-enhancing *pro-perspirant*—meaning it treats sweat as an active ingredient—that can give you energy, make you horny, or help you relax.

Sure, it's not exactly a miracle cure, or the discovery of a new species. It's just freakin' deodorant. But it's unlike any that's ever been used, a significant improvement on a mundane, un-improvable product. And they dreamed it up in what, a few months?

Which made me wonder what F-212 might do with something larger, like the music industry. Or with all the "off-line" toys Vuleta showed me that, because of confidentiality agreements, I'm not allowed to talk about. And then I can't help but wonder what they might be able to do with challenges where the bottom line reflects less on profit and more on humanity. For instance, would it hurt to ask F-212 to spend a few days lifting the hood on something like the oil industry? Or Darfur? Or to do a big, fast, and doable brainstorm about the Sunnis and the Shiites, surges and diplomacy? Who knows, maybe they already are.

When I asked Vuleta if they also did an advertising program for the Diageo and deodorant projects, he waved me off. Advertising isn't the point. It's the power (read: monetary value) of the idea that he's interested in.

For instance, Starbucks. Vuleta has a whole spiel about how Starbucks has lost its core focus, overproduced in-store adjacencies (non-coffee items), and under-delivered on its promise as a mystical coffee mecca. He wrote a three-page manifesto on the subject. In fact, F-212 has also done some unique and still-proprietary product development in the coffee category, replete with some pieces of print art and videos that, to the naked eye, look just like ads.

Turning Good Karma into Brand
Droga5

If there is a special wing in hell reserved for ad people, and I am almost convinced of its existence, David Droga, the creative chairman of the Publicis-owned advertising boutique Droga5, will not spend a millisecond there. Indeed, the Australian-born, New York–based Droga could spend the next fifty years making cigarette ads, peddling booze and handguns to toddlers, and doing recruitment ads for a polygamous West Texas cult, and he'd still be on the karmic plus side.

Which is understandable since one of his ideas will potentially save millions of lives and another is attempting to reinvent public education.

This isn't to say that Droga, the former worldwide chief creative officer wunderkind for the Publicis holding company, is averse to engaging with real, profit-hungry conglomerates. Indeed, his agency's current client roster includes the names Coca-Cola, Microsoft, MTV, and Adidas. It's just that his sexiest, most renowned branding feats to date have been in the name of—gasp—good.

I first read about Tap Project in the pages of *Esquire* magazine in 2006. *Esquire* had profiled Droga5 for its annual "Best and Brightest" issue, presumably (initially) because it had been impressed by the online video phenomenon the agency had created with "Still Free," a seemingly amateur film that showed Air Force One being tagged with graffiti on the tarmac at Andrews Air Force Base. Several million views and countless news features later, it was revealed that the video was a fake, made by Droga5 for the clothing entrepreneur Marc Ecko. *Esquire*'s editor in chief, David Granger, then challenged Droga to come up with something entirely new that demonstrated what some might call his delusional mission of leveraging brands to create moments that can shape our culture.

Droga didn't come back with a piece of film or an ad. He came back with a vision: create a brand out of something that everyone needs but is free. Tap water. Then, for one day a year, get every restaurant and bar in the world to sell it for $1 and give 100 percent of the profits to UNICEF. Why UNICEF? Because more than a billion people around the world do not have access to clean water. Because thousands of children die each day from diseases generated by tainted drinking water. And because UNICEF has been fighting this problem for decades.

According to Stevan Miller, director of corporate partnerships for UNICEF, whom I saw in Cannes, "In thirty seconds he [Droga] presented an idea that was brilliant. Within an hour I pitched it to our chief marketing officer, saying UNICEF had to do it."

Within months, two ads announcing the project ran for free in *Esquire*. In March 2007, hundreds of New York City restaurants participated in Tap Project, raising more than $5 million for UNICEF. Others helped raise money and awareness. Celebrities including Sarah Jessica Parker and Rachael Ray came on board. Donna Karan designed clothing and glass for sale in her stores.

For World Water Day in 2008, Droga took Tap Project national, doing a most un-advertising-like thing: sharing the opportunity with many of the best agencies in the country. More celebrities donated time. Major corporations donated money and media space. More than a thousand restaurants in forty-nine states participated. According to UNICEF, because of Tap Project, within eighteen months more than ten million children would have access to one more day of clean water.

In Cannes in June 2008, I watched Miller and Droga launch plans to a packed audience at the Palais des Festivals for Tap Project 2009, which will roll out in more than a hundred first-world cities around the planet. Their goal: reduce the number of people without access to water by half (one billion) by 2015.

"This single idea," Miller said, "will literally save millions of lives."

I met with Droga at Droga5's Lower Manhattan loft space several months before his presentation in Cannes. Droga's assistant, Mindy

Liu, who has a gorgeous tattoo on one clavicle that reads, "There is a dark and troubled side of life," and, on the other, "There is a bright and sunny side of life," led me into his corner office, which was decidedly sunny. It's a typical downtown ad-guy office in a typical downtown ad-guy space. Exposed white brick. Spare and comfy. Littered with ads living and dead. Droga was friendly and energetic, especially for someone who had just gotten back from delivering a speech in Dubai titled, interestingly, "Growth at the Expense of Creativity." I had one last question about the genesis of Tap, whether he'd been sitting on the idea or if he had simply risen up to meet *Esquire*'s challenge. "The idea for Tap only came about after the challenge by Granger," he said. "I would be too embarrassed to share the other ideas I had. Although, when we launched the agency in '06, we were very public about wanting to devote some of our time and thinking toward social and environmental issues."

The *Esquire* connection led to another opportunity for Droga. In the spring of 2007, a fellow "Best and Brightest" alum, the Harvard economist Dr. Roland Fryer, and the New York City Department of Education chancellor, Joel Klein, were seeking ideas from advertising agencies to help reinvent public education. *Esquire* recommended Droga, and after an extensive review Droga's idea rose to the top.

Droga's idea, still very much a work in progress, is called the Million, and its goal is nothing less than to reinvent public education.

Motioning for me to join him at his desk, Droga spun his monitor around and showed me, click by click, case-history-style, the latest on the Million.

The mission: turn academic achievement into a brand; make it desirable, tangible, and rewarding.

The insight: the most powerful way to reach students is to connect with them the same way as they connect with one another.

The solution: the world's first communication device (with an assist from Verizon and Samsung) designed specifically for students.

While other programs around the country have experimented with cash as a student incentive, Droga's recommendation was to use what many people above the age of seventeen consider the bane of humanity—the cell phone. The goal of the Million is to give a cell phone to every one of New York City's million public school students. Why? Droga's answer was to click play and allow a short film that was still being tweaked to demonstrate the ideal version of the process. Kids would use the phone, which would be disabled during class hours, to access learning applications and information regarding assignments, research, and school calendars. Kids who scored well on tests, met attendance requirements, and demonstrated improvement in classroom participation would be rewarded with additional free airtime and a number of incentives provided by commercial partners (an aspect of the plan that has many raising a concerned eyebrow).

To date, technically, the Million is more like the Twenty-five Hundred. It was launched in 2008 at three schools in Brooklyn, with more to come in 2009. But already, according to the Department of Education, there have been improved results in many key categories. According to Fryer, "We've started to get calls from Mexico, Chicago, and Houston inquiring about how they can have the Million in their schools."

I asked Droga about the topic of his speech in Dubai and his plans for growing Droga5, which recently opened an office in Australia. "I don't want to simply be the clever boutique. I want it to grow on a large scale, but of course not at the expense of creativity."

The agency has done a lot of great work for paying clients. But still. As industry critics are quick to point out, its most celebrated campaigns are for not-for-profits, and the third (the aforementioned Ecko "Still Free" video), while a critical success, is still a one-hit

YouTube wonder. In addition, its highly publicized and much criticized online youth-shopping/entertainment experiment, Honeyshed, hasn't exactly set the retail world on fire. And despite Droga5's doing projects for large companies, a blue-chip, agency-of-record anchor brand is still lacking on its roster. Plus, downtown office space (not to mention the salaries of some forty eclectic disciples) doesn't come cheap, either. As we spoke, I wondered how long of a leash Publicis might give its well-publicized yet modestly successful experiment.

Yet as Droga reiterated his beliefs that brand ideas "can have massive influence and impact and create things that aren't disposable, that will be around in fifty to a hundred years," and as he shared piece after piece of outstanding and risky work for clients like TracFone, the New Museum, and Steinlager beer, I couldn't help but think that with time, the big, enlightened brands will come.

Besides, I'm sure some muckety-muck at Publicis is aware of the value of having an innovative, globally celebrated, socially responsible creative star to shine upon a cynical industry.

Got (Insert Annoying Parody Word Here)?
Goodby, Silverstein & Partners

No matter what agency I worked at during my time in advertising, there was always another, better agency where my co-creatives and I would rather be. The It Agency. The shop that was producing the work we most admired, for the clients we most coveted, in an environment that appeared to be downright desirable.

Fallon, Mullen, Riney, Wieden, Cliff Freeman, Chiat, Ammirati (at the beginning), and Crispin (at the end) are just a few of the places I lusted after, agencies whose names began and ended so many of my whiny, frustrated, pathetic sentences over the years.

"But if this were Wieden . . ."

"Fallon would have been able to sell that idea."

"Ammirati would have resigned the business before subjecting itself to a review."

As if I knew.

But of all the agencies I admired, my favorite and longest-running crush was on Goodby, Silverstein & Partners in San Francisco. Not taking anything away from any of the above or any of the dozens of great shops not mentioned, it's just that to me, Goodby was different. Beginning with its brilliant "Got Milk?" campaign (now in its sixteenth year for the California Milk Processor Board), to its work for everyone from Polaroid, *The New Yorker,* Chevys Restaurants, and Norwegian Cruise Line to Hewlett-Packard and Rolling Rock, Goodby never seemed to rely on the wacky, flashy, forced creative vibe that so many agencies went out of their way to project. To me, Goodby was always smart and cool, funny and somehow humble.

For twenty-five years they have been like the Coen brothers of advertising, producing smart, award-winning work that you wish you had done yourself. Goodby projected integrity, intelligence, and confidence rather than arrogance, bullshit, and insecurity.

To me, Goodby was the ultimate idea factory.

More than twenty years after my man-crush on Goodby began, on the first day of the summer of 2007, I finally landed a date. It had been an uncharacteristically tumultuous few months at Goodby, which is now owned by the Omnicom Group. After losing its showcase Saturn car business and faced with the prospects of substantial layoffs in January, it had gone on a stunning new-business tear, winning more than $2 billion in less than a month. This included Sprint ($400 million in billings), Hyundai ($600 million), and the National Basketball Association ($40 million), as well as a number of additional assignments from existing clients.

I visited Goodby's offices on California Street on a Friday morning, and even though this was a summer Friday and this was adver-tising, the halls were buzzing. At one point after the new-business wins, the agency cofounder Rich Silverstein said they were hiring two people a day, and since then the agency had grown from four hundred to more than six hundred employees.

After finishing up with a creative team, executive creative direc-tor Jamie Barrett explained how Goodby had managed to refresh and reinvent itself. From regional boutique to TV-driven powerhouse to global super-agency. And now digital impresarios. Somehow, seem-ingly overnight, Goodby had figured out interactive without buying a digital shop or opening up a sub-brand called, say, Goodby 2.0. How had the perennial Agency of the Year finalist/winner become *Advertising Age* magazine's Digital Agency of the Year?

"It's very ironic to us that we're being held up as this progressive agency that has figured out digital," Barrett said, "when two years ago we were kicking ourselves, saying, 'We're fucking dinosaurs, we're always gonna be these thirty-second TV guys.'"

Rather than farm out its digital work, or gobble up an interactive shop, the agency looked inward.

"The only thing we did is we refused to accept that fate and tried to do it well, even though we never did it before, and we tried dif-ferent combinations," said Barrett. "We felt that agencies weren't formed to concentrate on one medium. We believe that digital is just another platform. In fact, anyone who considers themselves a tradi-tional or a digital agency are just being marginalized. I mean, why would a client with substantial resources and needs want to work with an agency that has limited capabilities? To arbitrarily say we can't do digital seemed self-defeating. At one point we were consid-ering sub-branding, but then we just got busy, and before we knew it, 50 percent of our work was interactive."

Because I had spent a lot of time working at places that couldn't detect a paradigm shift if its epicenter was directly under the ergonomically perfect wheels of their Herman Miller office chairs, I asked him to elaborate on the process that led to the interactive transformation.

"We [Barrett, the cofounders, Rich Silverstein and Jeff Goodby, and the partner and creative director, Steve Simpson] thought, why can't we play? We're relatively smart people who know how to solve problems—why can't we do this stuff? Partly that is stubbornness, and partly it's not wanting to go to the trouble of sub-branding ourselves. If you start doing that, they're ultimately going to have to work together. So rather than create some clusterfuck, logistical nightmare later, why not figure it out now?

"What we did, and we're still in it, is, if you've done terrific interactive work, we'll hire you, but as a *creative* person. If you've done terrific television, we'll hire you as a *creative* person. We made the assumption that a good creative person can get any creative challenge done."

That's not a particularly sexy creation story, I told him. No "aha!" moment, no proprietary process?

"People ask Jeff and Rich and Steve and myself, 'How did you do it?' and we usually answer we just came in every day and wanted to do better. None of us would be so pompous as to say we had a vision for it. Recently I was part of a workshop about the future of advertising. Everyone seemed to want to be anointed a visionary. But 99 percent of us aren't visionaries. We get where we're going because we dive in and enjoy it and stumble forward as we go. Just stay curious and let the business stimulate us to go forward, and if we have more success than failure, we get to be the *Ad Age* and *Adweek* and *Creativity* Agency of the Year."

Because interactive seemed to transform the industry overnight, I asked if he gave much thought to what the next big shift might be.

"None of us have the answer to what it will be like five years from now. What's important is that we be good at it."

Maybe this is how a small great agency becomes a big great agency, I thought. It's led by people smart enough to admit that they don't know when the rest of the industry seems to be drowning in its own visionspeak.

Before I left, I asked Barrett if there might be a piece of work or a campaign in progress that I could observe as a fly on the wall. "Well," he said, "we've got this awesome campaign for a new-business pitch that we're presenting in New York next week, but I can't discuss it." As he spoke, my eyes wandered to the tissue drawing that covered the wall behind him for the new-business pitch that they would ultimately win and that I'm still not allowed to discuss. Every few weeks Barrett will give me an update, and according to the client my fly-on-the-wall status is still pending.

A year after my first visit, I spoke with Barrett as he prepared to go to Cannes. In the interim, Goodby was again named *Adweek*'s Agency of the Year, and its work for Hewlett-Packard's PC division was named *Advertising Age*'s Campaign of the Year.

The last thing I asked Barrett (besides for a status report on the mystery client) was, what is the most interesting trend in the industry right now?

"Don't know that I know," he said. "If there is one, I know I'd want to stay away from it. By definition a trend means 'been done' to me. So I'm not sure the value in keeping up with them, unless it's to determine what *not* to do."

Torched If They Do, Torched If They Don't

We are looking to brands for poetry and for spirituality,
because we're not getting those things from our communities
or from each other.

— *Naomi Klein*

Advertising is the rattling of a stick inside a swill bucket.

— *George Orwell*

The Passing of the Placebo

The chief marketing officers at Worldwide Olympic Partners companies like Coca-Cola, McDonald's, and Kodak could not have been
pleased. On April 9, 2008, four months before the Beijing Games,
on a beautiful San Francisco blue sky morning, the Olympic torch
run that they were sponsoring (as part of overall commitments in the
hundreds of millions of dollars) was not going well.

Actually it wasn't going at all.

There were an estimated ten thousand people lined up outside
of AT&T Park and along the planned route, some of whom wanted
to simply glimpse the legendary torch, but most of whom wanted to
either protest or support the policies of the Chinese government.

After a short delay, a torch-bearing runner briefly emerged from the ballpark, but instead of proceeding along the Embarcadero, he slipped into a nearby warehouse on Pier 40. Turns out that his torch was a placebo. This is because after watching the surging, poster-waving crowds and sensing that the civic event once associated with global unity and peace was about to turn ugly, if not violent, San Francisco's mayor, Gavin Newsom, decided to make a change. He ended that leg of the run before it really began, and the torch (actually two different backup torches) finally emerged some two miles away on spectator-free Van Ness Avenue.

Newsom's strategy, and, I imagine, that of the mega-sponsors and the leaders of the most populous nation on the planet, had seemingly become: the fewer people who see the torch, the better. Which was a far cry from the good old days, when the torch run generated oodles of feel-good brand equity (in the case of Budweiser, fodder for a goose-bumps-inducing, award-winning torch run reenactment commercial) and an odd kind of global pride, and the Games themselves were a premier and risk-free advertising opportunity.

When I had the opportunity to work on ads for AT&T's sponsorship of the 2000 Summer Games in Sydney, I was thrilled. What's better than doing big-budget, 800-number-free commercials that will be seen by a global audience, not to mention every headhunter and creative director in the business?

But this time things were different.

Going into the 2008 Games, sponsoring advertisers had to know about China's oppressive pollution, deplorable human rights record, and smothering censorship of news, information, and ideas. Of course, the Olympics and its corporate sponsors weren't responsible for these crimes, but they were surely on the corporate and cultural radar. But still, one imagines markets rationalizing what an opportunity an Olympiad in Beijing represented for a brand: a showcase before the century's leading economic power on a global stage that celebrates friendship and peace through sport. Plus, they must have figured, if China's credentials were good enough for the International Olympic Committee, not to mention the executives at NBC Sports, they must be good enough for (insert mega-corp here).

Or not.

The protests that began in London and Paris before moving on to San Francisco were only the beginning. There were subsequent incidents in Indonesia, Australia, and Argentina. In Japan, local sponsors backed out of the torch run, citing phrases like "brand risk" and "brand damage." Before the torch reached Chinese soil in Hong Kong, three would-be Danish protesters were put on a plane out of the country, and officials braced themselves for the arrival of that radical threat to the state, Mia Farrow.

It was a fascinating time for aficionados of human rights causes, global marketing issues, and watching huge corporations squirm. The corporations squirmed because this time there was no easy out for a company. In the past, if there was even a minute chance that any aspect of a major corporate marketing effort would make a company look bad, ass- and face-saving protocol mandated the killing of the spot, the pulling of the campaign—and, in drastic circumstances, the termination of the $90-million-plus sponsorship.

So why, with people rising worldwide to protest political and cultural oppression in Tibet, China's relationship with Sudan amid the genocide in Darfur, and the Chinese government's human rights record at home, didn't Coke, or McDonald's, or Kodak run away from the controversy faster than you can say lead-tainted Happy Meal tchotchkes?

The answer, of course, is money. Because while backing out of an Olympic sponsorship while the entire planet was watching might have temporarily placated much of the politically correct free world, it would also have had the opposite and longer-lasting effect on several billion people in the planet's largest market, emerging and otherwise: China. And the Chinese government and Chinese expats everywhere were making it increasingly clear to those who were primed to oppose their showcase Games: cross us and you will be severely punished in the marketplace.

Look at what happened to the French-owned Carrefour supermarket chain after it publicly supported pro-Tibetan rights. Outraged Chinese protesters came out in the thousands and boycotted Carrefour's stores around the world. Essentially, they were protesting the protesters. Rather than rising up and renouncing their country's policies, Chinese consumers, determined not to let their Olympic pride be tarnished, rose up with nationalistic vengeance against Carrefour and anyone else brave enough to mess with them.

Plus, the sponsorships themselves were at stake. Entire marketing programs, many planned years in advance, revolved around and depended on a successful Olympic launch. And while the games and the athletes in theory are the reason for the Olympics, for better or worse the modern Olympics wouldn't be quite the same without sponsors. For instance, during the 2006 Turin Winter Games, Sally Jenkins wrote in the *Washington Post,* "There were just 2,500 athletes here, compared to 10,000 guests of the 11 top Olympic sponsors—including Visa, Coca-Cola and McDonald's."

When groups such as Dream for Darfur charged sixteen Olympics-sponsoring companies with "moral cowardice" and planned a series of protests at various corporate headquarters and urged people to turn off commercials during the Games, the corporate response was mixed. For their part, some of the 2008 sponsors, including Coke and McDonald's, issued statements expressing regret for the situations in places like Tibet and Darfur and decrying acts like genocide, censorship, and senseless executions. Kodak went so far as to write to the United Nations expressing concern about Darfur. But no one said anything explicit or damning about China. No one demanded policy change, or the initiation of dialogue, or threatened to pull out of the Games. Most echoed the sentiment of this statement by the Volkswagen spokesman Andreas Meurer: "We are supporting the Olympic idea and do not see it as a requirement to solve these political problems."

The only high-profile boycott came from Steven Spielberg, who had been hired as an artistic director for the opening and closing ceremonies but in a statement said that because of "continuing suffering in Darfur . . . I find that my conscience will not allow me to do business as usual."

But while Spielberg took a stand, and even jeopardized the opening gross in China of his film *Indiana Jones and the Kingdom of the Crystal Skull,* most corporations continued to contend that the Olympics shouldn't be politicized and that politics and their brands should not cross paths, anyway.

Ultimately, brand beliefs were weighed against bottom lines, and guess which won?

Rather than offend the world's second-largest and fastest-growing market, not to mention their shareholders, Coke chose to temporarily have "the Coke side of life" associated with genocide, McDonald's allowed "I'm lovin' it" to be linked to censorship, and GE ran eco-friendly "Imagination at work" advertising during the most polluted Games ever.

Too much money had been invested, and much more future revenue was at stake.

Perhaps because of this and the determined resistance of the Chinese people, the protests did not gain momentum as the Games approached. If anything, the issues that many had hoped would dominate the Games were given lip service by the networks and ultimately eclipsed by the unprecedented spectacle of the Games themselves. A record U.S. television audience watched an opening ceremony that, Spielberg or not, was universally considered the most spectacular ever.

Chinese officials attempted to placate the human rights community by designating a small corner of a Beijing park an official protest area. But many complained that their applications went ignored or were denied, and other than a brief initial mention of its existence the protest area was forgotten.

So rather than suffering because of their association with the China Games, sponsors like AT&T, GE, GM, ExxonMobil, United Airlines, McDonald's, and of course NBC itself benefited from record viewership. Thanks to Michael Phelps and an economy that was keeping would-be vacationers at home, more than 200 million Americans watched the Games during prime time, guaranteeing NBC an ad-sales profit of more than $100 million. Online audiences were similarly impressive.

Besides Phelps and the sluggish economy, perhaps American viewers watched in record numbers because, rather than protesting the country that is fulfilling its goal of being the most economically dominant on the planet, they wanted to get a better understanding of it. Maybe we like to watch what scares us (and watching the opening ceremonies, I was both artistically amazed and ideologically unnerved by China's determination to make a statement). Or maybe, for the most part, we just don't give a shit about Tibet, or Darfur, or China's polluted rivers, or censorship.

We'll never know what Olympic marketers could have gained or lost by taking a strong public stand. This time they clearly won.

But one hopes that before the leaders of a global brand plunk down $100 million on their next high-profile sponsorship, they'll seek the advice of an ideological consultant, if not their consciences.

Citizen Raj

Coincidentally, the day after the Olympic torch run debacle in San Francisco, I spoke with Robin Raj, cofounder and creative director of Citizen Group, a socially responsible, nontraditional ad agency based in San Francisco, whose clients include the Sierra Club, the Natural Resources Defense Council, and one of the few global organizations that stood to benefit from the Olympics controversy: Amnesty International.

Indeed, thanks to the Citizen Group–developed work for projects like the global musical event "Instant Karma: The Campaign to Save Darfur" and the live satellite-enabled watchdog Web site Eyes on Darfur (eyesondarfur.org), Amnesty has become the most outspoken organization in the world regarding the human rights situations in Darfur, Tibet, and China.

Having your work win a Clio or a Gold Lion at Cannes may be cool, but having it help prevent genocide is a little different.

In theory, I was checking in with Raj to follow up on projects we'd discussed when I'd visited several months earlier. But because of Raj and Citizen's long-term involvement with Amnesty International and the fact that the demonstrations had taken place within shouting distance of his agency, I had to first ask about the torch run.

"Yes," he said, "I saw the protests, and no, I'm not surprised. After all, the Chinese are leading the world in executions, censorship, and pollution."

"Did you do any kind of campaign for Amnesty around the torch run?"

Raj exhaled and paused before speaking. I'd imagined the stereotypical activist as a wild-eyed, fast-talking, high-energy, frequently raging zealot. But Raj is totally Zen. Calm and understated in manner and speech. "Not for the torch run," he said. "But we are absolutely gearing up for the Olympics, starting in July."

"Don't you think that it's sort of ironic," I said, "how on one hand all of these major sponsoring corporations are hamstrung by the protests, concerned about things like brand risk and brand damage, while on the other the situation presents a rare opportunity for non-sponsoring, low-budget citizen brands to make a high-visibility value statement, for considerably less money, sometimes without even having to run an ad?"

Raj waited, then finally said, with the slightest trace of pleasure, "Yes. It does present a rare opportunity."

For Raj, there was no dramatic epiphany. No Jerry Maguire–like moment in which he realized that despite the money and success he'd had in advertising, creating numerous award-winning campaigns at places such as Hal Riney & Partners and Chiat\Day, he didn't want to spend the rest of the best years of his professional life making ads for things he didn't necessarily believe in. The way he tells it, it was more of an accumulation of moments, of smaller epiphanies—for instance, a moment of soul-searching in an Orange County airport while waiting to trek out to an office park to present one more ad about one more promotion for a fast-food client—and occasionally the hollow feeling that a talented person in a position of power gets when he starts questioning the meaning of, well, everything.

Founded by Raj and the director Steve Fong, the art director Kurt Lighthouse, and the media strategist Kelly Konis, Citizen first made its mark on the world after the attacks of September 11, 2001. According to Raj, he was in a studio recording a voice-over for an industrial video with the actor Gabriel Byrne. Byrne mentioned that in an effort to help his local community heal, a group of students at his daughter's school had gathered the night before and sung John Lennon's "Imagine." Byrne told Raj that there wasn't a dry eye in the house.

"Gabriel told me that he thought that the song could make a difference," Raj explained. "I told him that it would be great for Amnesty. Next, Gabriel spoke to Jann Wenner [of *Rolling Stone* magazine], who spoke with Yoko [Ono]. Who gave us the rights to the song."

Within months a film crew traveled to four continents and recorded hundreds of children singing the song. Then artists, including Jack Johnson and Willie Nelson, recorded the song for animated public service announcements. This was followed by print ads and billboards and online messages. The campaign ultimately ran in sixty-five countries and raised awareness of Amnesty International's mission to unprecedented heights.

After the success of "Imagine," Ono granted Amnesty rights to John Lennon's entire solo songbook for its next effort, "Instant Karma: The Campaign to Save Darfur." For that, more than fifty artists, including Christina Aguilera and the bands U2, Green Day, and the Black Eyed Peas, contributed tracks to the CD, which was just one media aspect of the global awareness-raising campaign. According to Raj, the CD has already earned more than $5 million. "The money from the CD will help Amnesty keep a lot of projects going, including the Citizen-created Eyes on Darfur site," which, via high-resolution satellite imagery, allows human rights proponents around the world to literally keep an eye on a group of especially volatile and vulnerable villages in the region.

While Citizen's work for Amnesty is impressive and admirable, the reason I had initially sought it out was its mission of "bringing together the disciplines of advocacy, entertainment, and marketing" on behalf of clients (mainstream and purely altruistic) that it had labeled "Citizen Brands." A Citizen Brand, according to the agency's manifesto, "aspires to be part of the solution, not just part of the problem. The people behind them recognize that we live in an age of increasing transparency and increasingly conscious consumers. Citizen Brands understand the 'double bottom line' . . . that is, to do well by doing good."

Since Citizen Group had been in existence long before the concept of corporate social responsibility and sustainability had become fashionable, I asked Raj if he felt any resentment. "Not at all," he answered. "If anything the sustainability momentum surprised me in a positive sense because it's going to require that kind of concentrated energy and egoless effort to make systemic change. Competition and *coop*etition are good things for the movement."

But what about the companies that are less than sincere in their sustainability efforts? "Well, lots of corporations are embarking on green, but the depth of their commitment and the pace should be questioned." For instance? "The greenwashers. The instances where companies with bad records do ads that tout their token sustainability story to take the edge off others. Like Pepsi selling Sun Chips [where one of its eight factories is solar powered] yet still mostly selling sugar water with corn syrup. Or Toyota constantly promoting the Prius, which is good and forward, but how do they explain the Tundra? Then there is flat-out greenwashing."

According to the Web site the Greenwashing Index, the term "greenwashing" is a version of "whitewashing," or painting over a problem. Its origins can be traced to a 1986 essay by the environmentalist Jay Westerveld about the hotel industry's practice of placing green "save the planet" cards in bathrooms, urging reuse of guest towels. Westerveld contended that profit, not social responsibility, was at the core of such efforts.

Today, it's hard not to watch a television program, read a magazine or newspaper, or look at a billboard or bus kiosk without having a green message thrown in your face. Editorially, virtually every mainstream magazine and news program regularly produces some version of "The Green Issue" that is filled with ads for such unlikely products as SUVs, dishwashers, oil companies, coal companies, and corn chip makers, all touting their social responsibility and claiming to have saved some aspect of the rain forest, the ozone layer, and the planet.

For instance, the Greenwashing Index, which is run by Enviro-Media Social Marketing with the help of the University of Oregon, regularly monitors ads and allows people to vote online about their degree of truth. Not surprisingly, a billboard that reads, "Coal, Pennsylvania's Clean Green Energy," got particularly low grades for truth and accuracy. A commercial featuring Kermit the Frog singing "It's not easy being green" for the Ford Escape hybrid SUV got mixed reviews because, while it was at least promoting a hybrid vehicle, it was still the product of a big-three auto company, and the truck was shown smack in the middle of a fragile forest environment. In a more heinous example cited by the *Wall Street Journal*, the United Kingdom's Advertising Standards Authority concluded that commercials by the Malaysian Palm Oil Council misleadingly claimed the industry was good for the environment:

In one ad, which appeared on satellite channels across Europe, Asia and the U.S., a man jogs through a natural rain forest, interspersed with shots of palm-oil plantations and wildlife. "Malaysia palm oil. Its trees give life and help our planet breathe," the voice-over declared. The problem: Oil-palm plantations, which produce a vegetable oil used in products such as margarine and soap, have often been planted in illegally cleared natural rain forests. In neighboring Indonesia, where Malaysian palm-oil companies own large operations, plantation development is destroying the natural habitat of species such as the Sumatran elephant.

The same *Journal* article reported that in Norway, unlike in the United States, the government has made it illegal for any car advertisement to claim that its vehicles are "green," "clean," or "environmentally friendly" for the simple reason that "all car production leads to more, not fewer, carbon emissions."

In the United States, the Federal Trade Commission (FTC) oversees advertising claims. It recently began hearings to determine what can qualify as a green ad claim. The FTC last revised its advertising guidelines in 1998, and it's a good bet that by the time it gets around to phrases like "carbon neutral" and other catchphrases for the many alleged shades of green currently being tossed about, there will be an entirely new lexicon at the disposal of greenwashers.

Which means that for now, the policing of greenwashers is basically up to citizens and consumer watchdog groups like the Greenwashing Index and the environmental marketing organization TerraChoice, which recently released a study called "The Six Sins of Greenwashing," finding that 99 percent of 1,018 common consumer products randomly surveyed for the study were guilty of some form of greenwashing.

The Six Sins of Greenwashing

- Sin of the Hidden Trade-Off: for example, "energy-efficient" electronics that contain hazardous materials; 998 products and 57 percent of all environmental claims committed this sin.

- Sin of No Proof: for example, shampoos claiming to be "certified organic" but with no verifiable certification; 454 products and 26 percent of environmental claims committed this sin.
- Sin of Vagueness: for example, products claiming to be 100 percent natural when many naturally occurring substances are hazardous, like arsenic and formaldehyde (see appeal to nature); seen in 196 products or 11 percent of environmental claims.
- Sin of Irrelevance: for example, products claiming to be chlorofluorocarbon-free, even though chlorofluorocarbons were banned twenty years ago; this sin was seen in seventy-eight products and 4 percent of environmental claims.
- Sin of Lesser of Two Evils: for example, organic cigarettes or "environmentally friendly" pesticides; this occurred in seventeen products or 1 percent of environmental claims.
- Sin of Fibbing: for example, products falsely claiming to be certified by an internationally recognized environmental standard like EcoLogo, Energy Star, or Green Seal; found in ten products or less than 1 percent of environmental claims.

One of the most visible and controversial instances of a company going green is Wal-Mart, which made headlines and outraged environmentalists when it hired Adam Werbach, the former president of the Sierra Club and current president of the green consultancy Act Now, to champion its sustainability effort. While many in the sustainability movement renounced the move as an act of betrayal, including some green clients who immediately fired Werbach, others saw his move as potentially visionary: Rather than mashing one's head up against the opposition, why not enter into a dialogue with and enlighten them? Not coincidentally, Citizen Group was instrumental in helping Werbach and Act Now implement and market their sustainability program via a series of print ads and online materials. The key to Wal-Mart's effort, Raj told me, was the way Werbach met the corporate challenge of being environmentally progressive and progressively profitable.

"Hopefully, as demand for this kind of effort grows and acceptance grows," Raj explained, "there will be change on a global scale. The naysayers are behind the curve. Every presidential candidate, to some extent, is for clean energy. It just comes down to policy."

In addition to Wal-Mart and Amnesty, Citizen Group has done sustainability-based marketing campaigns for clients such as Pabst beer and the Philadelphia Eagles and a green initiative for Major League Baseball. This last included communications materials and Web sites for all thirty teams about how and why to go green. But, Raj noted, "They haven't yet greened. They're greening. I've learned a lot from people like Adam about how to be a true activist. It takes time. It's not as wham bam as we're used to in advertising."

Before I left, I asked Raj if a market economy based on the consumption of more, more, more could ever be truly sustainable. "I'm not against consumption," he said. "But the key isn't consuming more, it's consuming better."

It was raining when I left Citizen's office space on Pine Street. I'd hoped to take the BART train out to the airport, in part to save money, but also, after speaking with Raj, I thought it was about time I started to green my ass. But I was running late, and shit, there was a cab right there. I waved it down and got in. As we drove to the airport, I thought about ethics and compromise, white lies, gray areas, and greenwashing, capitalism, and democracy.

As I got out of the cab at the airport, I noticed an official-looking seal on the door that I was about to close.

It said that this was an official "Bay Area Clean Energy Natural Gas Taxi."

Approaching the terminal, I wondered what the Greenwashing Index or the government of Norway would make of the tagline for the company behind the program: "North America's Leader in Clean Transportation."

Reunion

An Unbranded Moment of Cultural Importance with a Shared and Authentic Sense of Community

Ten years after I walked out of N. W. Ayer for the last time, in June 2008, I tracked down and e-mailed a group of former Ayer employees. I told them that I was writing this book, some of which would be about my memorable and confounding years at Ayer, and that I wanted to ask them . . . what? For their perspective? To corroborate my account? Tell me how horrible/wonderful it was? To play the blame game?

I wasn't sure.

And my e-mail—which was filled with questions such as "Why did America's first and oldest agency fail?" and "Who or what was most responsible?"—didn't help garner a lot of forthcoming, attributed responses. The e-mail made it seem as if I were writing a juicy, accusatory tell-all titled, as one off-the-record executive called it in a letter to me, "Fall of the House of Ayer: A Tragedy in Five Acts." And while the story of my time at Ayer was fairly straightforward if not unfortunate—young guy bit off more than he could chew and went down in flames—those of others were far more tragic, litigious, and contentious. Their memories clearly reflected this.

For instance, one former colleague, also under the promise of anonymity, recalled one of Ayer's later, short-term leaders: "When a poseur takes the reins, spends precious cash on golf lessons for the staff, hosts dress-up days, and parades knee-high-boot-wearing hookers through the executive halls on Friday . . . then goes off on a binge . . . it's easy to see why that ship lost its rudder."

And Andrew Donnelly, who worked with me at Ayer during the early 1990s and is now a popular stand-up comedian living in L.A., offered this: "Seeing the head of account management rollerblading through the halls of the 34th floor was either a symbol that things were getting considerably better or about to get a whole lot worse."

Some blamed a string of bad management choices that began in the late 1980s and lasted through the millennium. Others blamed management for being late to the game in building a global network at a time when every major player needed one, and then spending too hastily and foolishly playing catch-up. In a matter of hours, mostly from off-the-record colleagues, I learned more about the feuds, politics, arrogance, hubris, sexual escapades, and tactical mis-fires at the agency than I did in my eight years inside its walls. Who knew?

A few days after I'd sent out my e-mail query, I had lunch on Hudson Street with John Bowman, now executive group planning director at Saatchi & Saatchi New York. Bowman is an optimistic, effusive man who started his career in the traffic department at Ayer in Philadelphia before following the company to New York in the late 1970s. In New York he worked his way from traffic, to copy-writer, to the head of account planning. We'd worked together for years on AT&T, US West, and a number of new-business pitches.

As soon as we sat down, Bowman told me that he had no desire to play the blame game. The most negative thing he'd say (and I certainly wasn't pressing) was "I loved the art that was Ayer and the art that Ayer made, but I came to hate the cacophony."

Instead, he chose to tell me a story that says much about what advertising was and what it has become. Because Bowman is a pro who has been speaking before groups for years, he even has a title for it: "Paying Back Joe Larkin." According to Bowman, one day when he first started out, Larkin, a senior executive at Ayer, asked him what his dream job was. "I said creative. So he let me shadow his creatives." Bowman tore a piece off the edge of our paper tablecloth and dropped the thin sliver in front of me.

"One day Joe Larkin came to me and dropped a piece of paper just like this on my desk and said, 'What would you do if it was a battery?' DuPont had just invented a paper-thin battery. I went home and told my wife, 'Someone wants to know what I think!' He helped me realize my dream. He was very sick then. His last day before he left and died, soon after he had me transferred into the creative department. At its best, Ayer was a family. To this day when I go to work, I think about what it was like back then and wonder what I can do to repay Joe Larkin for what he did for me."

Sappy, yes. But because I know Bowman, and saw him gracefully perform under the most stressful of circumstances, I believe him.

Several hours after my lunch with Bowman, I had oysters and drinks at the Grand Central Oyster Bar with the man who fired me from Ayer and who had asked me that day ten years earlier whether I wanted to be a great adman or a great novelist. In addition to firing me, Stephen Feinberg, now chief creative officer of the Seiden Group, was the creative director who supervised and improved just about every worthwhile piece of advertising I created at Ayer. He had been a supportive creative supervisor of mine on everything from Pep Boys to US West. We hadn't exactly gone to war together, but we did stand shoulder to shoulder on Omaha Beach. As with many of the others, especially those still in the business, Steve seemed guarded at first. He wanted to know what I was after, what exactly I was looking to get. "Context" was the best word I could muster, because I wasn't sure. What I knew from talking to Bowman and some of the others is that it felt good to talk about something that had consumed so much of our lives. I told Feinberg that I remembered his young daughters schlepping in from Westchester to keep him company and draw on sketch pads during many of the mandatory weekends we had to endure under the Fenske regime (later, at Y&R, my daughter would do the same). They're in college and beyond now. Then he told me how he first came to work at Ayer when his agency, Cunningham & Walsh, merged with it. He connected the dots on how he came to meet his first partner, his first boss, and the woman who would hire me after leaving Ayer and become my boss for six years at Y&R, and many others. Personal histories I knew nothing about when I worked there.

We were too busy then, glancing over our shoulders and furiously spinning the wheels of the never-ending idea machine.

Less than a week later, more than a hundred former employees of America's first advertising agency gathered on the second floor of O'Brien's Irish Pub and Restaurant on West Forty-sixth Street. I was late because I was coming from the opposite of a dead-agency reunion, a party for a brand-new agency, Howald & Kalam, owned by two friends and former colleagues from Y&R. The first party was in a downtown loft, where house music played, the drinks were free, and waiters made the rounds with trays of sushi and other gourmet hors d'oeuvres. The principals, Ahmer Kalam and Rachel Howald, were beaming. They were on the cusp of something. There was a kinetic sense to the party, and as I looked at them, one word came to

mind: "possibility." Of course there are two sides to the possible, failure and success, as well as the constant atmosphere of risk, all of
which, of course, represents the thrill of such a venture.

If the first party was about beginnings, the Ayer reunion was
about what comes after the end. For starters, you pay for your own
food and drinks. And you do a lot of hugging and, as is the case with
most reunions, talking in the past tense. What I remember about my
last days at Ayer is that we were all miserable and worried about our
jobs. Our careers. When I started at Ayer, the concept of "What's
next?"—for me, the economy, the emerging Internet, and the
world—was thrilling. By the time I left in 1998, it had become
daunting.

"What's next?" was about to be replaced by "What now?"

Soon after that, in 2001, "What now?" would become "What
happened?"

But on this night the talk was all positive. There wasn't a lot of
bitterness. I imagine the most bitter and bruised had ignored the
Evite and stayed home. Sure, a few of us were intent on emphasiz-
ing what we were doing now, and business cards were exchanged to
prove it.

We all came to this party because we were part of something
that for better or worse had consumed such a large part of our lives,
and it was important to recognize, if not come to terms with, that
fact. For years we had laughed, cried, joked, shared late-night sushi,
had conference calls in rental cars, and traveled the world with one
another.

Then, for five, six, eight years, nothing.

The mission statements of many of the idea factories that I've visited in the last year are remarkably similar: create moments of cultural importance that will give the people who use their brands a

unique sense of belonging and community. As I looked around the back room at O'Brien's on West Forty-sixth Street, as people hugged and laughed and talked about a place gone more than six years now, it occurred to me that even though the physical space was gone, this reunion for N. W. Ayer, America's first ad agency, had become exactly the kind of event that the new idea factories aspired to create: a moment of cultural importance with a shared and authentic sense of community.

Then I had a horrible thought about our reunion: a really smart brand would've sponsored it.

The Care and Feeding of the Next
Great American Hucksters

This is not brain surgery. You can learn brain surgery.

—*Mark Fenske, former boss of the author, former creative star,*
current associate professor, the Brandcenter
at Virginia Commonwealth University

Huckster U.

The director of the program never graduated from college. There wasn't one PhD thesis to be seen, published or in progress, by any of its faculty. And before walking through the door to his afternoon portfolio class, one of its featured professors, a former boss of mine, announced to me with Sweeney Todd–like glee, "It's time for the disemboweling."

Welcome to the Brandcenter at Richmond's Virginia Commonwealth University (VCU). One part art ad agency, one part rogue MBA program, and one part laboratory for experiments in twenty-first-century branding, the Brandcenter is widely considered the nation's most demanding, progressive, and acclaimed graduate program in advertising.*

---

*This, of course, is subjective, as there are several other quality ad schools that time and funds prevented me from visiting. But in 2007, *Creativity* magazine named the

It is also, in every way, the exact opposite of the preparation that I had for a career in advertising.

Which is precisely why I wanted to visit. I wanted to see what type of person would choose advertising not just as a major but as a profession. Had advertising indeed chosen them? Was making ads for denture cream and breakfast cereal a bona fide calling?

I'd also come to the country's best ad school to find out if advertising could indeed be taught, to see where the future of advertising is coming from, and to determine if we should be mortified or excited.

Finally, I came to Richmond because it presented a chance to wrestle with some demons from my own beginnings in the business.

In recent years, the Brandcenter was known throughout advertising as the creatively driven Adcenter, the talent factory from which many of the most gifted and acclaimed creatives of the last decade have emerged. But the mid-January 2008 opening of a new $9 million facility designed by Clive Wilkinson (the mastermind behind the Mountain View, California, Googleplex headquarters and the ad agency Chiat\Day's controversial and revolutionary modular workplace in Playa del Rey) presented an opportunity to give the program a name that more accurately reflected the brave new world of branding and the program's substantially broader and ever-evolving curriculum.

This includes a strategic-planning track (communications strategy), a new track in building a better client (brand management),

---

twelve-year-old program the country's best ad school, *BusinessWeek* ranked it among the world's top design schools, and, more important, based on portfolios I'd screened and people I'd met over the years, I'd always felt that the Adcenter/Brandcenter was the best in the country, too.

and a track that encompasses all things interactive (creative technology). The new building and new name were the administration's way of announcing that the acclaimed creative factory is now a full-service, 360-degree branding factory. In addition to providing a more diverse curriculum, the new tracks allow students to work in teams that attempt to replicate the real-world agency environment.

"In MBA programs, students don't have the opportunity to work with writers, planners, art directors, and account service people," Don Just, head of the brand-management track, told me in his office after class one day. "They're not exposed to the full breadth of the advertising process. Here they work in groups that mirror what's going on at the best agencies today. They are constantly exposed to dozens and dozens of projects with teams outside their discipline in environments they can't control."

In the real world, creatives and clients are always at odds. Even more than account people, clients are blamed for everything wrong in a creative person's life. Boyfriend left you? "Goddamn stupid client." Late on your rent? "Well, if only the friggin' client would've just understood that having a talking anemone is brilliant . . ."

If the clients of the future could better understand the creative side of things, and see that we're not all a bunch of commerce-averse, artsy prima donnas, and if the creatives of the future could see that clients are not soulless dweebs, then theoretically the process would be less contentious and the work would be much better.

In a perfect world, in theory, this made infinite sense.

But in twenty years in advertising I'd never seen anything that remotely resembled such a place.

Is Too Much Verisimilitude a Good Thing?

A tour of the Brandcenter's new digs with its director and professor, Rick Boyko, the former chief creative officer of Ogilvy & Mather, revealed the fusion of two eras in architecture and a literal link between advertising's history and future. The reimagined 1870s brick building that now houses the offices for a faculty that has more than a century of award-winning agency/client experience is the former carriage house for Richmond's swanky Jefferson Hotel. Attached to the carriage house is an ultracontemporary geometric structure of light and vibrant color that contains most of the student-friendly space.

"I thought this would be semiretirement," Boyko explained as we checked out a new focus-group room that will be used by the future agency planners of the communications-strategy track. "But the last four years I've worked as hard as ever." The focus-group room looked perfect, better than most professional suites in which I'd logged countless hours, watching people slowly kill my hard work. But Boyko wasn't pleased. The sound system that was to link the observed with the observers on the other side of the glass was not working, rendering the room, for the time being, useless. I offered that it could still be used as a focus group for mimes, but Boyko didn't hear me or didn't want to. Not only was Boyko, a former art director, involved in every aspect of the planning, design, and construction of the new buildings (right down to the stylish urinals in the men's room, which he proudly showed me and which I felt obliged to photograph), but he donated $1 million of his own money toward it, and he wanted it perfect. Which is the opposite state of the conditions at most of the real-world agencies (including every one I ever worked at) that the Brandcenter aims to replicate. To truly nail the agency vibe, I thought, they should plant a couple of bitter, disillusioned middle-aged dudes bitching by the gourmet coffee machine.

As we walked through the student lounge (partially financed by Yahoo!, foosball and Ping-Pong tables on order), twentysomethings skated past on Heelys sneakers, while others stretched out on plush couches. Next door to the lounge is a huge brainstorming room in which two students were playing chess on an enormous, curved poured-concrete community table. Nearby, a group of four was discussing plans for later that night.

It seemed almost idyllic for a college or agency environment, but the laid-back vibe was deceptive. The semester had only just begun, and soon the projects would be coming fast and furious. At the Brandcenter, as at many contemporary ad agencies, all-nighters and weekend work come with the territory. Hence the full shower and changing room. Hence the lockers, dining areas, and doors that are open 24/7 for students.

It occurred to me that this was not a place a student went to find herself or to experiment. Unless she had $17,000 a year to throw away. In fact, an administrator told me that morning that any student receiving one grade of D or less, or two Cs, was expelled from the program.

"Kids come here," Boyko said, "with a distinct sense of what they want to do with their lives."

Come to Work Stupid Every Day

I've visited quite a few universities in the past several years, and while every experience has been enjoyable for a different reason, the students here had by far been the most amiable and inquisitive. They went out of their way to introduce themselves to me in the lounges, at the cafeteria tables, before and after classes. They wanted to know who I was and, more important, the only two questions that ever seem to matter in advertising: what have I done, and what was I working on now.

While waiting for Boyko's class Building Brands in International Cultures, a second-year student in the art-direction track scooted over a few seats, introduced herself, and said, "This is much, much harder than Yale [undergrad] ever was. It is intense, and the workload is relentless." But she believed that the long hours and not insignificant financial commitment were worth it. "It's a different kind of intense. It's painful, but there's also an adrenaline rush that comes with it. You learn about the industry, then you go about trying to change it by doing something that's never been done."

One of the first presentation slides in Boyko's first class of the new semester was a tenet from Dan Wieden, cofounder of the legendary Portland (and now global) agency Wieden+Kennedy: "Come to work stupid every day."

As I stared at Wieden's words, I thought how that line could have applied to my career, only my version of it would have a comma and another period.

"Come to work, stupid. Every day."

Boyko's class was in an auditorium on the first floor of the rebuilt carriage house. As a provocation, he used a remote to showcase on a large pull-down screen a variety of some of the better promotional efforts being done worldwide. There was a video for the NIKEiD build-your-own-sneaker program and one for a video game featuring Burger King's creepy (yet apparently appealing to its young male demographic) animated king character. Next came a three-minute video downloaded from YouTube that dropped a series of sociological bombshells about the changing demographic of the marketplace, mostly insights about emerging India and China.

Not once during Boyko's presentation did I see anything that remotely resembled a print ad, out-of-home ad, or traditional TV commercial. And unlike every agency multimedia presentation I've ever seen, his came off seamlessly, without the slightest technological glitch.

Also of note: before playing a video, Boyko would ask the class if anyone had seen it before, and no matter how obscure the source, medium, or country of origin, no fewer than five and sometimes as many as twenty hands went up in response every time.

Before you attempt what's never been done, it helps to be familiar with everything that has.

"Now more than ever," Boyko told his students after playing an empowering, Web-based piece for Dove soap that was a big hit at the previous year's Cannes festival, "the brand steward isn't the corporation or the agency, it's the consumer."

A few minutes later, he told them that this past week his former employer, Ogilvy & Mather's New York office, had laid off a hundred of its thirteen-hundred-person workforce. "But," he said, "not one job in the interactive division."

To further illuminate his point, a quotation from another ad legend, Bill Bernbach, came on-screen: "Live in the current idiom and you will create it."

This messaging sequence seemed to be consistent with the educational mix that I saw served up throughout the program during my stay: share and discuss real-world examples, add applicable inspiration from people who have done it, and thereby issue an inherent challenge for the students to make it happen on their own, smarter terms, today.

To someone who has lived much of it, the wisdom rang true and seemed to have real value. But I wondered, looking around at the students, if these were the kinds of tropes that would actually sink in, or if this audience, despite its hunger and talent, was too young and inexperienced and filled with their own ideas for most of it to make sense.

I decided that it all depended on the student, that the more conscientious individuals in the program would absorb the cocktail of facts, wisdom, and new-media opportunities and distill it into ideas and an approach that could potentially change the industry. And I imagined that for others, even the most talented and ambitious, it was meaningless without context, that wisdom wasn't something to be imparted, but something to be gained by trying and failing to do whatever it is that's burning a hole in their guts.

Redefining Vanity and the Many Shades of Green

Projects for students in the strategic-planning track under Professor Caley Cantrell (formerly of the Martin Agency) included creating a series of presentations that revealed original perspectives on the issues that can shape a brand's future. On the day of my visit with her students two teams were scheduled to make multimedia presentations on their latest assignments.

Even more so than with the students in purely creative tracks, the strategic-planning students were inquisitive and outwardly and unapologetically ambitious and entrepreneurial. Unlike the creatives, many of whom believe that their ideas are an art form (more on this later), or at least much better than anything an old hack like me could have done, the planning students thought of their ideas and their experiences as calculated means to monetary and professional success.

Before they began their presentations, I asked them the obvious question: if, upon graduation, they all wanted to work as agency planners. After all, VCU strategic-planning graduates were already at many of the better agencies, including Goodby, Silverstein & Partners in San Francisco, Chiat\Day in Los Angeles, the Richards Group in Dallas, and Leo Burnett in Chicago. Their answers surprised me.

"Not especially," said a tall, confident second-year student who had already gone out of his way to introduce himself to me, several times, earlier in the day. "We feel that we can take this, what we're learning here, and go way beyond agencies. Insights and strategy can transcend advertising. They can be applied to any business model. I mean," the twenty-three-year-old continued, "a twenty-three-year-old did Facebook. When you see something like that, you feel that for this generation, anything is possible."

I had expected to see inspired but conventional student work, but instead I was shown two presentations that were as polished and insight driven as anything I ever experienced inside an agency. The first, delivered with practiced ease by three students, explored contemporary definitions of feminine beauty and then laid out a provocative and unexpected (especially from twenty-three-year-olds) conclusion that, if anything, revealed a huge and controversial opportunity for marketers willing to embrace and celebrate "cosmetically enhanced" beauty. Everyone plays up to natural beauty, they contended. But no marketer truly spoke to the desires, fears, and opinions of the unnatural beauty. At first, as with most good ideas, I was uncomfortable with their premise. But the more I considered it—and their numbers that reflected an exponentially growing liposucked, tummy-tucked, rhino-plasticized population—it made an astounding, if disturbing, amount of sense. It certainly wasn't an insight or a category I would ever have wanted to execute against, but if someone were to embrace it, I bet he'd make a killing.

The second presentation, called "Get Your Green On," was less sensationally provocative but equally insightful. The green movement is a topic that has been and continues to be discussed ad nauseam, so at first my expectations were low. But when the students laid out their premise—that green means totally different things to, and is acted upon differently by, each demographic (for instance, sixty-year-olds have a distinctly different definition of global warming from twenty-year-olds) and that great things will come to the brands that understand this best—I sat up and opened my notebook.

Having seen both presentations, I made a focus-group-worthy observation of my own: of all the demographic segments that they researched and discussed, the students reserved their harshest criticism for their own generation.

Prelude to a Disemboweling

The most telling thing about the ad school that seemingly has everything is the one thing it is lacking: anything that even remotely resembles a television commercial. Instead of storyboards and headline-driven print ads, at the Brandcenter I saw Web stories, photo essays, viral-video concepts, brand communications platforms. Cartoons.

Here, anything that can make someone take a second look is an ad, and what had previously passed as an ad is a pariah. No one seemed to understand and advocate this more than the students. "They're not that interested in TV at all," Boyko said.

I found this hard to believe. I'd been away from making ads for less than two years, and at my agency (which, admittedly, was huge and not terribly progressive) TV was still the most important thing to have in your portfolio, and on your agency's show reel. And last I checked, TV still captured the lion's share of total media expenditures. Has it changed that much?

"Yes and no," Boyko answered. "Clearly the work is heading in a new direction. But sometimes I have to tell them that, you know, you're still gonna need some ads in your books, some spots on your reel."

"Do you miss it?" I asked. After all, Boyko had been chief creative officer at a legendary agency, and at one time thought he might be asked to replace Shelly Lazarus as Ogilvy's CEO. "Do you miss the pace and energy of the agency life?"

He shook his head again. "I was done."

During my final years in advertising the most rewarding aspect of the job wasn't selling one of my ads, or winning a piece of business. It was trying to help younger people whom I liked make sense of the process, telling them what (and whom) to watch out for and what steps were needed to make their idea better and maybe even the one that wins. While there's only so much creative and ethical influence one can have even at a large agency, I imagine for an advertising person of a certain age and status, a leadership gig at a place like the Brandcenter represents an opportunity to exponentially increase the scope and degree of one's influence.

Why spend years trying to change an agency when you can help shape an entire industry, without worrying about having a knife stuck in your back?

"Some people might think I'm out of the business," Boyko said. "But I'm not. Sometimes when I travel on behalf of the program, I'll be in L.A., San Francisco, New York, Boulder, and Chicago and see people that I taught, who came out of our program, making their mark on the industry."

While we were talking, the Brandcenter's associate professor Mark Fenske stopped at Boyko's door and stared at me. Fenske, of course, is also a former boss of mine. The Gatekeeper of the Nincompoop Forest. The man who turned N. W. Ayer and the lives of many of its employees upside down.

Prior to visiting Richmond, I had written Fenske, asking if I could sit in on one of his classes, and was told in his return e-mail that, because it was the students' first day back, I could not. It wasn't a good time. However, he'd be happy to meet me for a drink, *after* class.

We shook hands. Of all the personalities I have met in advertising, Fenske is easily one of the most intriguing, intimidating, and perplexing. He wanted to know about my schedule for the rest of the day, and if we were still on for drinks. "Sure," I said. "But still keeping me from sitting in on your class?"

He groaned. Fenske frequently groans, and no two are ever alike. Sometimes it can express disgust, contempt, and even occasionally curiosity. From my past experiences I likened this groan to the "This ad sucks. How dare you waste my time with such mediocrity?" variety.

I glanced at Boyko. He knew that I knew Fenske, and I could sense that he knew there was a loose-cannon factor associated with his star professor talking to a writer that might not bode well for the institution in which he had vested so much. Boyko shrugged. Not his call.

"Okay," Fenske said, not entirely convincingly. "Give me a half hour to talk to them, then you can come in when they're gonna present their work."

Later, when I saw him heading into his class, he smiled and said, "It's time for the disemboweling."

If Clients Can Be Taught to *Get It,*
Who Will Be Left to Blame?

When I spoke with Don Just, head of the client track at the Brand-center, it was easy to see why in past years students had voted him their most difficult and favorite professor. If he looks less like a professor or flashy ad guy and more like the president of a bank, it may be because he once was the president of a bank, as well as the former CEO of the Martin Agency (Wal-Mart, "Virginia Is for Lovers," and a little account called Geico), the acclaimed shop that put Richmond on the advertising map and has played a major role in the development of the Brandcenter. With a résumé like this, one would think that Just would be satisfied if not entitled to coast, to share his wisdom with students gathered at his feet. But this was hardly the case. In just his second year heading up the client track, he appeared driven to build it into something special, far beyond the stereotypical creative factory.

"We are not a portfolio school," he explained. "We want to redefine what the space is by providing value that MBA graduates are not trained to do. We are focused on innovation and collaboration. Because the great clients, the clients who get it, understand the importance of the creative side."

For Just's second-year students this included an independent-study program developing marketing strategies with real-world clients. This year he also introduced an innovation lab that will culminate in his students creating a series of publishable white papers on topics such as the future of retail. But don't expect to see footnotes in the *MLA Handbook* style. At the Brandcenter, what's been done is not nearly as valuable as what's yet to come, so the case histories of the past are less valuable to Just than the fresh insights of the present. "I want them to invent their positions," Just said. "To focus on anticipating what will happen and share their original thoughts on it. Not cite things. We are," he said, "creating the futurists of our industry."

Of the first small group to graduate from the client track in 2007, half went to the agency side or a consultancy, and half went to work for clients.

Leaving Just's office, I imagined a future situation in which a Brandcenter-educated creative/account/planning team pitches a Brandcenter-educated client who is being advised by a Brandcenter-educated consultant, and I wondered if it would be the ideal or nightmare dynamic.

I suspect that someday soon we'll find out.

Worlds Collide

I tried sneaking into Fenske's Advanced Portfolio class while he was lecturing, but he immediately made me part of the lesson. "Right now," he told them, "you do not yet know what you want to do. The risk right now is showing your work to someone who doesn't get it. Do you want the job knowing that someone who works there thinks that your best stuff isn't good? I had that at N. W. Ayer & Partners when I worked with Jim. My best stuff wasn't what they wanted to do. And this was a problem."

I sat up. I nodded. It sure was a problem. Sitting there, I thought of a recent Fenske bio I'd downloaded before the trip. It mentioned Wieden+Kennedy, where "he learned how to aim high." It mentioned Nike, the Bomb Factory, and Van Halen. It even said that after graduating from Michigan State University, he "almost became a missionary, but 'displayed a genuine lack of aptitude for sinlessness.'" What the bio neglected to mention was his time at N. W. Ayer. So what he'd just told the class, based on my presence, was notable because he was suggesting that the problem wasn't solely the fault of Ayer, or the people at Ayer, or its clients.

There was something confessional in his tone. And as with everything I ever heard him say, like it or not, it rang true.

"You want to make sure you are at a place that appreciates your best," he continued. "And even then, there will be times when people still won't get it. Which usually means you're onto something."

Next he segued to morals and advertising with integrity.

"Can you keep yourself from doing something that intrudes on people's privacy?"

And, "You have to ask yourself, when you get an assignment or a new client, do I want to do *that* for a living? [For instance] I won't do lottery ads. I think lottery ads are shameless. Beer, not so."

The students were listening closely, but I wondered if his words could make as much sense to them before they embarked on their careers as they did to me, several years removed from mine. Twenty years of knowledge and experience and cynicism from where they are today.

Before the break he brought his talk full circle, to vocation. "You want the opportunity to do what you want to do: Write a script. A film. A cartoon. Last year someone did a cartoon that was one of the best things I saw here. I came upon him late one night and looked over his shoulder, and it blew me away. Other people I showed said, 'That's not advertising.' I said, 'Yeah, but did you notice how you *leaned in*?' "

That's advertising.

Maybe that's the confluence of art and advertising, I thought, the ability to make people *lean in*.

We sat in chairs on a rooftop lounge during a fifteen-minute break. I wanted to talk ads, but Fenske wanted to talk books. Fenske is an avid reader and a poet. On a suggested reading list on his Web site, he cites more literary works than pop culture or advertising books, which is consistent with his opinion that it's all art.

"Liking what Bukowski writes and believing whether or not he did it are two different things," he told me, referring to a Bukowski quotation I'd e-mailed him a few days earlier. "Drinking, screwing, and writing all day—you can't do all three, but it's fun to read about." Then he told me that he thinks Flannery O'Connor is brilliant. I mentioned the deft use of religious symbols in one of her stories, and he said, "Don't get me started on religion. How can you be a writer, how can you write a book, if you think there is nothing else? Don't get me started." Did I say there is nothing else, I thought, or is he just saying that? I'd been with him for only ten minutes. I wasn't ready to get him started.

A few minutes later, as if to make me feel better about my modest career, Fenske mentioned a campaign he said I'd written for General Motors twelve years earlier that was something that "Wieden would buy today." This did make me feel better, but mostly because I had no idea what campaign he was talking about.

Before we went back inside for the second half of his class, he asked about this book and where my visit to the Brandcenter would fit in. After I was through explaining, he groaned. "I hope it's not gonna be another fluff piece about this place."

Which brings us to the disemboweling.

Back in class Fenske had the students spread their work out for review on the rows of long tables before them. He asked them to pick the best of the four or five ads they'd created and explain why it's good and why they like it. The first, a young blond woman already blushing, held up a fake ad for Miracle-Gro plant food that showed in the lower-right-hand corner of the page a giraffe's head that clearly cannot reach the miraculously tall leafy plant on the top left. Not exactly the future of advertising, I thought. But cute, clever.

"What is the news in this?" Fenske asked. The young woman struggled with an answer. When she finished, he groaned before launching into a set piece about the necessity of including something newsworthy, something provocative that the consumer did not know, in your ads. "Do you mind if I do this?" he said, already starting to tear the young woman's meticulously composed yet unsuccessful ad in half.

What followed was not so much a critique of the twenty or so ads on the table as a platform for Fenske to use the ads to impart wisdom. Other than the student who happened to be on the hot seat at any given moment, the rest didn't seem to hate it. In fact, most were transfixed, uncharacteristically alert for twentysomethings in a classroom environment, scribbling notes in journals that looked curiously familiar.

Work may literally have been shredded and egos may have been bruised, but they seemed to consider it a small price to pay for the insights being dispensed with Taoist gravity.

This is a good place for Fenske, I decided as I got up to leave. Lecturing, enlightening, and occasionally humiliating young men and women is much more effective and rewarding than doing the same to forty-year-olds.

Earlier, I had asked Ashley Sommardahl, the Brandcenter's assistant managing director of student affairs, if graduates experienced something of a letdown when they started an entry-level job at a less-than-idyllic real-world agency.

"Actually," she said, "there's less of a chance of a letdown in the real world after leaving such a progressive environment, because they're recruited by the best." Indeed, there is a growing VCU alumni network in place at the country's top agencies. And at a re-cruiting fair at the school after graduation last year, there were 125 recruiters for seventy-five students.

One of the primary issues facing the Brandcenter is how it will handle growth. The new building means higher bills and more stu-dents to help pay them. Will the increased number of students translate to a watering down of the talent base, a lessening of the ad-missions standards? Are there enough jobs in adland to accommo-date so many graduates? Indeed, are there that many exceptionally creative people on the planet, period? And what about the increas-ingly polished competition emerging from other well-regarded programs like the Creative Circus in Atlanta, the Art Center in Pas-adena, and Miami Ad School? For instance, according to Amanda Vendal, creative/planning recruiter at the Richards Group in Dallas, which has had a relationship with VCU since the Brandcenter opened, "For a very well-rounded art director it's hard to top the best students from Art Center." And while many praise the Brandcenter students' ability to "hit the ground running" and to play well with others, some recruiters prefer portfolios where it's easy to discern in-dividual (rather than group) ownership of an idea.

"Talent and instinct are a big part of it," says Linda Harless, cre-ative manager at *Adweek's* 2007 Agency of the Year, Goodby, Silver-stein & Partners. "But I think that you can teach ways to bring it out and polish it."

But just when I thought that the future of advertising was going to be churned out by Brandcenter-like institutions and that it would be next to impossible in 2009 for someone to rise up through the creative ranks after honing his skills writing, say, about gallbladder surgery, wine, and high school sports, not to mention laying block in a mental institution, Harless tells me Jon Wolanske's story. Wolanske was thirty-one and had never written an ad when the Goodby re-cruiter Zach Canfield discovered him doing stand-up comedy in a

San Francisco performance space. Canfield thought that Wolanske's humor and narrative gifts would translate well into a job in advertising.

Some days, Goodby receives as many as five hundred portfolios and job requests, many from places like the VCU Brandcenter. But on that day Canfield did something that I suspect even Mark Fenske would approve of: he looked for magic in unexpected places.

Exiting the Nincompoop Forest

Advertising is a paradox because it attracts some of the most creative minds in the world, rebels and idealists, original thinkers and gifted artists, and asks them to produce something that will convince people that they need to buy or do something that they usually do not want, need, or care about. On top of that, these creative minds will be forced to operate under conditions that are the enemy of most art: mandatory guidelines for elements that must or must not be said or shown. And once it is submitted, the fate of the work they so passionately crafted, whether it will live or die, is often put in the hands of others, of clients and consumers.

I had been meaning to ask Fenske about his contention that advertising is art. Actually, I'd wanted to ask him about it fourteen years ago. I wanted to ask him this afternoon in class, and now, sitting at a table at the Irish bar Sine in Richmond's Shockoe Slip area, I wanted to ask again. But I didn't.

Later that night, while we talked at various Richmond bars, and even later on the steps of the Thomas Jefferson–designed capitol building, I still thought about it. But again, instead of discussing ads, we talked about books and history. At one point, in a bar across the street from a former home of Robert E. Lee's, Fenske remarked that we had spoken more in this one afternoon and evening than in the entire year we had worked together.

I said this was true. At first he had resisted me, and because of that I had resisted him.

Another question I'd been asking everyone during my visit to the Brandcenter was whether advertising can be taught. Which is a stupid question, I realize. Can advertising be taught? Can writing be taught? Can goodness or humility be taught?

However, this did occur to me while sitting in Fenske's class, watching his students watch him: The ultimate value of a teacher isn't just teaching rote principles and facts for memorization. It is recognizing an innate and untapped ability that resides within a student and helping him or her determine whether it is something he or she might grow to love. Plato wrote in *The Symposium* that one of the greatest privileges of a human life is to become midwife to the birth of the soul in another. My sister Karen, with an assist from the creators of *Bewitched,* did this for me. I'd like to think that Fenske did the same with the kid drawing a cartoon late that night.

More important than wondering whether something can be taught is the fact that people care enough to try to learn it.

While I was writing this, I shot Fenske an e-mail, asking a few too many follow-up questions, including, finally, a request for his response to the art question. His typed reply was akin to a groan. He said he'd give it some thought, but I realize now that his answer doesn't matter anymore.

It doesn't matter whether I think advertising is art. What matters is whether its creator does.

Afterword
Who Do I Think I Am?

During the year and a half I spent researching and writing this, I was often asked, usually by people who knew me in my past life, "What are you doing here? Didn't you write a novel? Didn't you gleefully leave this world behind?"

The simple answer was that I was writing another book. Not another novel but, ironically, a book about the world I had supposedly gleefully left behind. Many who worked with me found this curious and funny, and not just because of the irony, but because, really, who the hell am I to write a book about advertising?

What the hell does Othmer, he of the workmanlike creative career and creeping cynicism, know about the perpetually changing landscape of adland?

After all, I never had my name on the door of an agency. Never ran a big-agency creative department. *Adweek* never published a picture of me dressed in black, with a ponytail and sunglasses, beneath the headline "Hot Commodity." I never reaped an IPO windfall, created a famous Super Bowl spot, or wrote a phrase that would become part of the vernacular, like "Just Do It!" or "Think Different" or "Where's the Beef?"

But for twenty years I made ads. One out of fifty probably ever made it out of the agency. Maybe one out of five hundred ever made it on the air. But some were smart or funny or surprising enough to make bad meetings good. Others made clients with one $300 million foot out the door step back inside to reconsider. Sometimes I sold the proverbial big idea. Sometimes all I did was say something that made someone else's big idea seem even bigger.

And sometimes I was simply a halfway reasonable, adult mind in an industry that wasn't always.

Here's what happened: in twenty years I went from earnest, wide-eyed junior copywriter to big-agency golden boy to disillusioned, bitter corporate burnout, then, briefly, back to golden boy, then to capable veteran, and finally back to corporate burnout, but this time without the bitterness or disillusionment. Because really, there is no reason for a rational adult to be disillusioned with advertising. With medicine, or art, or the Peace Corps, maybe. But saying you're disillusioned with advertising is like saying you're disillusioned with politics, or the porn industry.

What did we expect, fulfillment?

During my career I survived some fourteen rounds of layoffs, downturns in the industry and the economy, takeover threats, IPOs, sixteen creative directors, thirteen CEOs, the demise of one great agency, and the ongoing collapse of another.

For this I was given more money than I ever would have made in my father's well-intentioned career of choice for me: mason's laborer and, if I played my cards right, bricklayer.

Because of advertising I got to travel the world and meet many smart, talented, and powerful people, from CEOs and artists to four-star generals and Carrot Top.

Because of advertising I got to follow and occasionally lead and make hundreds of friends for life.

When I left advertising a few months before my novel was published, I was indeed ready for a change. But it is important to note that I never hated advertising or felt that I was above it (in fact, I was often humbled and awed by the superior ad talent of others). I had just felt for the first time in my life that I ought to be doing something else, something I wanted and needed to do more.

Then, while doing press for my novel, a funny thing happened. While some questions were about the book, most were about advertising. Why was it such a huge part of our culture? Was it responsible for globalization? The downfall of our youth? What's the most despicable ad you ever made? The most despicable thing you ever saw?

My answers surprised me. Rather than rattling off witty renunciations of my past and the industry that had employed me, I found myself publicly defending advertising, and then, later, privately thinking about its role in my life and our culture more deliberately and sincerely than I had in the previous twenty years.

The simple answer to my friends in advertising is that I had come back to the scene of the crime because I was writing a book. A guy's got to make a living, right? The real answer, of course, is much more complicated, and if I had an answer for their questions, I probably wouldn't have been there to begin with.

During my time on the road I spoke with hundreds of people at dozens of agencies. Creatives. Planners. Account execs. Digital wizards. CEOs. Consultants. I sat at conference tables, looked at reels, and stared into speakerphones as people pitched and bitched, getting excited and frustrated by ideas in real time. "Embedded" is a word I'd taken to using to impress people, if only because it made me feel Anderson Cooper–ish.

I was fascinated by what they do and, more important, why they did it. Why do any of us do what we do, and is it a job, a profession, or a vocation?

Is it a calling, or a finding?

At first, when I tried to wrap my head around the entire advertising industry, it made my brain hurt. The mere thought of the myriad possible futures for digital advertising or media tended to make me curl up in the fetal position in a dark, brand-free room. I felt under-qualified, inadequate, analog. But when I approached the business one conversation at a time, one campaign or agency visit at a time, it made me feel somewhat better, if only because I came to realize that most of us don't have it all figured out yet—the industry or our vocation—either.

Is this book comprehensive? Hardly. It is simply an attempt to better understand something that has been such a large part of my life, and our culture, for so long.

One impression at a time.

Acknowledgments

Thanks to everyone in adland who gave me their time, insights, guidance, and support, including Ann Hayden, Ernie Schenck, and Roy Elvolve; to David Granger and Ryan D'Agostino at *Esquire*; to Jacob Lewis and Jeff Garigliano at *Condé Nast Portfolio*; to Mark Stein at Portfolio.com; to Elisabeth Eaves and Hana Alberts at Forbes.com; to all of my former creative partners, especially Kenny Evans, Jeff Griffith, Aaron Smith, Corey Rakowski, and Kleber Menezes; to Joey Spallina at Tone Farmer; to Ben Goldhirsh and Zach Miller at Reason Pictures; to the Williams brothers, Tom and Dave; to Sylvie Rabineau at Rabineau Wachter and Sanford; to Bill Thomas, John Pitts, Alison Rich, and Melissa Ann Danaczko at Doubleday; to David Gernert, Erika Storella, Courtney Gatewood, Stephanie Cabot, Will Roberts, and everyone at the Gernert Company.